I0601460

Civilizing the Texas Frontier

Civilizing the Texas Frontier

The Love Story of
Mr. and Mrs. James Lowry Smith

Bill McCarron
Afterword by Myrna Loy Smith

STEPHEN F. AUSTIN STATE UNIVERSITY PRESS
NACOGDOCHES ★ TEXAS

Copyright © 2013 by Bill McCarron. All rights reserved. Printed in the United States of America. No part of this book may be used or reproduced in any manner whatsoever without writter permission except in the case of brief quotations embodied in critical articles or reviews.

For more informaion:
Stephen F. Austin State University Press
P.O. Box 13007 SFA Station
Nacogdoches, Texas 75962
sfapress@sfasu.edu
sfasu.edu/sfapress

Book Design: Laura Davis, Troy Varvel
Cover Design: Laura Davis

Distributed by Texas A&M University Press Consortium
www.tamupress.com
1.800.826.8911

LIBRARY OF CONGRESS CATALOGING-IN-PUBLICATION DATA

McCarron, Bill
Civilizing the Texas Frontier / Bill McCarron - 1st ed.

p.cm.

ISBN-13: 978-1-62288-024-9

1. Texas - Amarillo 2. Texas - History 3. Texas - Daughters of the American Revolution

Contents

Illustrations

Preface

The story begins with my being given permission by my wife and her two sisters to clean out the drawers and cabinets in my late mother-in-law's house in Fort Smith, AR, in March 2003. I was to sort materials into piles for the sisters to evaluate. One of the last recesses I examined was a ceiling-level cabinet in the study where I found three old bread-size tin boxes that had likely been stored there and forgotten for nearly 60 years.

The contents were letters, diaries, autograph albums, scrapbooks mainly from the early lives of James Lowry Smith and his future wife, Marie Motheral Bynum. It took a year just to organize the rather haphazard contents found in the boxes into some form of chronology. While reading all the material, I quickly saw how the written words brought to life the numerous anecdotes my late mother-in-law, Katherine Bynum Cobb Baker, had related about her aunt and uncle—Sissie and Papa Jim as she referred to them—based on her childhood growing up in Amarillo, 1912-1925, and on the genealogy of both families that she had traced. Perhaps, I thought, there was an essay or two here about late nineteenth and early twentieth-century life in Texas since Jimmie Smith had grown up in Salado, 1863-1882, and had gone to Colorado City as a bookkeeper for a large stockmen's mercantile firm from 1882-1888. There, he met the niece of the firm's owner, a 20-year-old woman named Marie Bynum from Horn Lake, MS, in fall 1884. They courted by correspondence and married in 1886. By early 1888 they were both located in Old Town Amarillo where he operated a branch mercantile business. Except for a brief four-year interlude in the late 1890s, they lived in Amarillo for the remainder of their lives.

As I read and re-read and began to piece together their lives, I realized that the frontier life they lived early on in Colorado City and Amarillo revealed a civilized pattern beyond the usual Texas history of saloons, bordellos, cowboys, and gunfights. To give but one startling example, the first time Mr. Smith and Miss Bynum called each other by their first names was over the telephone in late 1884! Wow, this instrument had only been demonstrated by Alexander Graham Bell in 1876 and here it was on the Texas frontier.

What subsequently developed was the story of their lives, but one surrounded by what one would *not* expect on the primitive Panhandle-Plains frontier—one of the last frontiers in the continental United States: brick and adobe buildings, an efficient private banking enterprise, and rapid delivery of the U.S. mail, to name but a few of the civilizing influence they experienced and contributed to. To reach such a conclusion, I had to look into a variety of records at various libraries, museums, and special collections throughout the state. I found myself trying to piece together a jigsaw puzzle where I didn't know the full picture and had to search for the puzzle pieces.

This book is based chiefly on primary sources (letters, business ledgers, diaries, autograph albums, memorabilia, personal historical accounts, etc.), with secondary sources (newspaper accounts, journal articles, an occasional book) only used to fill in the blanks. Consequently, a bibliography is unnecessary; all the sources can easily be accessed in the Chapter Notes. To cut down on endnotes, I have used parenthetical documentation wherever possible and have omitted notation whenever a source is mentioned in the text. The faults of this book are my own. The largest difficulty I faced was following the example of historians before me who always use the past tense. By profession, I am an English teacher who is used to writing literary criticism in the present tense. Also, as I worked on the project, I always felt I was looking over the shoulders of Jimmie and Marie as they lived their extraordinary lives—so, on occasion and where appropriate, I have slipped into the present tense to make a few events more real. These two people brought civilizing influences to nearly every event they touched and they deeply loved each other and the people in their communities. And, most extraordinarily, unlike many Texans, they did what they did in quiet ways where they called attention to others and not to themselves.

This book would never have been possible without the help of some extraordinary people and some excellent research institutions. I am indebted to my late mother-in-law and her mother for preserving the Smith correspondence and other memorabilia. Also, the late Cile Robertson Ambrose of the Central Texas Area Museum in Salado who welcomed my initial research with an open heart. The Salado Historical Society also made available some of their materials. Mayor Jim Baum graciously showed me Colorado City and the staff of the Heart of West Texas Museum gave me open access to their records. UT-Austin's Center for American History houses the Mary C. Jones Collection that opened my eyes to the many historical accounts she had collected about Colorado City. Guy C. Vanderpool, initially Betty Bustos, and then Warren Stricker of the Panhandle-Plains Historical Museum provided valuable access to early materials on the Smiths in Amarillo. Gayle Brown and Rob Groman of Amarillo's Public Library Special Collections went far out of their way to show me files, records, and newspaper microfilm from early Amarillo. The Rev. Howard Batson and his secretary, Carol Brian, generously let me poke through all the early Church records at First Baptist Church, Amarillo. Ann Bynum Whittenburg opened up the files of Marie's brother and her grandfather, B. C. D. Bynum, and let me duplicate whatever I needed. I am deeply indebted to Carol Monroe, past Regent of the Esther McCrory Chapter of the DAR in Amarillo, for her generosity and encouragement on all levels. The splendid staff of the Southwest Collection at Texas Tech headed by Monte Monroe and Tai Kreidler, but especially Patricia Clark, Randy Vance, and student workers Sarah Goff, Gaurau Jain, and Brittani Kane who brought box after box of materials on James Lowry Smith's lifelong business partner, John A. Walker, for me to examine. Finally, Christine Smith Andrews began cataloguing numerous original family artifacts—chiefly on Professor James Lowry Smith and his wife, Julia McDowell Smith, and their families—in November 2009. Thanks to Christine and her husband Ben, I was made aware of these materials in July 2010. These materials were originally preserved by James Lowry Smith's two sisters, Mrs. Roxalee Smith Andrews (1870-1941) and Ms. Julia Catherine Smith (1875-1954). Christine continues to add papers to her Ancestry.com web site: http://trees.ancestry.com/tree/13911684/person/.

The late Kay Coleman (1917-2010) and the late LeBecca Paddock (1917-2010), great nieces of Marie Bynum Smith, knew Marie in her later years and generously shared their insights in personal interviews. Myrna Loy and Berry Smith, current owners of the James Lowry Smith House [designated the Smith-Rogers House, a Texas Historical Landmark, in 2009], opened their home to me and shared valuable information about that special place. I am most grateful for Myrna Loy's written recollection published as the Afterword to my book. Countless other folks helped at such places as the Bell County Museum, the Belton Chamber of Commerce, the Cameron Chamber of Commerce, and the County Clerk offices of Bell and Potter Counties. A special note of thanks to Bill Kinnison and MaryBelle Brown of the Salado Historical Society. Due mainly to their efforts, a Texas Historical Marker on Professor James Lowry Smith was placed next to his grave marker on July 16, 2011. Without the diligent work of Kimberly Verhines, and her staff, including Lauren Hawkins and Troy Varvel—but especially Laura Davis—this manuscript would not now be a book. In that regard, a special note of thanks to Mary Lenn Dixon of the Texas A & M Consortium and Editor-in-Chief of the Texas A & M UP for her valuable advice throughout the book development process. And God bless Aron and Doris Abrahamsen for their prayers and encouragement during the process of writing this book. Also, Justine Alessi who believed in this book even when I faltered. For good advice and encouragement along the way, I owe thanks to: Gray Bohon, James Lowry Smith Cobb, Matt Cobb, Ricky Dobbs, Sean George, Bo and Dee Grimshaw, Judy Head, Tim & Kate Head, Marty Jacobs, Doris Kemp, Malcolm D. McLean, Mary Mendez, Beth Purcell, and especially the late Charlie Turnbo.

Without the skilled scanning and word processing work of Ms. Kim Jefferies and Christina Jones, secretaries in the Department of Literature and Languages, my manuscript would have faltered. My thanks also to my sisters-in-law, Sarah Cobb Baker and Mary Motheral Baker, for their Bynum stories and their encouragement. Finally, and most thankfully, I acknowledge the love of my own life, Adele Baker McCarron, who has been my research assistant and advisor throughout the whole process. I dedicate this book to her and to our grandchildren.

For

My Wife and Grandchildren

Chapter 1

Salado
1863-1882

The Salado that James Lowry Smith, Jr. knew as a teen-ager was a former frontier town well on its way to being a civilized community in Central Texas. Mr. Jimmie, as he was referred to by the young women of the town, was the second oldest of nine children born to Professor James Lowry Smith and his wife, Julia McDowell Smith. Young Jimmie was born in Independence, TX, on March 12, 1860 just as his father was concluding four years as Principal of the Preparatory Department for Baylor University while that school was in Independence before eventually moving to Belton (eventually, University of Mary Hardin-Baylor) and Waco in 1886.[1] Professor Smith was a homegrown product who received both his BA (1858) and MA (1860) from Baylor.[2]

Smith senior probably spent two or three years teaching at Cameron Liberal Institute, Cameron, TX, during the early years of the Civil War because one reference lists him as a member of Company H, First Regiment, 27th Brigade, T.S.T., Milam County in 1862.[3] Whatever the case, Baylor President Rufus Burleson wrote a letter to Colonel E. S. C. Robertson recommending Smith for a position at Salado College.[4] Smith's father, William Berry Smith (alias "Camelback" Smith) was known to impresario Robertson ever since both fought with Sam Houston during the Texas War for Independence.[5]

So, at age 36, Professor Smith became Principal Smith and was entrusted with the leadership of fledgling Salado College in 1863. He would serve in that capacity for the next 11 years before stepping aside to teach at other places, including a school in nearby Belton. In fact, Smith signed on to head up Belton Collegiate Institute where he was asked to "take charge of the school and employ teachers" in December, 1876.[6] Smith would once again take up the Salado College reigns for 1879-1880, the concluding year

Jimmie and Archie Smith, ca. 1868

for the original 20-year charter of Salado College, though the institution would survive for another 10 years or so before eventually being turned into Thomas Arnold High School in honor of British Victorian poet Matthew Arnold's father who was a premier educator in England in the nineteenth century.[7]

Salado was a small, sleepy agricultural town in the 1850s. Indians had disappeared and the spring-fed Salado Creek through the center of town provided ample water for its inhabitants. The surge of Salado began in 1859 after Elijah Sterling Clack Robertson (in effect, the owner of the town who had built a stately 20-room antebellum mansion a decade before) set up a literal land grant basis for a school to attract newcomers. Plots of a 100-acre grant were sold off by the enterprising heir of the Roberston Colony to finance a two-story limestone building which was completed in 1861.[8]

With a faculty of six or so men and women, representing the disciplines of Latin, math, music, science, and practical subjects such as husbandry and bookkeeping, Salado College quickly acquired the reputation as the "Athens of Texas." Salado College was originally the equivalent of what today we would call a preparatory school, but by the early1870s it was granting bachelor's degrees. It was a private college, non-sectarian, and supported strictly by tuition paid by local students and by those who came from all areas of Texas and some nearby states and resided in the homes of Salado's rapidly growing numbers of families. Whenever the College needed funds, it was usually Colonel Robertson who came to his College's aid.

Into this thriving agrarian and educational community came James Lowry Smith, Jr., whose diary entries, complete for each day of 1878 and partial for Jan-Oct, 1880, reveal a developing Texas seen from the eyes of an 18 to 20 year old who is already mature beyond his years.[9] The diary for 1878 is literally a veritable farmer's almanac where the young Smith annotates the development of five basic crops in order of their planting: wheat, oats, corn, millet, and cotton. The diary is a weather barometer and thermometer with every Norther, freeze, ice accumulation, and soil depth of rain faithfully recorded. One learns when the cotton had to be replanted because of a spurt of subnormal temperatures, and, on the same day, the wheat reaper stopped because, on second thought, the crop was too green (May 15), and the next month when a fierce wind blew down the developing corn (Jun 19). One might surmise that such entries are dull

James Lowry Smith at 17

and boring, but most are far from it because young James infuses many of the entries with wryly humorous observations, many of them centered on himself.

For Jan 8, Smith writes: "I went down to the farm to see if geese were eating up the wheat. I had been told that they (the geese) were there. No geese there at the time. I was the largest 'goose' in the field." During all of 1878, "Pa," or Professor Smith, was teaching in Belton, leaving on horseback each Monday morning and returning on Friday evening. Frequently, William "Archie" Smith or James accompanied their father, returning immediately afterwards to assume joint chores on the family farm. On one such return trip on Jan 13, Smith regrets that he "fell down in the Lampasas River and was not slow in getting home." Four days later he and Archie had rebuilt the storage shed on the farm. Archie was pitching straw and Jimmie spreading it when the roof collapsed under too much weight and "down came Jimmie straw and all."

In mid-February the final acreage was "brushed off" and ready for planting. Young Jim gives "three cheers at the top of my voice though I don't think anyone heard me" (Feb 19). The brief entry for Mar 12 offers a case of humorous juxtaposition: "Am eighteen years old today. Hauled a load of wood." In fact, the most recurring diary notations are on two items: hauling wood for the fireplace and the kitchen stove and, for 15 days, in May through September, "chopping" or "picking" cotton. Occasional bad weather gave Jimmie a reprieve from agricultural toils. On April 27 he attended Justice Court in Salado and notes that "there were 11 cases, only two disposed of, though there were seven or eight lawyers present."

Picnics played an important role, particularly in the lives of Salado's young people. One May 1 picnic was especially noteworthy because of the humorous description involved about one of the vehicles: "The place selected was Wilkerson Valley. There were about thirty went. We all put away mountains of grub and rivers of lemonade. There was a wagon in the crowd that looked real circus like. The wagon was a new one, with four spring seats, and two spans of horses with plumes on their bridles." Later the same month, a Mr. Walden came again with his reaper but was late in arriving and the final three uncut acres had to wait until the next day. Smith concluded, "I wished I had never seen any wheat by the time the days' work was over" (May 27). Occasionally, Smith's latent humor could take a sententious turn. The sole entry for June 22 is about painting a fence: "Whitewashed (The wall I mean)." Three days earlier a severe storm had wreaked havoc with a portion of the corn: "It was all blown down (never to rise again)." As expected, July 4th signified a big celebration—a barbecue with an estimated 2,500 people present! Alas, the affair concluded with a small accident: "As we were going home, a wagon ran on to one of our buggy wheels and mortally wounded it."

Smith catalogues all his trips to nearby towns, including one to Belton on September 7 to have a haircut or, as he puts it, "to have my wool clipped." In mid-October he returned to Belton for a day at the Bell County Fair and comments, "The Belton Silver Cornet Band furnished music (such as it was)" (Oct 18). Smith's clipped understatement is probably well deserved because four entries in the 1878 diary reveal that Jimmie, his brothers Robert and Forrest, and 12 other young men comprised the Salado Cornet Band. In addition, as other entries reveal, Smith's musical talents extended to piano duets (Apr 8, 1880 and May 5, 1880), the guitar (Jun 12, 1880), and later the organ. This more civilized aspect of Salado culture is in strong contrast to several proverbial town uproars that Smith catalogues. The rigid rules of Salado College forbad firearms, alcohol, and rough-necking anywhere near the school's location on College Hill. Nonetheless, during an early January, 1878 "Mayor's Court" one Nathan Cawthon "was fined $5.00 for swearing in the street and Randolph Robertson was fined $25.00 for carrying a pistol" (Jan 8). One very functional civilizing addition to the Salado landscape was a suspension footbridge across Salado Creek. Jimmie and Archie were in town picking up a new wood-burning stove for the Smith household when Jimmie observed: "Some fellows were on a bender and cut up considerably, shooting, hollering, and riding the bridge" (Nov 23).

More notorious forms of lawlessness occasionally surfaced. Strictly by coincidence, young Smith had ridden south of Salado on July 21: "Pa started for Austin again. I went with him to Round Rock to bring the horses back. Sam Bass died this evening—he was shot Friday evening." And on July 22: "Went to see Sam Bass but he was in his coffin." Then Smith immediately undercuts the historical significance of the moment by adding: "Stoped [sic] at Corn Hill to see Miss Alice. Got home just at dark." Then in October, Smith writes, "Bill Longly [sic] is to be hung today in Giddings" (Oct 11). Indeed, Longley was the second-most wanted man in Central Texas because he was a "notorious desperado who is credited with having killed twenty-two men."[10]

Such shocking descriptions of Texas outlaws stands in isolated contrast to the daily rigors of running a family farm, an undertaking that illustrates civilized agriculture at its best. In fact, a survey of the U.S. Census for 1870 and 1880 reveals the expected: most Saladoans listed farming as an occupation. However, one closely related civilizing influence that marked Salado as a forward-looking community was the Grange. Salado's 1873 Grange #1 was the first community chapter in Texas, due in large part to the efforts of Major Archibald J. Rose, a Civil War veteran who settled in Salado in 1870 and was a dominant force in Salado for the remainder of his life, including serving on the Board of Salado College.[11] His home is now an historical location on a hill outside of the downtown Salado area. Thanks to Colonel Robertson and his comrades such as Major Rose, Salado hosted the Bell County Fairs in 1874 and 1875 before that event found a permanent home in Belton.[12] A surviving program from the five-day-long 1875 Fair provides a list of competitions that few county fairs today could ever match.

Rates of admission were: adults, per day 50 cents, children under 12, 25 cents; children under five, free; horses, each, 25 cents; carriages and wagons, 25 cents each. Prohibited were gambling, lotteries, trials of skill, games of chance, and racing for money, intoxicating liquors; in addition there was an "ample police force" to regulate everything. The highest award was $10 for Best bale of cotton; $2 for Best bushel of meal made from different kinds of corn; $2 for Best pound cake and $1 for Second best; $10 for Best buggy horse; $5 for Best pair of aged mules; and a special diploma for Best threshing machine; and one for Best Roper; and, last but not least, a silver cup for the Prettiest baby, under one year old. Advertisements abounded, including those for several dentists; E.S.C. Robertson & Son, Dealers in General Merchandise, with a large stock of Bagging and Ties; Eppstein & Co. Kentucky Whisky Depot, Rockdale, Texas, Agents for Anheuser Lager Beer; and Dr. W. Barton, Special Attention to Diseases Peculiar to Women and Children.[13]

Beyond prizes and rewards at a county fair, however, was the pragmatic necessity of a good set of crops to supplement Professor Smith's limited income as a teacher. The combination of a spring-fed creek and good alluvial soil accounted for it. Just east of the so-called Balcones fault lies rich land:

> The Black Prairies to the east of Salado are underlain with
> limestone, limy clays, marls, and shales. The soil here is

granular for good aeration, circulation of moisture, and easy penetration by roots of plants, not to mention ease of working with farm tools.[14]

In 1878, the Smith's corn crop was finished with replanting on March 28 and the cotton was finally in by April 2. A few days later, Archie and Jimmie "broke up a piece of land to plant millet" and the seed was sewn and harrowed in on April 11. Then followed a ritual of days devoted to such crop cultivation tasks as "ploughing over the corn for the first time" (Apr 6), hoeing corn (Apr 19), and "thinning the corn" and checking the "scorched ends of blades" because of another unseasonably late frost (Apr 23), but, thankfully there wasn't enough cold "to do any damage." In the meantime, cotton was ploughed, weeded, chopped. Most of June was devoted to harvesting oats and wheat. And it was a community affair with one farmer having a reaper and a "Mr. Walden a thresher" (Jun 10). Statistics dominate as Smith and his older brother calculated the yields of each owner: "We helped John Smith thrash wheat. He had 15 hands employed including the hands with the thrasher. Made 100 bushels off of 9 acres" (Jun 11). Jim Markham's farm yielded "85 bushels on 8 acres" while Samson Williams made "just over 89 bushels" from the same acreage (Jun 13). That year's Salado record for wheat yields per acre, however, belonged to 18-year-old Jim and 20-year-old Archie who "had 14 acres and made 315 bushels" (Jun 12). The next week was devoted to hauling two loads per day at around 30 bushels per load.

Supposedly, a farmer never has time for a summer vacation. Well, not in 1878 Salado. Despite the fact that railroads were still three or four years away from making their entry into Bell County (but, alas, to Belton and never to Salado) and that roads were only wagon trails at best with few if any bridges across the Lampasas or Nueces or Navidad Rivers, young James and his father set off on a two-week trip by horseback to the Gulf Coast. The trip, covering July 31-August 18, was to visit aunts, uncles, and a grandmother in Jackson County.[15] The total distance traversed round-trip was approximately 370 miles. At the end of the first day's ride, Smith notes in brief diary entries: "Ate dinner at Possum Creek. Camped 2 or 3 miles below Taylor. Found plenty of water on the road." On August 1: "Dinnered at Hogeye. Camped three miles below Bastrop. Water scarce." The two passed through Flatonia and spent the night of August 4 with a Mr. Culpepper. Smith's annotations are optimistic: "Culpepper has four grown (single) daughters. All good looking." Finally, on the 5th they crossed the Navidad at night and arrived at dark at their destination. Always on the outlook for something new, Smith remarked "All hands [relatives] went to Aunt Kate's for dinner. Became acquainted with a very pretty lady that was there, Miss Lorena Mathews" (Aug 7). The very next day the same Miss Mathews was at the home of a Mr. Bolings "on the bay."[16] However, his attention was soon diverted because Jimmie and his companion met the Misses Ruth and Susie Ward in a home just across the Jackson County line in Calhoun County (Aug 9). Young Mr. Jimmie admired their looks but put his hands over his ears because "they can claw the ivory and howl." Cake, wine, watermelon, peaches grace the tables for the next three days before James and his father have to depart for the return trip to Salado.

The northerly route home was slightly different. He headed for Texana and spent one day at a slow pace because rains had drenched the region forcing Jimmie to "travel 8 miles in water two to twelve inches deep" (Aug 14). Several dry days follow and young Smith observes, "Camped three miles south of Cistern. Filled my canteen out of the cistern from which the place gets its name" (Aug 16). After finally fording the San Gabriel River, he located a watermelon patch where "I helped myself" and got home ahead of his father who was some distance behind the son "about an hour after dark" (Aug 18).

So how did Uncle Henry, Aunt Kate, and Uncle Ed Clary[17] know the Smiths were coming to their area? By letter, probably; by telegraph, possibly. As two early diary entries reveal, Salado got linkages with the outside world in January. For January 15, Smith writes, "Today they have carried the telegraph poles a short distance beyond the town of Salado. So in a few weeks the telegraph line will be ready for business. I do not know whether or not they will have an operator in this town." The lines would link south to Round Rock and north to Belton. On March 2, Smith declared, "Today the telegraph poles were erected through town."

Another recent frontier phenomenon was the advent of barbed wire. Smith goes to some lengths to relate how existing fence has barbed wire strung inside of it to keep cattle out of the farmland. The strings of such wire did not preclude other modern additions to Salado culture; twice Smith mentions playing in pick-up games of something called "Base Ball" (Feb 23 and Mar 2). Not satisfied with catching an occasional fish in Salado Creek, Smith and his younger brothers seine the ponds of the creek, on one occasion netting 50 lbs. for a fish fry (May 13).

Still, the issue requiring almost constant attention in 1878 was the farm which beckoned after the hiatus to the Gulf Coast. Nine successive days in August (21-30) contain the sole entry of "picked cotton," with only August 21 containing the actual amount (143 pounds). By early September the wagon loads were ready to cart to Colonel Jones' gin. This facility, run by a Colonel Tom Jones, "did a thriving business, and after 1870 when cotton became an important agricultural factor in Central Texas, Colonel Jones was the first of the Salado millers to add a water-power gin to his mill…a wooden screw-press gin [that] was a great step forward at the time."[18] Looking to the future, young James "bought 200 bushels of cotton seed from Col. Jones, gave four-and-a-half cents per bushel and hauled them to the farm shed in four loads" (Oct 8). Late October marked the climax of the harvest returns, and Jimmie's summarized entry for October 25 is most revealing:

> Hauled 80 bushels cotton seed & 4 bales cotton from gin.
> Had afternoon to rest in. So the crop is wound up with 800 bushels
> of corn, 6 bales of cotton, 315 bushels of wheat,
> 4 tons of millet, and a good stack of oats, to say nothing
> of peas & popcorn.

The following day turned much colder and was a perfect day for butchering the fattened hogs.

So what beyond emerging technologies (telegraph and modern cotton gin) and emerging diversions (a Gulf Coast excursion and baseball) would indicate that James Lowry Smith was relishing civility as a counterbalance to the rigors of manual agriculture? The most obvious and unusual trait was an 18-year-old who could hold mule reins or a hoe by day, yet write a diary every night! Young Mr. Jimmie used a variety of names to refer to social events: a sociable, a singing, a party, a frolic, an evening—never a dance—at the homes of leading Salado families. The most frequently mentioned residences were Creekmore, Rosenbaum, Barton, Rose, and Tyler. (The latter three are preserved today as Texas State Historical sites).

Welborn Barton, M.D., served as a Trustee for Salado College for many years,[19] was instrumental in locating the Masonic Lodge over the newly constructed Baptist Church in late 1878, and taught primary class Sunday School.[20] He served briefly as a surgeon for the Confederacy during the Civil War and is reputed to have made some of his own surgical instruments. He once summoned young Smith to his house for a "singing" but with accompanying instructions for Jimmie to bring his guitar (Jun 12, 1880).

Besides his agricultural expertise, A. J. Rose fought Indians and Jayhawkers in West Texas and is considered one of the foremost crusaders for better Texas schools and teachers, free textbooks, and vocational education. He went on to be President of the Board of Directors of Texas A&M, 1891-1896. He once summoned Smith to his home to help him clean out his cistern (Nov 9).

O. T. Tyler was a native New Englander, a Texas state representative, and was a county commissioner; hence, he received the appellation "Judge" even though he was not a lawyer.[21] He was Mayor of Salado in 1868[22] and President of the Board of Trustees of Salado College for a time. He also donated the land for the construction of the Baptist Church.[23] James Lowry Smith visited the Tyler home frequently, once carrying Dr. Barton's daughter, Sallie, to a party there (Jan 10, 1880).

In any event, evening parties dot the pages of the 1878 and 1880 diary at the rate of at least one per month over an 18-month period. There were four violins for an evening soiree at Rosenbaums (Jan 21). A double party marked the night of June 16, 1878, first "up to Maj. Rose's," then "went down to Mr. Caskey's." The night prior to his Gulf Coast trip, young Jimmie notes: "Went to a party at Prof. Faupel's," the music teacher at Salado College and the tuner of Salado pianos (Jul 30). The New Year's Day of 1879 (and the sole entry in the diary for that year) was marked by an invitation to "A party at Judge Tyler's." On a cold night in January, 1880, Mr. Jimmie escorted Helen Rose to a "teacher's meeting at Dr. Barton's" (Jan 29). Later that year another double social event occurred with "a picnic at the old campground" followed by "singing at night at Capt. Barbee's" (May 8).

A tall, handsome young man, slender but muscular, Mr. Jimmie had plenty of practice harnessing the family wagon to haul loads of wood, wheat, oats, corn, cotton, and millet by day. By night, particularly most Sunday nights, he hitched up a team of horses and, in his oft-repeated word, "carried" various eligible young Salado women to "preaching," chiefly at Salado College where services were held until the wooden-framed Baptist Church was completed in late 1878. Transportation was provided for the Misses Anderson, the Misses Brenham, Miss King, and the Misses Halley, though the most frequent wagon guests in 1878 were Helen Rose (five times) and Addie Barton (three times). The only young woman receiving more attention was Miss Laura Sherman of Belton, a frequent dinner guest at the Smith household and high on the agenda whenever Mr. Jimmie went to Belton with his father or to shop or to get a haircut. The name Miss Laura Sherman appears an even dozen times in the 1878 diary. For example, Smith notes on February 18: "At night carried Miss L. S. to a sociable at Mr. Creekmore's." And in late summer: "Went riding with Miss Laura Sherman in the evening" (Aug 25). And as winter approached: "Went to preaching at night and went home with Miss Laura Sherman" (Nov 11). There is also an intriguing factor among the three most frequently mentioned women Mr. Jimmie lent his attentions to: they are slightly older than Jimmie and they are all Salado College graduates: Helen Rose in 1875 and Laura Sherman and Addie Barton—the only graduates in 1876. Obviously, young James Lowry Smith had an eye on the minds of these young women as well as the shape of their figures.

What the Bartons, Roses, and Caskeys all share in common with the Smiths is that they were devout Baptists. Professor Smith had become a charter member of the original Salado Baptist Church in 1864, having transferred his membership from Independence.[24] The original pastor was an old friend of Professor Smith's, The Rev. George Washington Baines, President of Baylor-Independence, 1861-1863, and the great-grandfather of President Lyndon Baines Johnson. Baines, in consort with Maj. Rose, Prof. Smith, and Judge Tyler, was responsible for the fledgling Salado Baptist Church's initial growth between 1868 and 1877. Baines turned over the Church leadership to the Rev. George W. Green in August, 1877 when Baines became an agent for the Education Committee of the Baptist State Convention.[25] Baines, however, was apparently always in the background because young James Lowry Smith mentions his name several times in late portions of the 1878 diary.

Indeed, young James was mature beyond his 18 years when it came to Church functions in civilized Salado. Sunday School attendance was a weekly occurrence and only in mid-September does Smith chide himself: "The first time I have missed going to S. School when Pa is in town for a long time" (Sep 15). Nonetheless, Smith did manage to make the 11 o'clock preaching by the Rev. Green. What is more, Smith's diary frequently annotates the services of visiting clerics. On April 22 he notes, "J W. D. Creech preached" and on June 2 that "Rev. Mauel of Belton preached." In between the foregoing dates, young Smith is not averse to voicing his opinion about an ineffective Church service: "Do not remember the man's name that preached but I think it was the longest sermon I ever heard" (May 25).

Despite what would become a life-long devotion to his beloved Baptist faith, James was not without an ecumenical side. Twice in March and twice in September of 1878 he went to preaching at the Campbellite Church (nineteenth-century predecessor to the Church of Christ). And on July 7 he notes: "Attended Sunday School & preaching to a faith known as Christadelphian faith," and he followed Baptist Sunday School on December 8 with a "preaching at the College. Mr. Glass preached (Methodist). The first time I ever heard him." Then, in classic Smith humorous understatement, he adds, "Formed a good opinion of him." A week earlier, Smith had followed the same ecumenical format of Baptist Sunday School, then he went "to the College to hear Dr. Conner preach, but he did not come. Mr. Hinton filled the appointment."

Nonetheless, it was the Baptist Church in Salado that grew by leaps and bounds, perhaps because construction of a permanent facility was well underway by mid-1878. Prior to individual churches being built, Salado denominations had used Salado College on a rotating basis. Young Smith faithfully catalogued crucial events in late 1878. According to Smith, the Baptist Church opened its double wooden doors for the first time on October 19: "The first sermon was preached in the new Baptist Church at night. Was present. A protracted meeting commenced." Indeed, Smith reports, the very next day "a massive meeting was held at the Baptist Church for the purpose of organizing a Sunday School at that place." A week later Smith proudly reports: "Went to the Baptist Church. Sunday School organized complete—75 people in seven classes" (Oct 28).

Often, the demands of farm activity and rigors of churchgoing achieve a humorous juxtaposition. On October 30, Smith pencils: "Archie and myself ground our axes, preparatory to wood hauling. Went to Baptizing in the evening. There were four Baptised. Elder Green did the work." On November 2, Smith "had the mules shod," but the very next day finds him again at Sunday School and Church service: "M. V. Smith of Belton preached. 'Twas the best sermon I ever heard." More protracted meetings ensued and by November 15, Smith calculated that "some 54 have joined the Church so far." On November 24, Smith apologizes for being "late to SS," but at least "G. W. Baines preached at 11 and Rev Green preached at night. After five weeks, members joined now 59."

If any one month brought James and his Salado to the forefront as a true civilized community, it was December, 1878, and, in particular, the Christmas holidays. Farm, Church, and social life coalesced in a series of diary entries separated only by dates. Misfortune marred the opening of the holiday season because young Smith states ruefully on the 13th: "Lost a five dollar bill (out of my pocket)." That amount in 1878 was equivalent to the sale of 50 pounds of cotton! The next day was cold and clear and Smith boldly states: "A fine day for killing hogs." This ritual is noted four other times in diary entries during the year. December 15 marked a new event in the life of the newly constructed Baptist Church: "'Twas decided to have a Christmas tree. A committee of arrangements was appointed. Twelve in number, myself one of them." The very next day he went to Belton and bought a winter overcoat and cap than he, "Took dinner with Miss Laura. Had a good dinner too." He was back on the farm on the 16th where the entire day was spent outside in the frigid air where Smith bravely "Bored all the post holes [for a new fence] before dark."

Archie Smith went to Belton to escort Pa home for the holidays on the 20th while the next day, "A part of the Brass Band met and played at night." By late on the 22nd, the Christmas tree arrangements were complete, but, ominously, Smith notes that a close friend suffered an injury that he did, however, recover from: "This eve George Caskey was shot accidentally." On Christmas Eve, Smith senior and junior decked the Baptist Church Christmas tree with presents, though Smith admits it was "cold enough to freeze the ears off a brass monkey." Nonetheless, there was a "full house" at the event and Smith and his close friend, Wesley Ray, "were the ones to get things off the tree." For the young farmer it was back to chores on December 27 as he began a set of repairs to the smoke house; still, he had free time in the evening to entertain Miss Laura who had come down from Belton. Two days later there were "Children's meetings, speeches, and essays read" after "Rev. M. V. Smith preached the Dedication Sermon at the Baptist Church."

At the end of his diary, Smith includes several copied poems about such topics as maidens who have never been kissed and misers who cheat everyone. These lyrics are mostly laced with typical Victorian sentiment. However, such additions were characteristic of educated life where students kept adages, songs, and sayings in the form of a commonplace book. These late entries support the contention that Smith's next two years in Salado were diametrically opposed to the farmer's almanac of 1878. In January, 1880 Smith was enrolled at Salado College and had undertaken a variety of intellectual pursuits.

The entries Smith writes spanning January 1 through June carefully delineate the studies he pursued. After noting a two-week hiatus for the Christmas holidays of 1879, on January 8 he writes: "Went to School. My studies at present are English Grammar, Mental Philosophy, Geometry and Bookkeeping. Spell in both Dictionary and Spelling Book." One might take pause at the latter two entries and wonder why a young man on the verge of his 20th birthday would be studying spelling and highlighting the spelling matches that occupy many of the diary entries that spring semester. The answer is that Salado College was many things to many people. Originally, the College provided a preparatory school curriculum, something James Lowry Smith, Sr., would be an expert on based on his four years' expertise running Baylor Preparatory School in the late 1850s. Not until the 1870s did Salado College begin a true collegiate course of study.[26] The allure of Salado College was that it provided the rudiments of a classical education that permeated all levels of the curriculum.[27] Thus, courses of study were keyed to the needs of individual students and Spelling and Grammar could be studied by Archie Smith who wanted to remain a farmer or mixed with more advanced subjects such as Mental Philosophy in James' case. In fact, Mr. Jimmie was a model student who could "spell down" the competition on numerous occasions. Only late in the term did he finally err or—in his own deliberately humorous reflection on his own abilities: "Mist a word in Sp today. First time in a long time" (Apr 12).

Above and beyond the listing of academic subjects, young Smith takes careful note of his competition. On February 23 he writes: "Started University Algebra. Those in the class are Archie, Ed Guthrie, Bea Rose, Sallie and Emma Barton, and myself." Jimmie defeats all comers, including the vaunted Sallie Rose, in a spelling competition on May 19, though he admits that the study of "Natural Philosophy" [Science] "commenced" on May 5 is more challenging than he anticipated. He had better luck with Trigonometry where "he worked all the examples for the first time" (Apr 5) and with Surveying, an elective initiated on May 14, because his theoretical study was re-enforced by his work on the family farm. The subject that most caught his interest, however, was the Bookkeeping where he successfully "posted my books again" on January 24 and on several succeeding occasions. Indeed pursuit of this very subject would stand young Mr. Jimmie in good stead for the career path he eventually chose.

In its early days, Salado College had strict rules about the interactions of young men and women. In fact, years later Helen Rose Mackey recalled: "We were in our own places in time to answer roll at 8 o'clock. We were not allowed to talk to the boys from the time school commenced in September till the Christmas holidays."[28] Evidently, the rules had relaxed considerably by 1880 because Mr. Jimmie mentions the co-ed classes frequently, engages in spirited classroom discussions with young women from the Rose and Barton families, and even escorts several different young ladies to evening lectures at the College. In fact, based on Smith's diary entries for 1880, it would seem that College Hill was the hub of an extended wheel that had spokes in many different directions. James reports going to the College in late 1878 for a "calisthenics exhibition" (Nov 2). Get-togethers with the Salado Cornet Brass Band occur regularly over a four-year period from 1878-1882. Young Smith was the instigator in erecting a "gymnasium pole" on the campus for physical fitness training (Apr 3, 1880) On two different occasions during the same time period, the adventurous Smith attended a meeting of "The Spiritualists" at the Williams house near College Hill (Mar 28 and Apr 4). On April 30, Smith took time off to attend the trial of outlaw John Bonner which resulted in a hung jury. And in the meantime, he was in charge of counting Sunday School attendance at the Baptist Church, reporting, for example, that 141 of 173 attended on the first Sunday in April.

In the midst of James' busy academic and social life in early 1880, a family tragedy occurred—the death of the youngest Smith sibling, the infant McHenry Smith just before he was to reach 18 months—after a series of harrowing events stretching over a two-week period of late February and early March. The first mention of McHenry occurs on February 5 where Smith simply records: "McHenry is very sick; been so for two weeks." Almost daily updates follow. What is most indicative is the attentiveness of key members of the Salado community. For example, the following day Smith notes: "Dr. Barton stayed all night," followed by Mrs. Barton the next night. On February 22, Dr. and Mrs. Barton visited again. He "came into the room and had us sing 'Shall we meet beyond the river.'" McHenry was diagnosed with pneumonia and during the next week displayed an up-and-down battle with his illness. For example, on the 23rd Dr. Barton was sent for again because McHenry was thought to be dying but he "recovered a little." A Mrs. Tomison and Barton sat up all night on the 24th. Four women joined Mrs. Smith the following night and two more on March 1 as McHenry seemed to rally.

Professor Smith, obviously distressed, "dismissed school for the rest of the week on McHenry's account" on March 2 because the pneumonia was complicated by "meningitis of the brain." Despite the continuing crisis, daily life had to go on in a town where chores needed to be accomplished, including planting the spring garden of beets, cabbage, and beans and young Smith himself joined the Grange the same week. In the meantime, Helen Rose spent a night at McHenry's bedside, as did several other unnamed women. During the next five days, things deteriorated and McHenry died "at half past four" in the afternoon of March 7. At his deathbed in the final hours were at least seven people, including Archie, James, and Addie and Sallie Barton. McHenry was buried the afternoon of the following day.[29]

The family with the closest association with the Smiths—given the repetitions of encounters—was that of Welborn Barton, M.D. The 1880 diary (with the vast majority of entries confined to the first five months), Mr. Jimmie visited or escorted Miss Sallie Barton some 15 times. Most of the occasions involved "carrying" Sallie to preaching on Sunday night, though In January alone, Jimmie took the apparent apple of his eye to a party at Judge Tyler's (Jan 10), to an evening meeting "up at Maj. Rose's" (Jan 18), and on a night when the "moon shown bright as day" he admits he "lingered at the gate of the Barton home" (Jan 27).

Spring brought even further adventures such as a get-together at Capt. Barbee's with Miss Sallie in tow (Apr 10), a "picnic" along Salado Creek (Apr 21), and this humorously understated encounter at a Leap Year party at Major Bostick's: "Miss Sallie offered her attentions which were received" (Apr 23). Equally noteworthy is James' frequent mention of Dr. Barton's son, Bob, several years Jimmie's senior, but whose comings and goings are tracked in the diary entries. He notes when Bob left for medical school in Louisville to follow in his father's footsteps (Sep 1, 1878) and when he returned to Salado "by stagecoach" (Feb 28, 1880), and how the two spent a long evening eating hard-boiled eggs and engaged in conversation about Bell County medicine (Mar 3 and Apr 8, 1880). The premier social event of 1880 Salado marks the final entry in Smith's diary volume: he and Sallie were two of the eight "waiters" at Bob's marriage to Sallie Hamblin on October 6, 1880.

Whatever Salado was in the last quarter of the nineteenth century, it was most certainly a place that encouraged the exploration of different options. On May 9, 1880 Smith notes in his diary that Major Penn was scheduled to preach the dedication sermon at the Baptist Church in Georgetown, but that a sudden illness prevented him from doing so even though Bob, Sallie, and others had traveled to that city for the event.

William Evander Penn was the Billy Graham of late nineteenth-century Texas: an itinerant evangelist, hymn writer, and preacher who made converts wherever he traveled.[30] One of the last entries in Smith's diary dates from August 20, 1880. He writes simply: "Went with Archie, Eddie and Richard Ray to Maj. Penn's camp meeting near Moffet," located north of Temple. One week later, Smith returned and notes on August 30: "Two hundred and seventy-two conversions." This nearly week-long encounter with Evangelist Penn would not be the final meeting between the dedicated young Baptist and Penn. Five years later Penn would reappear in Colorado City, TX on another missionary trip.

Smith, who had received the keys to the Salado Baptist Church because he had been chosen as bell-ringer soon after the Church had opened, has other church-related anecdotes in his diary entries. On September 1, 1878 Smith had noted that a "Parson Bush" admonished the congregation about irresolute game-playing and considered it an "unpardonable sin to play croquet." Such a stricture seems severe, even for the late nineteenth century, but then again maybe the Baptist preacher was a prophet because on May 8, 1880 Smith notes that Miss Lizzie Black "is very sick--caused from a knock received on her head from a croquet ball" at a picnic some 10 days previous. Fortunately for all concerned, she did recover. One can only wonder that the "shooting matches" that Jimmie mentions engaging in during the winter of early 1878 were somehow much safer!

Smith's autograph album records additional significant events in his life during 1881 and 1882, his final two years in Salado.[31] In fact, the 24 individual entries in Smith's album encapsulate the best in the way of civilized advice from his peers and elders. Smith prefaces his album with his own lead-in comment inviting "those of my friends" who wish to "write a line" and thereby cause "fond Memory to revert" to the pleasures of such an enterprise are welcome to do so. Smith concludes with an echo from Hamlet's most famous soliloquy whereby such inscriptions will endure when he and they "have laid off this mortal coil." Smith's own entry is dated Mar 9, 1882.

Mr. W. J. Caskey, the Baptist Church's Sunday School superintendent urged Jimmie to always pursue Christian principles (Jan 20, 1882). T. R. Russell inscribed a long tribute entitled "To My Old Grange Friend" on the same date. An 1880 Salado College graduate, Kate Crawford, saluted Mr. Jimmie on Christmas Day, 1881: "Glory to God in the highest." It only seems fair that since Jimmie signed Sallie Barton's autograph album in

April, 1880 that she would return the favor in the most extensive inscription of the dozen or so female entries that dot the album. She addresses her words to "Mr. Jimmie" and writes, she hopes, "with a burning pen," so that he will always recall the three theological virtues of hope, faith, and love:

> Have Love, NOT love alone for self,
> But man as men thy brothers all
> And scatter, like the circling sun,
> Thy character on all.
> Your Friend
> Dec 29th/1881   Sallie Barton

If any one thought in the album proved to be prophetic of Smith's later life, it was this sentiment of his then closest female friend. Smith's mother, Julia, begins her May 17, 1882 entry with the words "Jimmie, My Dear Boy, Tomorrow you leave us to take up your abode among strangers for a time." The time only amounted to two or three months as Smith went to the Island Business College, Galveston, to study Bookkeeping, knowing apparently that a job loomed in West Texas later in 1882. Fifteen separate circles surround the individual signatures of the Salado Cornet Band of May 22, 1882. Upon his return from Galveston, the Smith family threw a going-away party for their 22-year-old son. Several belles wrote in the album that they hoped his path would be strewn with roses and two of them were sad at his imminent departure: "Tomorrow you will bid our village and your school mates adieu" (Beatrice Rose, Aug 24) and "May your friends in the future be as many as those you leave tomorrow" (Lorinne Tyler, Aug 24). The final inscription, written on August 25, is by his older brother who would remain in Salado as a farmer while the adventurous Jimmie headed for the unknown West Texas town of then Colorado. Thus closed the Salado chapter in Smith's life, except for occasional future visits.

From the diary entries and autograph album, it is patently clear that Mr. Jimmie had carefully weighed the options for his future. He didn't want to be a lifelong farmer and, having witnessed his father's commutes via horseback to Belton in 1878 and his struggles to keep Salado College intact, he didn't want to be a teacher either. Instead, he opted for the business world.

Salado Cornet Band

Dear Brother,
Let kindness and honesty
be your guide.
Prosperity and Happiness
will be your reward.
W. A. Smith
Aug 25th 1882

J. L. Smith Autograph Alburm inscription by Archie Smith

Despite all of Jimmie's diary entries, the precise location of the Smith family home has been difficult to determine. According to old Salado historians, the Smith home was very close to the College. Felda Davis Shanklin recalls, "I well remember their Salado home on Smith Branch east of the College."[32] Another Salado historian, E. M. Hutchens, refers to the Smith home as "the hut of Eumaus," recalling the humble servant of Odysseus.[33] In his diary, Smith several times alludes to 'going up to Maj. Rose's home.' Thanks to MaryBelle Brown, the exact location of the Smith home has recently been pinpointed:

> Professor Smith purchased two lots from the town of Salado in 1865. These were Lots 11 and 12 shown on the original map of the town. Lot 11 lies east of College Block on Front Street. Lot 12 lies due north of Lot 11 across Front Street. The Smith's home was erected on Lot 12. A building housing a school for young children, too young to attend the College, was erected on the other lot.[34]

Indeed, thanks to Christine Smith Andrews' searching through the papers of Jimmie's sister, Roxalee Smith Andrews, extant property tax receipts from 1865, 1869, 1870, and 1872 confirm MaryBelle's findings.[35] As noted earlier, many of the early Salado homesteads still stand today as historical artifacts. However, there is not in Salado a finer monument than a simple granite obelisk tucked in an unobtrusive plot in the Salado Cemetery. The tombstone is that of Smith senior who died unexpectedly within six months of his son's departure. The words etched in the granite read:

James L. Smith

was eleven yrs.

President of Salado

College

Born in N.C.

A.D. 1827

Died

Jan 10, 1883

The memory of the just

Smells sweet and blossoms

in the dust

THIS MONUMENT IS THE OFFERING OF GRATEFUL AND SORROWING STUDENTS A SLIGHT TOKEN OF THEIR APPRECIATION OF THE MEMORY OF ONE WHO IN ALL THE BEAUTIES OF LIFE, WHETHER AS <u>CITIZEN</u>, PARENT, TEACHER OR FRIEND BEAUTIFULLY ILLUSTRATED IN HIS UNOBTRUSIVE CAREER ALL THE TRAITS OF THE CHRISTIAN GENTLEMAN AND SCHOLAR AND WHOSE INDIVIDUAL ANNALS WERE AN EPITOME OF THOSE BLESSED HUMANITIES OF LIFE, VURTUE, HONOR AND TRUTH

Chapter 2

Horn Lake, MS and Winchester, TN
1864-1884

Mary Motheral Bynum, the third oldest of seven Bynum children, was born on March 7, 1864 in Horn Lake, MS, a farming community a dozen miles south of Memphis, TN. Her mother, Katherine Walker Bynum, was the second wife of William Joseph Bynum, a bottom lands cotton farmer and frequent sheriff of DeSoto County, MS. Joe Billy, as the locals referred to him, had lost his first wife and infant son two years after their 1855 marriage.

Katherine Anne Walker was a local girl. How she and Joe Billy met and courted is unknown, but they were married "at 9:30 a.m., Sept 21, 1859, by the Rev. Samuel Cowan."[1] After the start of the Civil War, William Joseph Bynum signed on as a Private with Nathan Bedford Forrest's Company A, 7th Tennessee Cavalry on September 9, 1862. At the Battle of Byhalia, he received a gunshot wound to his right arm which produced a fracture of the humorous joint just above the elbow rendering the arm useless. Consequently, much to his dismay, he was declared incapable of further service and received an honorable discharge on July 23, 1863.[2] So severe was the pain that Bynum was continually administered morphine and became addicted. However, his nephew, Dr. D. W. Bynum, a University of Pennsylvania Medical School graduate, came to his aid and helped his uncle recover from the dependency.[3] Such a gesture was true and literal 'reconstruction' of southern wounds, though Joe Billy would be hampered by the injured arm for the remainder of his life.

The one item the Bynum parents were most attentive to was the education of their children, particularly Mary and her older brother by two years, William "Buddy" Bynum. Sometime in early 1879 Mary was

Marie and W. J. Bynum, Jr., ca. 1867

enrolled at Mary Sharp College in Winchester, TN. This woman's college would later be referred to as the "Vassar of the South" even though Vassar was actually founded 10 years after Mary Sharp.[4] This college, located some 60 miles east of Chattanooga, had been founded by two ministers from Vermont. The keystone was Rev. Z. C. Graves who was president of Mary Sharp from its founding in 1850 until its demise shortly after the Financial Panic of 1893.[5]

So, just before her 15th birthday, Mary boarded the Mississippi & Tennessee RR north to Memphis, then transferred to the Memphis and Charleston RR to Winchester. At Mary Sharp the youthful Mary soon learned that in addition to music and art, she would be required to study algebra, Greek, and Latin. Hence, the college was far from being a mere finishing school for post-Reconstruction southern women. In fact, it was named for Mrs. Mary Sharp, widow of a wealthy planter, who made a large bequest to the college, specifying a rigid curriculum as a requirement for the bequest's acceptance.[6] And sure enough, Mary struggled initially. Among the dozen or so preserved letters written to her by her parents is an early one expressing concern about her difficulty with mathematics: "I am sorry to hear you are not getting along with your algebra," wrote her "Paper" in October, 1879, "as it is a very important study. Will write to Dr. Graves as you suggested." Her father then admonishes his daughter gently about "avoiding too much pranking & foolishness with your class mates." Finally, he adds a P.S.: "I write tonight to Dr. Graves and will ask him to see Prof. Barrett about your algebra lesson."[7] Evidently, the solution worked because Professor Barrett eventually signed Marie's autograph album with a cheerful, though undated, personal note.

Probably the first letter sent to Mary in Winchester was a hand-delivered one of mother to daughter sent via a class mate, simply named Lizzie. In the packet, Mary's mother encloses "a calico shirt, an undershirt corset, 3 pocket-handkerchiefs, and two dollars for your pocket."[8] However, her motherly concern, as shall be seen below, also addressed Mary's academics since Katherine Bynum and President Graves' wife, Ardelia, exchanged several letters during Mary's stay at Mary Sharp because Mary manifested what Ardelia Graves referred to on several occasions as your daughter Mary's "noble spirit." Indeed, with the exception of three extant letters Mary herself wrote (two to her older brother and one to her parents, all in 1881), the primary sources are uniformly all contemporary letters written to Mary or about Mary or several letters to Mary's school mates where

Mary is mentioned and, somehow, acquired the letters from those friends.

The term 'headstrong' is probably a more apt word for what Mrs. Graves meant by Mary's manifestations of 'noble spirit.' One family story handed down is that Mary Bynum, at some point, decided to change her first name to the more elegant-sounding one of Marie and that she contemplated switching her religious affiliation from Presbyterian to Episcopalian because of the nearby attraction of male-oriented University of the South in Sewanee. Reportedly, Mrs. Bynum cautioned her spirited offspring, 'You can change your name to Marie, but you may not change your religion.' Partial proof of this anecdote resides in the margins of Mary's still-extant *Goodwin's Greek Grammar* and *Bingham's Latin Grammar* textbooks where her practiced Spencerian hand writes 'Marie Motheral Bynum' as marginalia some 14 times.

Another indicator of Marie's independent spirit is her autograph album where a variety of friends and faculty were invited to provide a message or inscription. In many ways, this album is a mirror image of Mr. Jimmie's Salado album. At least four of the entries from Mary Sharp students are those of women two or three years older than Marie. One particular inscription, that of 1879 graduate Ada E. Weber, of Cleveland, OH, reads:

> Dear "Max,"
> Although we have been together only about five short months, Yet in that time I have come to regard you as one of my <u>truest</u> friends. And now, as we are about to separate, allow me to wish for you a <u>true</u> and noble womans [sic] life. Do not only <u>dream</u> noble things but do them. Let that be the motto to guide you through life.

Marie Bynum, barely 15 at the time, had little idea how prophetic Ada's advice would prove to be. Her mother, Kate, was always encouraging her daughter during her years at Mary Sharp and wanted Marie "to have as good a chance as the boys" for an education because "Paper says you are the smartest child."[9]

In the interim, however, Marie fought to find herself at Mary Sharp. Advice was constantly forthcoming from another Mary Sharp graduate, Lucie Bennett who completed degree requirements in January, 1880, and had returned to her family home in Courtland, MS, some 50 miles south of Horn Lake. In some 16 letters written to Marie over a 15-month period between Feb 1880 and Mar 1881, Lucie was a veritable whirlwind of admonition: "I am so glad you are learning to love Dr. and Mrs. Graves. …You must abandon your willfulness and abide by her guidance."[10] Aside from occasional reminders to Marie about her obligations to study, however, the letters of Lucie Bennett uniformly display a disparaging tone and cruel ability to chastise Marie about insignificant matters. Several examples will suffice to reveal Lucie as the spoiled southern belle. While Marie was at home from Mary Sharp in the summer of 1880, she had received an invitation from Lucie "to come to a croquet party I have gotten up for you." When Marie was unable to attend because of family obligations, Lucie "sat down and had a big cry." However, Lucie consoled herself, bragging to Marie that "Papa and Mama have bought me an elephant piano and I don't practice any scarcely."[11]

Later the same fall, she wrote to Marie at Mary Sharp: "I have taken morphine for the first time in my life for the pain of measles" and, reviving almost immediately, she received as a reward "my own new room added on to our house by my parents." Then, in a fit of indignation, concludes the letter by telling Marie: "I am not at all satisfied with my new room."[12] In December, smitten with Marie's first cousin, John Walker, a student at Vanderbilt and from Colorado City, TX, where he lived with his mother and stepfather, Lucie wrote: "I would not like to live in Texas but would do so for as valuable a prize as he."[13] When Walker did not return her affections, Bennett grew testy and predicted to Marie that "The end of the world will come in 1881."[14]

While the petulant Lucie pined for Marie's non-attentive cousin, Marie herself was not without male admirers at Mary Sharp. Marie's classmate at the school, one Etta Moore, received a letter from her older brother, J.M. Moore, a law student in Lebanon, TN, in spring 1880: "…tell Marie I think of her often and dream frequently of entering" Mary Sharp College "for one kind, fair draught of her charming smile."[15] In fact, an earlier letter from Mr. Moore to his sister had shown he was particularly fond of good-looking Mary Sharp women.[16] Another correspondent of Marie's, a Miss Mattie Morgan, was a student at Wesleyan Female College in Macon, GA. In the fall of 1879 she had written that she regretted she did not go to Mary Sharp so she and "my old Maria could be homesick together."[17] The next semester she wrote, hoping she might meet up with Marie at the Peabody Hotel in Memphis in late June so that they could take the same train home with her to Horn Lake. She then summarizes the marriages of

Marie Mothereal Bynum at 16

several girlfriends and mentions how some neighboring college boys one night climbed a tree and "mewed like cats and it frightened the girls nearly to death." She concludes with the fervent hope that boys will woo her and Marie, but not in such a crude fashion.[18]

Marie, also unlike her privileged correspondent, Lucie Bennett, was counting pennies. Her father managed an occasional $5 in pin money, but a piano purchase was out of the question, particularly when the Sheriff of De Soto County had four other children still living at home. Even several surviving tuition receipts reveal a father's notation of 'money to follow' to complete payments. By modern standards, a total of $60 per term for tuition seems insignificant, but when one figures in the value of the dollar in 1880—and considers that board and room, travel, books, clothing, must likewise be added in--then the sum placed a demand on her family's limited income.[19] Marie's situation was soon compounded by the fact that her older brother was sent to the Agricultural and Mechanical College of Mississippi [Mississippi State University today] in early 1881 and had to work in the dairy barns to supplement his room and board.[20]

Marie's most frequent correspondent was her father. In late December 1879, he sent his daughter "Forty dollars" for board with "six dollars & 25 cents left over which I send you for a Christmas present "since "it will be your first Christmas you have ever spent from home."[21] Two months later, he sent two money orders totaling $75 for tuition and board and praised Marie's progress expressing "what great and fond desire your loving Father has to see his bright daughter Mary graduate with Honors & a first class college education."[22] When Marie was about to leave Mary Sharp that June, a caring father stated: "Your mother says pack up your clothes in time & not wait until you get ready to start" because you will forget something. In the meantime, he went on to say, "We are all in hope you will stand a good Examination."[23] And, always the encourager, Joe Billy considered himself blessed with her steady progress at Mary Sharp: "Daughter, I will say you are a faster learner and a better girl than most any daughter."[24]

Equally solicitous of Marie was the president's wife and college treasurer, Ardelia Graves, who faithfully acknowledged each postal order for her tuition and other expenses. Her comments on Marie over a two-year period bear witness to a young woman with enormous potential who, despite her tendencies toward stubbornness, is destined to become a "good student" because she continually manifests "a sunny and cheerful disposition."[25] A year later, Ardelia thanked the Bynum parents for the prompt rendering of tuition sent for the next term and stated, "Miss Marie wins golden opinions this session" and at long last seemed to be embracing the school's "rules & regulations."[26] Indeed, Mrs. Graves re-enforces her own considered opinion of Miss Bynum when she commented that Marie "has much less of that imperious and commanding manner that she had one year ago."[27] So much so that, by May, Mrs. Graves admitted having developed a "precious relationship" with Marie and completed the letter of mother to mother with a summary of Marie's official expenses.[28]

Mr W. J. Bynum

To Mary Sharp College, Dr.,

(The Session ending June, 1884.)

For Tuition of _Danytha Miss Marie_

| 5 | Months in Literary Department, | - - - - - | $30.00 |
| 1 | " " Musical Department, | - - - - - | 30.00 |

Amount, - - - - - $30.00

Cr. By Cash, _Sept 8th_, 18___,

Balance Due, - - - $3000

Received Payment in full $30.00

Mrs. A. C. Graves

Winchester, Tenn., _Nov 16_, 1886.

Treasurer.

Mary Sharp College tuition receipt, June, 1880

Indeed, Marie's own correspondence to her brother who was newly enrolled at A&M in Mississippi confirms her becoming a more adept and settled woman and capable of rendering sisterly advice: "I am very much pleased that it is a military school but I fear if you spend all the afternoon drilling and working that you will accomplish very little in your classes." In the meantime, she adds, "I will not go home next summer. I am going to graduate next summer a year and I will have to study and read all summer so I can make a respectable graduate" so that "my big Bud" will not be ashamed of his "little Sis."[29] In March, she stated that "I am expecting to take the measles every day. It is raging in the Normal School and the Drs. say we will have it." She concludes by asking Bud to send a picture of himself in uniform along with "an excuse" as to why he hasn't already done so.[30]

Interestingly, her younger brother Ben, born in 1869, frequently answered letters from his big sister by appending paragraphs to letters to Marie written by her parents. Marie evidently did fall prey to measles because Ben notes in April that "we got your letter today and you said you had the measles. I am sorry."[31] Ben also updated his sister on family news and queries. Older brother Wade had "four pigeons but lost one," but "I did get to go on a Buggy ride with Wade."[32] The following January, Ben wonders if Marie ever received the "sweetgum balls" he had recently sent and reports that "Uncle Matt," a state representative, is off to the legislative session in Jackson.[33]

In the best Bynum tradition, Marie always re-gathered herself from adversity and plunged anew into her studies and other related activities. She helped organize and run a gala presentation which had become an annual tradition at Mary Sharp. The *Argonauts Review*, based on the Jason and the Argonauts theme, included a ship that was erected on stage, under the artistic direction of faculty member Edwin Gardner and under the music direction of another faculty member, C. C. Guilford. On the program for the December 23, 1881 production was the "piano for 4 hands of Rossini's William Tell Overture," a vocal duet, a chorus and solo rendition of Guilford's own original composition entitled "Barbara," and Miss Marie Bynum's rendition of an Artemus Ward lecture, plus other poetic, solo, and literary recitations, concluding with an original score, "The Argonauts of 1882," also from the hand of Professor Guilford. The concluding four lines of lyrics are:

> This, Argoes vainly erst have sought;
> But we, with such a crew,

> Can seize the fleece and bear it home
> On ship of eighty-two.[34]

A review of the actual production credits "Prof. Edwin M. Gardner in his realistic delineation of the rich and quaintly ornamented galley Argo, apparently just coming to anchor in a land-locked harbor." Praise also accrued for all the Mary Sharp young "Argonauts," but especially for "Miss Marie Bynum's presentation of Ward's comicalities [which] was so well read that she was frequently interrupted by uncontrollable bursts of laughter from the audience, who applauded her to the echo."[35] So successful was this original review that musical director Guilford "gave the Argonauts a reception Saturday night." He even, as Marie puts it, "sent carriages around for us."[36]

Interestingly enough, both Guilford and Gardner had recently made additions to Marie's autograph album. Guilford had penned on Dec 21, 1881: "The darkest sloppiest day, if garmented in the light of your beauty will seem a symphonic poem." Gardner, later to become a southern newspaper illustrator of some note, had done an original drawing in the album on May 26, 1881.

The Christmas pageant kept Marie in Winchester for the holidays, but her Bynum parents did not neglect her. They had prepared a special "box" of smoked turkey, two fruit cakes, jelly, cocoanut cake, ham, chicken, and peaches and dispatched them to Mary Sharp.[37] As Marie wrote back, "The first thing I did when I reached my room today was to break in my box, but you had it fixed so nicely and securely, that it required the strength of all the room to get it open with a poker."[38] She then added a truly heartwarming note of thanks: "I have the best Papa and Mama of any girl. They are not rich and able to give me a number of costly presents, but what is infinitely more valuable to me—great love, and numberless little acts that tell how a daughter is thought of."

Soon after the new year, "Paper" Bynum sent his longest letter of the seven that have survived. It was filled with news from the Christmas dinner with Uncle Matt also present. He also wonders if Marie received the special bottle of cologne sent by four-year-old Sally, the youngest Bynum child. There is even a lengthy account of the escape of four prisoners from the Hernando Jail and their recapture six days later during a shoot-out on the Arkansas side of the Mississippi River where the Memphis Police Chief shot and killed a gang leader. Father Bynum concludes on what would

M. M. Bynum Autograph Album original drawing by her Art professor, Edwin M. Gardner

prove to be an ominous note, stating that he has just received a short note from Buddy at A&M in Starkville, but adds "we had become uneasy about him being silent for so long."[39]

Evidently, many of the letters from Marie's Mary Sharp years were undoubtedly filled with precautions about proper health care and recoveries from illnesses because the family members in Horn Lake constantly inquire about her well-being and share their own news of injuries and maladies. The family mare, Fanny, was obviously a recalcitrant horse because it once pulled back suddenly from Joe Billy, pulling his finger and dislocating it. Lucie Bennett, was a true hypochondriac, complaining ad nauseam about her coughs, headaches, rheums, insomnia, skin infections, and such. By contrast, Mrs. Graves only alerts the Bynum family when a serious medical problem occurs, such as the measles outbreak that affected all the young women boarding with the Graves.

The measles epidemic had caused the greatest problems to Marie's cousin, John Walker, who had to temporarily withdraw from Vanderbilt because the disease had severely affected his eyesight. He had returned to Colorado City to clerk for his stepfather, A. W. Dunn, a well-to-do stockmen's outfitter who had married Walker's widowed mother, Caledonia Pruit Walker, some years earlier. Caledonia's first husband, Lt. John Walker, was Katherine Walker Bynum's brother who had died at the Battle of Antietam on September 15, 1862, never having seen his infant son born July 6, 1862. In any event, Walker wrote to Buddy in August 1881, reporting that "he could write an hour or so without injury to my eyes." He doubted, however, he would ever return to Vanderbilt and might just have to continue clerking for Dunn because John "was pleased with this Texas country. The T & P RR will be completed to El Paso by Nov 1st. Over two miles of track is being laid per day. The entire state is in a whirl of railroad excitement."[40]

By contrast, young Buddy experienced "military discipline" and uniforms. He cites "12 boys who raised a fuss" at A&M and that "the Lieut. is holding courts martial" regarding the incident. He concludes by sending a brother's love to Marie at Mary Sharp.[41] Just before Christmas, Buddy wrote again to his sister stating he hopes his "Co. A" will win the "drill competition" because the winners will receive "a big Christmas dinner & flags to the fortunate company."[42]

Once again, however, come the new year, William Joseph Bynum, Sr. was a concerned father. He wrote his eldest son: "I am very sorry and uneasy to hear you were sick & had been in bed for four days." Bynum had just sent his son "eleven dollars" to supplement his sparse income from working on the A&M farm. He warned Buddy: "You must be very prudent & take good care of yourself [during] this bad weather, else you will relapse." The father continues with feeling distraught because "we have not heard from Sisy [Marie's nickname] this week" and fears that she, also, may be ill. He further urges his son to "write to her regular" and that he must conclude his letter because "Mother has a severe cold though she refuses to be confined to bed."[43]

In February 1882, John Walker wrote to Buddy again with regaling stories about a "wedding and a ball" during Christmas week in Colorado City and Walker wonders whether he will recover from "so many balls, sociables, dinings, etc. in our little town." Then, in a genuine gesture of bravado, Walker invites Buddy to "Come ahead to Texas to visit us" next summer. "You will do well to get near enough buffalo to kill them with your drill gun, much less your bayonet." In this "strictly prairie country, you and I will go out to Mr. Dunn's ranch [in Midland]" and "ride pitching ponies, rope cows." In fact, Walker concludes, "Think you can learn on such a trip such good initiating ceremonies for your green agricultural students."[44]

Unfortunately, Buddy never read John Walker's letter because he had died suddenly at A&M on January 26. One would think that such a tragic event would put William Joseph Bynum into a fit of despair. Instead, he has exchanged telegrams with Mrs. Graves at Mary Sharp: his informing her of Buddy's death and hers informing him that Marie is stricken with mumps. The day after his son's death, Father Bynum wrote the Mary Sharp treasurer a long instructional letter stating that his "son's body will reach here tomorrow morning & be buried in our family burial ground at Bethlehem Church. If you please, send me a postal every day & let me know how Daughter is getting along & should she get worse, telegraph me at once." He wants Mrs. Graves to console Marie about "the death of her Buddie," and even though Marie's mother is anxious for her to come back to Horn Lake, the father is reluctant to see his daughter abandon her studies. Mrs. Graves, in a letter dated the same day, expresses deep sympathy and goes on to state, "I have lost two children, a grown daughter and a son and well do I realize what such a calamity is in all its height and depth." Mrs. Graves adds that she has called upon her own family physician on the "third day" of Marie's bout with mumps, adding that she will telegraph when it is advisable for Marie to travel.

In an undated letter, Marie's aunt, Mary Peebles, consoled her: "You are now the oldest, and [it] is more necessary than ever that you should be self sustaining." Peebles follows the father Bynum's advice and urges her "not to come now [for] there is too much danger" and that the difficulty of travel is complicated by a "big snow on the ground." Eventually, Marie did return to Horn Lake and she evidently did write to her cousin John in Colorado City informing him of her brother's untimely death because in a March 12, 1882 letter to Marie, John states: "I have the last letter Buddy wrote me, dated Jan 10th, which I shall preserve as one of my most precious relics. Mama sends her most sincere and deepest regrets to Aunt Kate and family."

In a superb personal touch, President S. D. Lee, in the second year of A&M's existence, penned a Resolution to be included in the Faculty Minutes and also sent to William Joseph Bynum, Junior's parents: "Be it Resolved that we the Faculty and Students of the A&M College hereby express our deep sympathy for the parents of the deceased. Be it further Resolved that it is with Great satisfaction we bear testament to his uniform good conduct, modest worth and moral integrity."[45] On March 21, 1882, the late William Joseph Bynum, Junior's room mates shipped to the father "your son's trunk and clothing," and assured him that there were no debts outstanding, but that the room mates would keep the table, chair, and mattress until a later date.[46]

Marie Bynum never returned to Mary Sharp, and further correspondence from the year 1882 is non-existent. What has survived is a Teacher's Certificate from the Mississippi Public Schools dated January 1, 1883. The opening of the certificate reads: "It is hereby certified that Miss Marie Bynum known as a person of good moral character, and having passed a satisfactory examination (entitling her to this First Grade Certificate), is recommended and authorized to teach the branches specified below in any of the Public Schools of De Soto County, for twelve months from this date."[47] As it happened, the teaching credential was extended for several more years as Marie gathered up her first-graders and taught elementary school. Not until October 1884 did Marie take any time off. She was Buddy's surrogate replacement on a trip on the T & P RR to Colorado City where she would soon meet one James Lowry Smith, the head bookkeeper with Dunn's newly named Burns, Walker & Co., Wholesale Stockmen's Outfitters.

Chapter 3

Colorado City
1882-1888

Colorado City[1*], TX, was a robust frontier town in all the usual senses of the phrase. In the heyday of the mid-1880s, there were 28 saloons, numerous bordellos for cowboys and a few for ranch owners, gambling houses, a marshal who died in a saloon, another peace officer who was bushwhacked, and other disturbances. One graphic example is the Lancaster-Cooksey gunfight described by Judge J. H. Looney, one of Colorado City's first justices:

> After a trial in which one Henry Cooksey was heavily fined, and as Fred Lancaster was the constable, also the principle witness and was responsible for his conviction; as Lancaster passed one of the saloons, Cooksey called him in and asked him to take a drink with him. Lancaster says that he believed that Cooksey planned to kill him when he turned his attention to the bar to take the drink, but instead, he kept his gaze upon Cooksey; he says also that Cooksey drew a pistol and he, Lancaster, made a quick move, catching Cooksey's pistol in such manner that when the hammer came down, the flesh part of his hand between the thumb and his finger was between the hammer and the cylinder so that when Cooksey snapped his pistol, the fleshy part of his hand prevented the cartridge from exploding and gave him time to draw his own pistol, and he at once shot Cooksey thru the vital part of his body.[1]

To conclude from such an account that gunplay was an everyday occurrence in the Colorado City of the 1880s would be very misleading.

1 The original name for Colorado City was Colorado until 1939 when it was officially changed to its modern designation. The modern reference is used in my text, but the original "Colorado" is retained in the quoted material.

In fact, prominent merchant and ranch supply owner, Frank Burns, and others emphasize in their late-in-life reminiscences that Colorado City had less lawlessness than most frontier towns.[2] As for gambling, games such as Mexican Monte, roulette, and Faro were confined to parlors set up for that purpose.[3] In any event, Colorado City's main streets were not host to the likes of "High Noon" or "Gunfight at the O. K. Corral." One solid reason was that the sheriff of Mitchell County was the steadfast and able R. C. "Dick" Ware, the former Texas Ranger who probably put a bullet hole in Sam Bass and who, later in life, would be elevated to U. S. marshal.

Colorado City had a sound, civilized basis almost from its very beginnings in 1880 when James Lowry Smith's eventual uncle-in-law and Marie Motheral Bynum's step-uncle, A. W. Dunn, set up a tent-roofed, plank-sided store. His initial foray into Mitchell County merchandizing established him as the "Father of Colorado, Texas." Dunn, Coleman & Co. eventually became Burns, Walker & Co., but the power behind the throne was always A. W. Dunn. He ran the First National Bank, a separate enterprise from Burns, Walker; he served as the town's first postmaster; and he passed judgment on all the company's business dealings even though his name was no longer posted above the store.[4] In the most prominent Burns, Walker Co. letterhead, the name of A. W. Dunn is at the center, flanked by his partner, Frank Burns, and his stepson clerk, John A. Walker, on one side and the names of Zack Williams and rancher J. A. Peacock on the other.[5] Although prominent Colorado City historian Mary C. Jones notes that little is known of the actual stock supplies of early Colorado City merchants, Omar Cline provides an overview in his later history: "Dunn, Coleman and Company were advertising in one ad, under one roof the following: A banking and exchange business; dry goods and groceries; hardware, glassware, and crockery; wood and willow ware; arms and ammunition; and ready made clothing. They were also buying wool, hides, and cattle."[6] A recently recovered feature story from the 1880's Colorado City newspaper, *The Clipper*, provides the reader with a tour of the red-brick Burns, Walker store erected in the early 1880s:

> Accompanied by the handsome and polite business manager, Mr. J. A. Walker, we took a walk through the mammoth establishment of Burns, Walker & Co. this week, and to give respectable write-up of what we there saw would take two or three issues of the Clipper, so we can only attempt to mention a few of the prominent features of

the establishment. The building is 50 x 140 feet, two stories high, and is literally crammed and jammed full of general merchandise, consisting of everything in that line from a cambric needle to an Avery road wagon. The building is finished up in elegant style, with everything artistically arranged in perfect order. The business office is situated in the rear of the dry goods department. Near the centre of the building the book keeper's office and the business manager's office, in separate departments, all nicely carpeted and furnished in the most elegant manner. In addition to this there is a side office where customers had a comfortable and conveniently arranged office, with paper, chairs and everything handy for the transaction of any little private business they may wish to attend to while in the city. Their stock is immense in every department, and Mr. Walker informed us they still had large invoices to arrive. This house carries from $50,000 to $100,000 stock and competes successfully in prices with wholesale and jobbing houses of Fort Worth and Dallas. This is the largest establishment of its kind in the west, and its proprietors are men of high integrity, fine business qualifications, and first-class clever fellows.7

This factual newspaper account is re-enforced by phrases dotting the various letterheads of Burns, Walker stationery which describe the Company as "Agent for the Bain Wagon," "Stockmen's specialty," and "The largest and best-selected stock in North-west Texas."[8] The bookkeeper's central office had a stove in wintertime and a circulating fan in the summertime, indicating a limited amount of electrical power was available. What is more, the detailed pen-and-ink drawing on some of the letterheads reveal a cupola façade marked "Burns, Walker & Company" and, behind the building, several telephone poles are denoted. Among its foremost civilizing influences, Colorado City had an actual telephone exchange which allowed merchants, bankers, law officers, and homemakers to keep in touch with one another.[9] In fact, only larger places like Galveston (1879), Houston (1880), and Dallas (1881) preceded Colorado City in being able to claim a local telephone exchange.[10] A second, even more suggestive civilizing influence was the rapid conversion from tents and lumber structures to brick buildings. Perhaps the most pre-eminent edifice was the three-story Frenkel Opera House across the street at Second and Elm from Burns, Walker and a facility capable of holding 1,500 citizens for various entertainments from concerts to theatrical production.[11]

Colorado City got its name from the river that runs through it and, literally, from the bricks made from its rich red clay. By 1884 several hotels, including the St. James, Pacific House, and Rendrebrook sprang up, as well as the brick facades of bakeries, restaurants, homes, and churches. The population surged from a handful of settlers when A. W. Dunn arrived with his primitive store in 1880 to some 6,000 citizens by 1886.[12]

Several factors contributed to the rapid growth. First, thanks to a federal government that looked the other way, the some eight million buffalo that made an annual round-trip trek from Kansas to South Texas all but disappeared in the massive hunts between 1877 and 1881. Along with the buffalo, the Indians disappeared, particularly the menacing Comanches who depended on the buffalo for survival. Third, the rich prairie grasses consumed by the buffalo were now available to the burgeoning cattle industry. Numerous ranches sprang up from San Angelo west to Midland and eastern New Mexico and north through the Panhandle. Open range, longhorns, and cowboys were the staples of the day. The most significant factor, however, was not the geography, nor the changing ethnic population. It was the railroad, specifically the Texas and Pacific RR which had track completed to Sierra Blanca, Texas, by late 1881 where it hooked up with the Southern Pacific in January 1882.[13] This railroad was the only federally funded railroad in Texas, thanks to the entrepreneurship of the fabled Jay Gould who was its chief 'engineer.' For the first time, the southern United States—and Texas in particular—had a transportation link that fostered enormous growth. Thanks to negotiations and maneuvering on A. W. Dunn's part, the T & P ran parallel to Main Street in Colorado City, assuring that the town would be the focal point for the shipping of cattle to hungry eastern markets.

Dunn's stepson, John Walker, well-acquainted with his Bynum relatives in Horn Lake having visited them on several occasions while at Vanderbilt, was now firmly anchored in his stepfather's mercantile store, soon passing from clerk, to manager, to majority partner. Walker's eyes, still hampered by his bout with measles, were weak, but his mind and resolve were strong. He would soon become a capitalist, a premier merchant, and one of Texas' leading wholesale grocers for the ensuing 60 years.

The everyday eyes of Burns, Walker & Co. belonged to its resident bookkeeper, a salaried employee in his early-to-mid 20s who meticulously recorded each day's individual sales in a huge ledger, who sent out all the bills due to ranchers, and who calculated the expenditures and profits for the entire enterprise. That individual was James Lowry Smith, late of Salado, but by September of 1882 sitting in the "pen" (as he referred to his centrally located office) and entering the receipts handed to him by the "boys" (as he called the sales clerks), including chiefly a Sam Henderson, a Dick Boren, and an Ed Pruit. Young Smith had letterhead stationery which bore his name, but it was far less conspicuous than that of the firm's partners.

How Smith obtained his position is an unanswered question. The only records are the entries in his autograph album from late August 1882 with references to his leaving almost immediately. The lone Colorado City entry is from November 5, 1882:

> Jimmie
>> That your life may be long and happy and your sorrows be but
>> few is the sincerest wish of your true friend
>>> Anna Griffin

A possible link leading to Smith's employment might have been the 1881 visit of his Salado hometown pastor, George Washington Baines, who founded a Baptist mission church in Colorado City, a year before his death in December 1882.[14] Perhaps Baines recalled the First Baptist Church's trusted bell ringer and Sunday School statistician and recommended him to A. W. Dunn. Baines was certainly well aware of young Smith's contributions to the Salado church and community.

Whatever the case, Smith was a mainstay in the mercantile store, earning his $100 per month salary by working most nights until 10 o'clock tracking inventory, credits, and debits.[15] However, the life of a frontier-town bachelor, with his sales sheets and ledgers, was about to take a civilizing change beyond his fondest expectations.

The autograph album of Marie Bynum contains a poem, "To my Daughter," from her father. The closing lines of the opening stanza read:

> Come back on a bright tomorrow
>> And banish the clouds of to-day,
> Come cast off thy burden of sorrow
>> And laugh and be glad while you may.
> You are traveling, 'tis true to the sun's waning light

But look for the stars and forget the dark night.

The final two lines of the second and final stanza, followed by an October 24, 1884 date, are:

'Tis true by the dark flowing stream we must stand
But over its tide is the beautiful land.

No doubt Papa Bynum meant the Mississippi River and his own bottom-land farm outside of Horn Lake. For Marie, however, "traveling" would be to Texas where she would spend the next three months, and the "stars" and "light" would be her exploits—professional and romantic—in Colorado City and its environs.

Marie traveled north to Memphis, then across Arkansas, then to Fort Worth and the T & P RR bound for her uncle's home in the rugged west. Exactly when Marie arrived in Colorado City is unknown, but within a month there occurred a signature event that would herald her achievements in New York and Chicago newspapers. Sometime before Thanksgiving Marie visited Uncle Dunn's thriving ranch near Midland. Not merely satisfied to observe cowboys on quarter horses cutting out cattle, she joined in. The lengthy account of her exploits, entitled "The Cowgirl of the West," was penned by George M. Bailey, the flamboyant editor of *The Graphic* and appeared in the December 21, 1884 Sunday *New York Sun*. One can forgive Bailey's overly dramatic descriptions of "scampering antelope" and cowboys carrying "three or four revolvers" each and wearing "big white sombreros with rattlesnake skins twisted about them" for the heart of the matter, Marie's expert equestrian skills:

She insisted that if she could get a swift pony and a side saddle she would show that she could ride alongside the wildest steer and turn him. …A big brown steer reared up…and started off like a deer. Miss Bynum whirled her pony and started after the animal. She did her work bravely. The cowboys watched her with admiration. Her pony dashed alongside of the steer and the cowboys expected that, as the animal turned, he would catch his horns in her drapery or she would plunge over the pony's head as she turned with the steer. They saw her stop as the steer turned and balance herself like a skilled equestrian, and then head off the steer and turn him back.

Soon she came dashing back alongside the steer and landed him in the bunch that was headed for the pen.

That evening, according to Bailey, the cowboys paused from their evening meal of coffee and "jacked buffalo meat" and agreed among themselves to send Marie a gift in honor of her superb horsemanship. A few days later a gold ring arrived at Dunn's residence bearing the inscription "To Miss Bynum from the Texas cowboys." Aside from Bailey's exaggerated prose and the fact that easterners relished embellished tales of the wild west, the substance of the story is true. In an aside in one of his earlier letters to Marie at Mary Sharp, Papa Bynum had mentioned that only Marie seemed at ease on the spirited family filly named Fannie. Second, the ring episode is no fictitious addendum; the ring exists today as a family heirloom.

Exactly when James Lowry Smith, bookkeeper, met Marie Motheral Bynum, visiting schoolteacher, is not etched in stone. It had to be early to mid November because his first extant letter to her, delivered locally to Mr. Dunn's residence, was dated November 25, 1884 and in it he speaks of being "all alone at the store" and missing her good company.[16] They passed each other love notes (written on Burns, Walker sales slips) in observation/response or question/answer form, usually written in ink on his part and answered by pencil on her part. However, as a series of exchanges reveal, infatuation, even love, was an almost immediate occurrence:

> Him: Now my dear Marie I am sorry my remark caused you such <u>unpleasantness</u>— it was as you first thought, 'twas not meant at all—only a careless word lightly spoken. Have things changed?

> Her: No, it has not changed.

> Him: I wish you would feel towards me as I felt toward you last night when I was writing that letter.

> Her: Has that feeling changed so soon? You can <u>never</u> imagine how <u>I</u> <u>did</u> feel towards you, as I never felt for man before.
>
> (Dec 3, 1884)

Evidently, they managed to convey their feelings by telephone also. Later in their relationship, she would remind him in a letter: "I don't remember exactly when it was, but it 'twas through the telephone that I first called you 'Jimmie' and you called me 'Marie,' too." In the same letter, she recounts the night in early December: "…that memorable night of Dec 4th when our lips first met" (Mar 11, 1885). Such exchanges are symptomatic of the basis of a relationship that budded and blossomed fully over the next year of courtship correspondence, along with his visits to Horn Lake in May and December. Marie was the more frank of the two, the leader, it would seem, in the evolving relationship. For example, on February 10, 1885 he would admit by letter: "…intellectually, you are my superior. … You have an ambitious disposition—more so than mine."

In the meantime, however, the Christmas season loomed in Colorado City and it was a challenging task for both Marie and Jimmie because they had vowed to keep their attachment—soon to be their engagement—secret, and there were at least two beaux in the town who were suitors for her affection, an attraction garnered by Marie's winning personality and good looks. On December 7, there was a party honoring Marie at the home of A. W. Dunn. George Bailey wrote the next day that "Miss Marie Bynum's vivacity held all the boys in a state of admiration the entire evening" and then in unctuous prose so characteristic of journalist Bailey, he added he had to adjourn "to the emblazoned magnificence of his boudoir [where] angels of peace played about him in his dreams."[17] An unnamed San Antonio newspaper contained another Bailey byline of December 16 wherein are listed the names of all the cowboys (including A. W. Dunn himself) who sent Marie the gold ring as a remembrance of her cowgirl exploits.

The Colorado City chapter of the Knights of Pythia staged a December 19th Ball at the Opera House for all female visitors to the city. Once again, George Bailey singled out the woman he was pursuing, unaware that her love had been placed elsewhere: "Miss Bynum looked queenly in her magnificent gown of gold satin and lace and some of the boys requested us to say that she was the Queen of Hearts."[18] The day before the so-called "Literary Society" of Colorado City had gathered to hear Miss Anna Hammann sing a German version of "The Blind King" and a physician's child recited a poem. However, "the young men took a vote after adjournment" of said gathering "and the palm was awarded to Miss Marie Bynum."[19]

Bailey's public declarations were matched by the privately declared ones of Ivy Burney, the City Attorney for Colorado City. In a December

20 letter he begged Miss Bynum's forgiveness that a prior commitment prevents him from attending to her on a particular day. However, he promises to atone for this deficiency with a Christmas Eve visit to the Dunn residence because "everyone knows that Ivy likes to be with mistletoe and don't you forget it."[20]

Sitting alone in his office with late-night billing and paychecks to be written, James Lowry Smith was a frontier version of Bob Cratchett, though with A. W. Dunn and Frank Burns at the helm, his situation was far better than with a Scrooge or Marley of Dickens' time. The busy young record keeper's façade must have brightened immediately when the "Express man" suddenly delivered a "lovely little bouquet encircled by a horse shoe of arberviter, mistletoe, and berries" from the faithful Marie (JLS to MMB, Dec 23). Reluctant to show his affection publicly, Smith confided his intentions to only one other person, his mother in Salado. He received a reply from her in late December in which she expressed surprise but joy at her son's intentions to get married. She hoped his Marie would make a "good poor man's wife" and trust that her future daughter-in-law will display "economy and I must add industry."[21]

Such virtues were fortunately also inherited by the son because all the 90-plus letters that ensue over the next 14 months display the prudence of James and the forthright planning of Marie.[22] He claims he lacks "the vocabulary to fully express my deep feeling for you" as an eventual lifelong companion (Feb 20). Side by side in many letters is the ritual of quotation-marked baby talk that marked the lighter side of their civilized correspondence. Marie calls Jimmie her "boy" and he refers to her as his "little girl." He inquires if the picture of herself she sent looks "dis" [just] like her; she responds with "doin" [don't] you know it does. In several instances he humorously would like to give her a "whippen'"—not of the sadistic variety, however.

One trait Jimmie constantly displayed was selflessness. When he learned from his mother that his younger brother Robert was manifesting unruly behavior back in Salado, he volunteered to find him a position in Mitchell County that would help him mature once he arrived. Equal to the task of giving advice—a constant in Marie's letters—was her concern about the late working hours of her fiancé at Burns, Walker. She vows on several occasions that once they are married, he will be home each evening by 6, else she will come to the bookkeeper's office and collect him.

Another highly civilized facet of nineteenth-century social life was the personalized calling card each businessman had made up for distribution throughout a given year, starting with the requisite social calls at residences of friends, employers, and employees on New Year's Day. Firecrackers and Roman candles marked Christmas Eve, but festive buffets were a New Year's social requirement.[23] New Year's Day fell on a Thursday in 1885 and a lengthy Colorado City newspaper article highlights a singing group, the Pleiades, composed of "Misses Burney, Earnest, Shepherd, Coleman, and The Graphic" giving performances at residential stops, including the Townsend, Byrne, Swinney, Judge Smith, and Winfield Scott abodes. "Our last call," wrote Bailey in a rare sentence of straightforward prose, "was with A. W. Dunn's. Misses Bessie and Alta Peacock and Misses Marie Bynum and Anna Hammann were the young ladies who received, while Mrs. Dunn presided. Dunn rushed in at the last moment, having just returned from a Chicago business trip."[24]

Marie evidently had her autograph album out for display, judging by the many Colorado City entries, particularly for the first two weeks of January, preceding her departure to visit her uncle, Drew Pruit, in Fort Worth en route back to Horn Lake. Sometime during the morning of January 13, Jimmie dispatched a hurried note to his Marie stating, "You would not think hard or strange of me would you if I should not write in the album?" Marie must have prevailed despite his reluctance because the following rather innocuous message appeared, in stately Spencerian script, signed by J. L. Smith and labeled, almost prophetically Colorado, Texas, Jan'y 13th 1885: "Kindly consider me among those who have been made happy by your visit to our City, and be assured that to do honor to your bright smiles and happy disposition will be the chieftest delight of your friend of friends." Smith also has left a copy of his colored business card from 1885.

It also contains the names of three other Burns, Walker & Co. employees and stands in stark contrast, both in size and ornamentation, to the embossed elephantine elaborateness of his competitor for Marie's affections—none other than George M. Bailey. Likewise, Bailey has signed the autograph album *twice*: once in huge script: "Forever Yours Geo M Bailey Colorado, Texas Jan 1—1885." The second inscription is elaborate both in its poetic extravagance and in the original red pen Bailey used to form an intricate acrostic of his name and Marie's.

To My Cousin:—

Marie, oh may thy life's rich perfume cheer me
May its sweetness compass me forever.
For 'twill bring, if thou art ever near me,
Joy in life which naught but death can sever!
Shine a star of hope thro' clouds of sorrow!
Throbbing hearts will gladly see thy glimmer
And many a darkning day will seek to borrow
From thine eyes a fadeless golden shimmer!
Lend thou unto my heart, thy love, angelic maiden!
Guide thou me to Joy's eternal 'Aidenn'!

Your Cousin

Colorado, Texas, Jany 1st—1885.

M. M. Bynum Autograph Album Inscription by Geo M Bailey

Other inscriptions include those of Colorado City's most prominent physician, P. C. Coleman, who hopes his words will rise up, "The lady of the book to greet."[25] Bailey would eventually depart Colorado City to become a Houston newspaper editor and columnist. So, too, would his chief competitor, Alf Tolar, editor of the most successful Colorado City newspaper, *The Clipper*. Tolar has been cited for his gallant conduct at Gettysburg on July 3, 1863 where he was severely wounded. He was a dentist, businessman, and avid journalist who eventually left Colorado City to found the *Abilene Reporter*. He was later elected a state representative, and in recognition of his diverse contributions, Squaw Lake, Texas, was renamed Tolar in his honor.[26] Of the many civilized men in Colorado City in the mid-1880s, only a few would remain during the city's gradual decline. Dr. Coleman was one such remarkable individual. He fought hard and long to get Texas Technological College located in his beloved town. The winning contingency from Lubbock were so impressed by Coleman's groundwork in bringing a major institution of higher education to West Texas that they designated him as the "Father of Texas Tech."[27] Indeed, the case could easily be made that Colorado City was the proving ground for many Texas men whose renowned service in other parts of the state continued, including the aforementioned Ivy Burney who became one of Fort Worth's leading attorneys.

Miss Marie Bynum's nearly three-month stay in Colorado City was the subject of a *Clipper* article (the only other *Clipper* article of the numerous ones mentioned during the ensuing James Lowry Smith-Marie Motheral Bynum courtship correspondence that has survived). Alf Tolar concludes: "We extend our sympathy to several young gentlemen who seem to be afflicted by the loss of what was perhaps a source of extreme pleasure to them. If Miss Bynum's visit was as pleasant to herself as it was to the friends she made, we know that she will always have pleasant memories of Colorado."[28] In order to keep their blossoming romance a secret, Jimmie resorted to securing P.O. Box 135 in the Colorado City Post Office, stating—with humorous flourish—in a Jan 14, 1885 letter to her in Fort Worth: "So that my letters would not be mixed with the common herd, procured me a box today." Indeed, the lack of return addresses on all their correspondence envelopes generally assured that their budding relationship would remain their business alone.

For the next four months, written correspondence was their only contact. One thing they shared in common was a mutual love of music.

Marie Motheral Bynum, late 1884

In one of his first post-Colorado City-visit letters to Marie, Smith recounts that "Just two months ago tonight at thus very moment I fancy I was to sing the "Milwaukee Fire" but with poor success" (Jan 21). Interestingly, the subtitle of this song is "The Burning of the Newhall House" and it is based on a tragic blaze at the Newhall Hotel in 1883 in which 71 lives were lost, mostly women. For other songs, Smith had requested sheet music from New York City, including "Pretty Pond Lilies" (1884) and "The Rose You Gave Me Long Ago" (1884). In the absence of phonographs, these latest songs were sought often for recitation by the professional bookkeeper and accomplished amateur musician. Smith mentions also a Colorado City men's quintet called the "Jubilee Singers," then writes Marie that he has learned another tragic ballad from 1877 called "The Brooklyn Fire."[29] Not to be outdone, Marie wrote from Fort Worth that she and her Uncle Drew were in a "fashionable box" where they heard a concert by Clara Mannie.[30] Young Smith also learned through Bessie Peacock, John Walker's intended, that Marie was concerned that Jimmie was working too many hours with his account books and did not have any time for the piano. Humorously, Smith counters: "All right, you keep the books and I will go up and sew on buttons, mend my vest, and your dress too" (Feb 1).

At various times in 1885, Smith cited other civilized entertainments that graced the Colorado City scene. On March 26 he attended a performance of one of the great Victorian plays, Tom Tyler's "The Ticket-of-Leave Man." The touring company that performed was one of the most famous in America, Nellie Boyd's. Smith also highlighted the opening of a roller-skating rink at the opera house (Mar 9). The Frenkel Opera House's spacious interior also was the locale for a benefit concert on behalf of the recently constructed Episcopal Church (May 5). Although there was at least one ice manufacturing concern in Colorado City and even an ice cream parlor, the surface for the skating rink was undoubtedly wooden because on another occasion, with his hotel window open, Smith has heard crashes and bangs and hollers as the local citizenry got their first taste at skating on wheels.

The most universal form of public entertainment in the city also owed its origins to the entrepreneurship of the opera house's builder, Frank Lester. He constructed a set of tracks leading out of town across Lone Wolf Creek to a place called Phenix Park which included "a race track, a baseball park, a dancing pavilion, and another skating rink."[31] In fact, Smith mentions in one of his letters about the Colorado City club taking on a visiting baseball team from Abilene (May 2). As John Rix recounts, Phenix Park also included a "zoo made up entirely of West Texas animals, reptiles, and birds. …Buffalo, deer, antelope, Lobo wolves, coyotes, panthers mountain lions were also secured" and a "white wildcat was caught by a negro in Blanco Canyon and added to the collection."[32] There were also trap-shooting demonstrations and crack-shot pistol contests.

Thus, what one hears almost exclusively about when it comes to Texas frontier history is entertainment in the form of clicking wheels of fortune, kerosene-lit bordellos, and endless clacking of mugs and glasses in saloons. Looking beneath the surface, it is the live music in homes, professional drama productions in the opera houses, and a variety of athletic events that offer a counterpoint to the rowdiness of bar talk, fist fights, and gun slinging. True enough, at the supposed opposite spectrum from civilized forms of entertainment would be the rough-and-ready world of cowboys, cattle drives, and ranch life. However, the advent of the T & P RR marked a new turn for the cattle industry in West Texas. No longer was it the Goodnight-Loving cattle trail, for example, but rather controlled herds driven to the railhead in Colorado City. The open range still existed for the most part, but two entrepreneurial mid-westerners names Joseph F. Glidden and Henry Sanborn were busy demonstrating the value of barbed wire in deflecting the mad dashes of longhorns in Sherman and San Antonio and at ranches in the Mitchell County environs and in the Texas Panhandle where Sanborn and Glidden had their own full-enclosed demo ranch, the Frying Pan.[33] The cattle industry was rapidly moving towards modernization.

Insofar as Mitchell County alone is concerned, in 1882 there were 35,000 cattle, 13,000 sheep, and 1,000 horses.[34] The population of Colorado City was a sparse 700 in 1881, but it increased twelvefold in the next four years.[35] So, too, did the cattle and sheep. Conservative estimates list at least a dozen cattlemen within a 75-mile radius whose net worth was in the six-figure category.[36] The history of ranches, cattle barons, and cattle brands has been written about in numerous books. The point here is to show, in small ways, how James Lowry Smith and the people he knew influenced or were influenced by the rapidly emerging changes in the cattle industry. In the year 1885, young Smith had four different residences. He was at a Mrs. Johnson's boarding house when Marie arrived. In late February he switched to the Rendrebrook Hotel and two weeks later to the Pacific House because its accommodations were "nicer."[37] By September, he would be quartered above the store to save much-needed money for his impending marriage to Marie. The Pacific House board and room consumed 30% of his $100-a-month salary and the space above Burns, Walker was, presumably free.[38]

In any event, Smith's Pacific House room mate was a man named Frank Vaughn. In response to Marie's request to learn more of the man, Smith wrote on July 26: "You asked who Frank Vaughn was. He is working for the stock ass'n, gets $150 per mo. He watches all the cattle shipped from this country to see that the members of the ass'n have none stolen from them. He is a jolly good boy." So jolly that James and Frank, on at least one occasion, rode together: "Last night was so pretty and inviting," he told Marie "that Frank and I took a long horseback ride" (Aug 23). Frank's work must have been demanding, to put it mildly. One early historian tells of enough cattle in the stockyards of Colorado City to fill 200 cars.[39] Ironically, the live cattle were shipped eastward to Fort Worth and St. Louis side by side with the dead relics of their predecessors on the rich prairie grasslands.

One might well ask why there are no buffalo bones on the West Texas prairies? Concurrent with the completion of the T & P RR, Colorado City became the "largest shipping point" for buffalo bones.[40] As Colorado City old-timer A. J. Payne relates, "I well remember two or three wagon loads of Buffalo Bones that would be brought to town from off the Plains with from 12 to 16 oxen pulling these loads, and same would be unloaded on the right of way of the T & P making a huge mountain of bones, and the wagons would go back loaded with food stuffs amounting from $1,000 to $1,500 to the load."[41] Thus, almost unconsciously, the largest recycling project in West Texas history yielded $22 to $23 per ton for bones before the price dropped and settled at $8. Old bones were ground into meal, fresh ones supplied refineries with calcium phosphate to neutralize cane juice acid and de-color sugar; choice bones went to bone-china furnaces for calcium phosphate ash and firm bones went to the button factories.[42] Hence, business boomed at Burns, Walker & Co. In fact, Smith himself notes in one of his letters to Marie that a good day's sales often reached $1,400 or more (May 2).

Although bookkeeper Smith never ventured directly into the cattle business, he did write about a sideline of mortgaging sheep in June 1885. Later that month he proudly reported: "Ivy [Burney] sold our sheep today at one dollar a head, throwing in the lambs. He went to camp this evening and ordered them brought in tomorrow" (Jun 26). The total amount collected on their mutual several hundred dollar investment was $650. Smith, however, was primarily the recorder of other peoples' transactions and if he gambled, it was not in the nearby saloons but only a humorous gentleman's wager in the store where Burns, Walker conducted the mercantile business and A. W. Dunn one of his profitable banking concerns:

> Next week comes "the tug of war" in the store. An invoice will have to be taken, our books balanced down, and a dividend declared. The Bank will declare a dividend this month also. Mr. Swinney has wagered Mr. Peacock a fine hat that the Bank would beat the store. If Mr. P wins, he promises me the hat. Think we will beat them by five or six per cent. (Jul 3)

Smith may have spent most of his time in his interior office "where I get the benefit of but little air" (Aug 1), but he did manage escapes on occasional outings to nearby ranches. One such occurred on April 21, 1885 when he and one of his clerks attended a picnic "at the CA Ranch which is about twelve miles off. …One of the cowboys came and asked if we did not want to see a circus; replied in the affirmative and repaired forthwith to the scene of action. The horse did some hard pitching but did not budge its rider." Rodeos were just on the cusp of becoming entertainment events derivative, of course, from everyday cowboy work. The first recorded performance was probably at Pecos two years before in 1883.[43] At the time, Jimmie Smith, having once earlier in his life ridden a pitching horse in Salado, was observing what would soon become the modern, civilized spectacle of the professional rodeo.

One other family event connected the bookkeeper to life on a cattle ranch and it came from an unexpected chance. True to his promise to his mother, Jimmie 'welcomed' his recalcitrant younger brother, Robert, to Colorado City in late March. Having no money to put him up, he had Robert bunk in the corner of his room. For over a month, the intrusive Robert pestered his brother about employment and about the secret letters he was writing nights by lamplight while Robert lay on a cot across the room. All visible evidence of Marie was hidden away. Finally, a jubilant James was able to write to Marie on May 10 that "Robert left yesterday for Mr. Peacock's ranch about fifty or sixty miles distant. After donning the necessary regalia, he had very much the appearance of a typical cowboy." No doubt it was John Walker's fiancée, Bessie Peacock, who had helped engineer this job at her uncle's spread, the Joe & Alf Peacock Concho Ranch and Cattle Company. Literally, Robert had been dispatched to boot camp in hopes that the training would give him direction in life which it apparently did because the next time Smith saw him Robert had grown-out hair, a beard, and was much more subdued (Aug 30).

With regard to ranching, a 25-year-old Victorian man writing to his 21-year-old sweetheart in Horn Lake, MS, would almost always avoid excessively graphic material. One noteworthy exception was a June 24, 1885 letter which vividly recounts one current and one past experience of the same dangerous encounter:

> A young man with whom I was well acquainted was brought in from the Magnolia Ranch this evening; he was killed by lightning yesterday evening at five o'clock. His body will be shipped to Fort Worth in the morning, where his people live. On one of the Round-ups about a month ago a negro was struck by lightning, the whole of his hat crown was torn off, his clothes were torn too and a white stripe made down his back, two holes pierced through the seat of his saddle and his horse killed instantly; also a white man and horse which were standing near. It seems incredible, but the darkey was only stunned and is today all right. This young man that was killed yesterday was putting up wire fence at the time. A negro was helping him and says he fell dead just as he picked up a strand of wire; said he heard no thunder or saw no lightning, but something like a little ball of fire fell off the end of the wire just as 'twas picked up. Suppose the wire had been struck some ten or fifteen miles away.[44]

If such an anecdote, as the one just related, indicated the dangers of enclosed ranges, an account of another cattleman's event illustrated the celebration of civilized achievement at its fullest.

If there was ever one occurrence that earmarked Colorado City as a civilized mecca, it was the Stockmen's Ball of March 4, 1885. It might appear heartless to juxtapose sudden death on the prairie against ebullient life at a premier, one-of-a-kind highbrow social event. However, as Smith conveyed to his Marie, Bessie Peacock was unable to attend because of the death of her nephew; Smith himself was one of the pallbearers at the funeral but had to attend the Stockmen's Ball for business purposes. To create a unique perspective for this crucial frontier undertaking, three accounts will be presented: a secondary account from a 1940 history, a reminiscence of a Colorado City resident who was a teen-ager at the time, and Smith's own subdued account. Based on accounts rendered by two Colorado City women, Mary C. Jones concludes:

> Grandmothers still tell their granddaughters of the Stockmen's Ball held in the Frenkel Opera House during the Cattlemen's Convention, March 5 [4], 1885. It is estimated that 3,000 persons attended at one time or another and it was necessary to brace the ball room floor with carpenter's trusses. The wealth of the cattle kingdom, which is to say the wealth of the state was represented on this occasion. Resplendent silks and satins, long sweeping trains and voluminous, puffed over-skirts, bejeweled fingers and glittering necklaces were features that those who attended never forgot.[45]

The Rix family had arrived in Mitchell County from Wisconsin in January 1883. J. A. Rix's description of the Ball itself is vivid and compelling:

> Colorado was the scene of the first Stockmen's Ball the winter following the completion of the St. James Hotel and the opera house, where the ball was held. This ball was sponsored by the wealthy cattlemen whose headquarters were in Colorado. A fifty (50) piece orchestra from St. Louis was engaged for the occasion and carpets were spread from the opera house to the St. James, in order that the ladies might not soil their evening gowns or slippers as they paraded from the ballroom to the St. James dining room, where a banquet was held. It surpassed any banquet ever held in Texas before or since. All of the cattlemen from far and near attended this ball. Diamonds, magnificent costumes, some spurs with 20 dollar gold coins for rowels all flashed and glittered in the dazzling lights reflected by hundreds of kerosene burning chandeliers. It is regrettable that photographers could not have been on hand to hand down to future generations the true colorings of the early activities of the old open range country.[46]

Smith's account of the event in a March 7 letter to Marie was far less splendorous, partly because of his remaining somewhat aloof from the proceedings. By his own admission, he was more an observer than a participant:

> Well, the grandest event of the season has just passed—the Stockmen's Convention, Ball & Banquet. I attended the latter two and found them very enjoyable. The Opera House was filled to overflowing, a splendid band of music, and all went as happy as a marriage bill. Will not attempt a description of either as the *Graphic* will doubtless do justice to the occasion in terms more pleasing. Wine flowed so freely that nearly every boy got too "full" for <u>utterance</u>. <u>Your</u> "boy" did not touch a drop though the lady to his left wondered at such proceedings and soon asked why. He is reforming isn't he?

Marie, already acknowledged as Smith's intellectual superior, obviously had tried to curb the young Baptist's occasional consumption of alcohol. He freely admits such in the next paragraph: "If I had never met <u>you</u> Marie, then it would not haven been necessary for her to have asked about my sobriety, for I would doubtless have partaken but not to the extent that did the other boys." By the way, the inexorable George Bailey evidently did parade the event in his tabloid because J. A. Rix notes that Bailey offended many of the women by failing to mention, as his competitor Alf Tolar did in *The Clipper*, the attire of any of the women. Then, again according to Rix, Bailey scoffed at one man's poor "cuff buttons and obvious limited acquaintance" with proper dress codes and derided another for his omission of dress boots and his wearing effeminate "leather pumps" instead.[47]

Ever the meticulous keeper of accounts, Smith also sent his beloved a copy of the program cover for the event.[48] The four committees shown on the cover represent a virtual Who's Who among 1885 Colorado City dignitaries, including bankers (Dunn, Swinney, Scott); cattlemen (the Robertsons, Mann, Peacock) and merchants (Burns, Shear, Pruit), and one of the west's most famous lawmen, Sheriff R. C. "Dick" Ware, former Texas Ranger and the man likely responsible for the capture of outlaw Sam Bass seven years previous. Colorado City must have been a bowl of light that March 4th evening, and perhaps so on other nights as well. One can speculate that some of the light was probably electric, though to what extent will never be known for certain. What is known is that one of the men whose name appears on the program cover (H. B. Smoot), along with a partner, organized a stock company on electric light service in the early 1880s. If so, as historian Omar Cline states, "Colorado City had an electric lighting system before Dallas."[49]

Based on Smith's own recounting of the Rendrebrook, Pacific House, and St. James, one could translate the scale of accommodations to a modern-day AAA rating of two, three, or four diamonds or nice, nicer, nicest. In fact, Smith relates one instance where the Pacific House served heart-shaped toast with an arrow through the middle, apparently on Valentine's Day.[50] And, just before his impending marriage, Jimmie wrote to Marie that he had engaged a room for himself and Marie at the St. James "where we will stop for a month or two" before setting up house "because that abode is most pleasant" (Feb 7, 1886).

Hotel preferences, however, needed to await the completion of courtship. Foremost on the agenda was the letter he was expected to write to Marie's father, formally requesting his daughter's hand in marriage. This type of letter demanded Victorian formality and was made more difficult by the fact that James Lowry Smith had yet to meet William Joseph Bynum. In what today seems like highly inflated language, the opening three paragraphs of the permission letter read:

> I do not doubt you will be surprised at the reception of this, for the writer, if at all, is very slightly known to you.

> This will be handed to you by Mr. Walker. Although I firmly believe that he and Mr. A. W. Dunn will be the means of sufficiently introducing me to you, it is nonetheless with delicacy that I enter upon the subject of this letter.

> Probably you may know that on your daughter's recent visit to this City I had the pleasure of meeting her. From a simple introduction sprang up an acquaintance which thereafter grew into love. I do not think I presume to say mutual love.

He then urged Mr. Bynum to contact Dunn and make whatever inquiries he thought appropriate regarding the letter writer's character. Then, in a frank turn, Smith commented on his own rather meager financial circumstances:

Proof Sheet Colarado and Brazos Stock Convention, March 4, 1885

"Will say that I have but little; however, believe nature has endowed me with the capacity and disposition to accumulate. ...Depend upon it, Sir."[51]

Smith had to wait seven weeks before reply from the man he hoped would be his future father-in-law. In the meantime, he did some scrambling to explore ways of increasing his income. A Colorado City friend named Steger made an offer to purchase the Shrader Drug Store in the city and invited James to invest in the business with him. Smith mulled over a possible increase in salary to $300 per month though he never revealed how much capital he would have to come up with (Mar 29). Smith had approached P. C. Coleman about his participation also, but Dr. Coleman, soon to be remarried, declined because such a venture would be "undertaking too much at once," though Coleman admitted it would undoubtedly be a "paying business" (Apr 5). At the same time it was nail-biting time, as Smith anxiously awaited the reply to his request for Marie's hand in marriage.

Unbeknownst to Smith until a later date, another branding iron had entered the fire and was heating up in professions of deep affection for Miss Bynum. The suitor was none other than the indefatigable George Bailey whose April 8, 1885 letter to Marie was effusive about his own worth—not Marie's. He expressed irritation that Marie had never written to him since her departure nearly three months before, but then admits that he himself has not written because "I did not know when you would be at home." Then, in a tone of high arrogance and supreme miscalculation, Bailey surmised: "It is a hard task now to convince friends—ladies and gentlemen—that we are not engaged. They will believe it in spite of anything I can say. It was a general impression that 'the editor' led the van, but I have heard that you expressed a greater liking for Cousin Sam than anyone else in Colorado."

Although the appellation "Cousin" was a common one for any close friend in the late nineteenth century, it sometimes assumed a more forceful presence, particularly when the writer was insistent. Bailey's concluding paragraph to his four-page letter indicated a hoped-for assignation. It contains more smoke-blowing than a prairie campfire: "Cousin Marie, I often wonder why it was that "the greatest girl on earth" has forgotten her Texas Cousin. "And I will make this letter brief until I find out how you feel toward me. Perhaps then, my communications can _possibly_ be made more interesting. From Your Own Cousin, Geo M. B."

Luckily for Marie, her Jimmie remained busy writing checks and making sales entries in his ledger at Burns, Walker and confined his letters to a ritualistic 10 or 11 pm timeframe after long days in the office were complete. In his April 14 letter he told Marie he had just written to John Walker who was in San Antonio getting his eyes attended to and that the firm expected Mr. Dunn and family to arrive back in Colorado City the following day. He added a most meaningful postscript: "By the way, today saw among Mr. D's mail a letter from your Papa; will guess it is the one asking about your "boy." If it is, believe he will show it to me,--would like to be his private secretary for about fifteen minutes."

At long last, James' good humor and sensibility were rewarded in an April 27 letter from the hand of Papa Bynum:

> Dear Sir
> In reply to yours of the 9th sent asking My Daughter Marie in marriage, I will have to say I have gained all the information I desire from Jn Walker and Mr. Dunn regarding you, which has resulted in every instance in your favor. I could more willingly give consent if you were not a stranger.
> Yet I feel that I have no right to withhold my sanction to the union you both desire.[52]

After several sentences about the hardship of the loss of a favored daughter and assured of the knowledge that young Smith will visit Horn Lake in a few weeks, Bynum concludes: "Trusting that nothing may ever occur in your life to cause you to forget that you have asked and received the dearest gift I possess, I am Very Respectfully, W. J. Bynum."

In almost total contrast to "Cousin" Bailey, the elated Smith wrote to Marie on May 2, and the letter reflects the full range of his emotional attachment, business interests, and even a social aside as he contemplates being eventually united with his devoted Marie. The letter opens with apologies to the love of his life:

> My Own Darling Marie:
> I do feel that I have rather neglected you for the last two or three days, though in my heart I know I have not meant to do so. No, my little girl, you are just as dear to me as ever and I could not be so happy if I were to grow indifferent towards you, the source of my purest and happiest thoughts.

Then, ever the man of business, Smith shares a sheep story about himself and the City Attorney:

> Have been sorely vexed and put to considerable trouble by a party leaving the country, upon whose flock of sheep Mr. Burney and I have a mortgage. We did not know of his action for several days afterwards. He had very bad luck with his flock last winter, loosing over half. Besides our claim, he had contracted considerable indebtedness, and saw that he would never pay out. To rid himself of all, he quietly left for parts unknown. Thus you can see Mr. B and myself must make what we can out of the sheep. …Will probably shear next week. The boys are poking all sorts of fun at me every hour in the day about being a "sheep man."

From Smith's sheep dealings in Colorado City and his later dealings with the same form of husbandry in Amarillo, one can conclude that wool was a valuable commodity and that Burns, Walker & Co. marketed wool directly to eager eastern markets. Apparently, as Smith goes on to say, John Walker had lost a bet to Smith and Frank Burns about even getting some profitable sheep business for the store. Consequently, Walker had to pay up: "Mr. Burns received a letter from John which says he will be at home Monday next with an exterminated mustache and stiff new hat for the boss."

The contents of this letter, as well as others of a similar ilk, reveal the fully civilized personality of a Texas frontiersman. First and foremost, he is devoted to Marie and looking forward to his upcoming visit to Horn Lake where he will, as he kiddingly put it, meet the "old Gent" (Mar 9). He does turn the adverse sheep situation into a profitable venture for Burney, himself, and Burns, Walker. He does continue with an unabated late-evening work schedule, but the ever insistent Marie vows that her James will have to be home for dinner when she sets the time and adds just before the bookkeeper headed for Mississippi: "You ask Uncle Dunn if he doesn't think you should do as I say" (May 4).

At the New Orleans Exposition a week or so later, he had his photograph taken and he there received a letter from Marie stating she cannot personally greet him there as planned: "I am so very sorry I could not meet you in New Orleans. 'Tis all cousin Lilla's and Ed's fault" (May 13). They had promised to escort her but got waylaid at the last minute. Nonetheless, the week-long stay in Horn Lake only served to advance their love. He recapped his return trip as soon as he was back in Colorado City: "I did not leave New Orleans at the time expected, and had to layover in Fort Worth, so did not reach this place until today. How very happy I was to find such a sweet letter awaiting me. I can never tire of reading it" (May 22).

James Lowry Smith at 25

To the modern reader used to cell phones, e-mail, and all the other forms of instant communication the lengthier and time-consuming exchange of personal letters might seem an antiquated novelty. Not so for a late nineteenth-century engaged couple. Almost a year after he first met Marie, James reflected, "What a blessing the art of writing is" (Oct 4, 1885). In point of fact, the nearly 100 letters each sent to the other during their 16-month courtship exemplifies civilized communication at its best. With no long-distance phone service, one either sent a telegram or wrote a letter or met in person. Perhaps the most important meeting place—and occasionally even now in many Texas towns—was the post office. Smith, alas, had to abandon the façade of the secretive P.O. Box 135 in Colorado City when the postmaster's daughter announced across the post office floor in mid April that 'Mr. Smith has another letter from his girl' (Apr 12). Humorously, the woman's name was Miss Hazzard. Again, six months later, Smith forgot to affix a stamp to his letter and the postmaster this time waved the guilty missive and called across the lobby for young Smith to remedy the oversight (Oct 4).

Nevertheless, the U.S. Postal Service of 1885 vintage—if the frequent internal references in their mutual letters are any indication—was superb. First, on at least a dozen occasions the newly composed letter referred to a letter being received bearing the writer's date of composition only two or three days before. Second, what do Marie's numerous empty envelopes reveal besides lost or expunged letters? The answer lies on the reverse side of nearly each envelope she mailed to Colorado City. First, starting on May 27, 1885, the post office in Horn Lake began adding the specific month and date to their stamp cancellations. Second, over the next seven months (minus the time of Smith's visit to Hot Springs, AR, in November and then Horn Lake in December), all 36 envelopes reveal a date-received cancellation in Colorado City on the envelope's reverse side! Four letters took four days to arrive; five took three days. However, the remaining 27 took only two days to go 10 miles north to Memphis, then 300+ miles across the state of Arkansas to Texarkana, then 200 miles to Dallas/Fort Worth, then 300 miles to Colorado City—a total distance of some 800 miles! What is even more amazing is that there are no references in the some 110 actual extant letters that a missive was not received or is missing! The efficiency of the consistent and timely mail delivery is a remarkable achievement in the civilizing of the Texas frontier.[53] Finally, several of Smith's letters contain mail car cancellations (supported by several mentions of his rushing to the railroad station with a letter in hand), indicating he bypassed the post office entirely.

Only one letter in the entire corpus of correspondence between Jimmie and Marie has a different format. The presentation has nothing to do with content and everything to do with the method of composing. The letterhead is that of J. E. Hooper, District and County Clerk, Mitchell Co., Tex, and the date is June 25, 1885. The opening paragraph reads: "I am at the Court House for a few moments and Mr. Hooper kindly offers me the use of his machine to write my girl a letter. This is my first attempt; don't you think I'm doing well?"

The invention of the modern typewriter coincided with the invention of the telephone in 1876. So, here on the Texas frontier, less than 10 years after the fact, both 'machines' are available for use. In addition, the first mechanical adding machine, driven by finger power and a crank, was not patented until August 1888; hence, Smith the bookkeeper had to manually calculate the sales slips and accompanying daily ledger entries at Burns, Walker & Co.[54]

Another demographic factor affecting the civilizing process was real estate values. As Cline reveals in his extensive study, "City lots that were bought for one-hundred-fifty dollars in 1880 sold for as much as five-hundred dollars in 1882."[55] Other records show a housing boom in July 1884: "We have some beautiful private residences in Colorado. They tell in unmistakable terms the taste and refinement of our people. In point of elegance, of finish and other surroundings, the brick cottage of Winfield Scott is the most conspicuous."[56] Scott rivaled A. W. Dunn, whom, according to Marie's letters also had a nice home, because he had a mutual interest in cattle and banking. The precise dollar figures of their incomes are unknown, but both Scott and Dunn were probably close to being Colorado City millionaires. Whatever the precise case, the rapid inflation of real estate over the first three years of the 1880s indicated a civilized growth. In fact, another historian from the early 1880s goes even further and estimates that "Investments in town property have been very profitable. Lots that were bought for $100 or $150 have been sold for $1,200 and $1,500 and as high as $3,000 without any improvements."[57] By the time Colorado City's population hit the 6,000 mark in late 1884 or early 1885, Mary Jones speculates that "lots of 25 foot frontage on Oak Street, the principle business street of the town, sold for as high as $6,000."[58]

An added incentive to visitors—potential landowners, distant cattlemen, and eastern merchants—was a rental hack facility available at both the town's livery stables. Folks could then take a whirl through the busy streets, even drive to a picnic area at Seven Wells, seven miles south of the city. This practice was akin, as bicentennial historian W. K. Smith, Jr., puts it, "to the rental car business of today."[59] However, the first indicator that an over-inflated real estate boom was crashing occurs in a mid-April 1885 letter of Smith to Marie. He writes that, despite his meager circumstances, he fondly hopes some small private abode looms in their future: "Must say that I like your suggestion of our having a little home of our own. A nice dwelling house well located was sold one day last week for $800 which first cost $1,500. Bargains like this can be found frequently today" (Apr 15). In the meantime, the exchange of letters between the two betrothed was supplemented by something only smooth and civilized delivery by rail would permit. On several occasions she sent fresh floral bouquets which he was careful to set in inconspicuous places or with the sender's name card removed so that the boys would not kid him unmercifully. In return, fresh produce began to arrive in season from El Paso, and Jimmie sent a parcel of grapes to Marie (Mar 10).

The courting couple's letters were filled with constant reminders on whose letters were how long and who had written whom most often. In late summer he gently chastised: "You have forgotten sometime ago I was without a letter from you for a full two weeks and had been writing you promptly all the while." Then, he just as promptly apologized: "I am sorry. Your heart and name are as dear to me today as they were six months ago" (Aug 23). These lines re-enforce a July correspondence where he has stated passionately, "Our lives are before us unbegun" (Jul 22). Her surviving letters, though few, mirror this type of repartee that at times assumes almost a humorous dimension. Just prior to his May visit, she had reminded him: "For Papa's sake, please wear one of your regular suits and ask Uncle Dunn if you shouldn't have a white Texas hat" (Apr 27). Still preoccupied with his own limited finances, he promises "We'll make up in love what we lack in diamonds" (Jun 15). She kids him about a single strand of silver hair she detected in his "raven locks" when he visited her in Horn Lake (May 29). Her letters to him were continually hidden in his pockets, drawers, files as he tried to keep the clerks in the store in ignorance of his infatuation for Marie. She, likewise, gets kidded by her younger brother, Wade, about how many more times she will read Jimmie's latest letter (Dec 13).

Despite the serious nature of courtship and the pressures of arranging a marriage date, making personal visits, and planning sufficient finances, a sense of humor was always present to lighten their moods whether the stress was personal or even religious. The original Baptist Church in Colorado City was destroyed by a cyclone in mid-1884, but the newly erected chapel, a box-like building, was his constant other home. In June he joked about having missed one service so that on the following day, "being a prominent person, I was sent for" even though "I am a long way off from being a preacher" (Jun 7). Young Smith even induced Mr. Dunn to attend services and when the great itinerant evangelist, William Evander Penn, set up a revival meeting, Smith was on hand. At one meeting Penn, as Smith put it, "gives clergy a black eye" (Sep 27), but during the two weeks or so Penn preached so powerfully that he is "the subject of conversation in every house and business" (Oct 11). Smith cheerily notes that "Bessie is converted" along with junior partner, Zack Williams, and that "even Mr. Burns is taking a considerable interest" (Oct 4). Interestingly, Penn had to opt for a building "near Tolar's *Clipper* office" rather than the Baptist Church because Penn was "attracting such large crowds" (Oct 11). Smith proudly told Marie, too, that his own organ-playing talents had been made manifest at such services.

The importance of organized religion as a tempering and civilizing influence on the frontier occasionally had an application to business practices. By mid 1885 the Methodist, Episcopal, and Baptist Churches were in full operation in Colorado City. Doubtless, some of the church members serving on the City Council were influenced by their clergy to enforce an ordinance about operating a business on Sunday. As Smith reported to Marie:

> The boys are today rejoicing over the passage, or rather the enforcing of the Sunday law. The Sheriff went to all the business houses, saloons, and barber shops yesterday evening and told them they <u>must not</u> open their doors from twelve o'clock that night to twelve o'clock tonight—not even to deliver goods which had been sold the previous day. Men have been rattling the store doors all day, but they will not be opened unto them. (Jun 12)

Marie, herself a Presbyterian by family practice, finally relented toward the end of their courtship period and agreed to become a Baptist convert, but not until after the impending wedding at the Presbyterian Church in Horn Lake. On her final letter to Jimmie in mid-February 1886, she admitted, "I do not regret my promise [to become a Baptist] for I do not

First page of letter, Marie to Jimmie, October 15, 1885

feel afraid of any lessons in obedience I *may* have to learn" (Feb 17). In fact, the entire courtship-by-corresponden*ce* period that lasted well over a year was best summarized in a comment Jimmie made in an apologetic letter the previous April: "Don't we have a wonderful time misunderstanding one another" (Apr 1).

Marie, still a first-grade Mississippi school teacher in charge of some 15 students, and James, a stalwart keeper of checks and balances, did not mention their mutual physical appearances in their letters—except on two occasions. He remarked in a June 9, 1885 letter that he was surprised to learn that "you have had your hair cut" and wonders if she, "like Samson" will "loose" her strength. At the same time, he admitted he has followed her lead and wants a more youthful look because "my mustache is coming out too much." No full-length photographs exist from this time period, so it is difficult to assess their exact sizes and shapes—aside from the passing prose comments made by Bailey in the *Graphic* that Marie is "the fragrant flower of Old Mississippi" and that Jim is simply "slim."[60] When she suffered from a summer cold, Jimmie wonders when the "blooms of health" will "again be budding"—then in an uncharacteristically bold query he asks, "How much do you weigh now? I'll guess___pounds. I only weigh about 173" (Aug 15). Marie, of course, never responded to his question.

One very pointed Colorado City story he does share in a September 13 letter is one he doubtless reveled in because it concerned the childish escapades of the city's second-most important journalist, George Bailey. Celebrating the departure of a Mr. Hodges, a visiting Baptist minister, Bailey went to ridiculous extremes:

> George got on a spree. He did not intend to get drunk at all—I think—but was over persuaded by parties who pretended to be his best friends, and he says they drugged him. This all occurred at night. Next morning he was taken before the magistrate and his fine assessed at $13.20. Some boys took chalk and put the figures 13.20 in every conspicuous place. Don't think Geo ever did a thing which he regretted more.

Sometimes in his own fond imaginings, Smith envisioned a future life with Marie at some of Colorado City's surrounding recreational spots. He mentions observing, unseen a preacher and his girl as "cooing lovebirds" at Seven Wells, an inviting picnic area (Apr 9) and, on a late August night he looks out toward "Lone Wolf Mountain. Now why would not weekly visits there be conducive to good health—say, make them every Sunday evening in a buggy to save getting lonesome…with a young lady, like you, who is also seeking health" (Aug 1). Such mentions of actual geographical surroundings are rare in his letters because, as noted, all the "cooing" is in highly Victorian vocabulary with its sweetness and charm.

One item of crucial importance to the acme of Colorado City's rise and to the slope of its gradual descent from cattle mecca to near ghost town was the issue of water. If ever there is an indicator of civilizing influence, it is the marked presence or absence of this most essential of all compounds. At its height, Colorado City received a steady water supply from a remarkable artifice. Contemporary Colorado City historian, Jim Baum, summarizes its history:

> Long after all the brick buildings were reduced to rubble and the saloon doors closed, one edifice, contemporaneous with all of them, remains standing—an edifice that served the community for nearly 120 years. It is the standpipe imported in sections from Pittsburgh and erected atop a hill with a natural gravity feed to the original cast iron pipes laid down in the city.[61]

The storage capacity of the assembled standpipe was 280,000 gallons. This system and its cost and debate of its worth are almost the sole subject of the City Council minutes as presented in the preserved ledger at the Heart of West Texas Museum.[62] Judge Looney notes that the pipe was financed by a $45,000 Water Bond for fire protection and consumption purposes.[63] In her own reminiscence, Mrs. John A. Mooar credits Dunn, Pete Snyder, and her own husband for ordering the plating and erecting a water standpipe that "stands second to none in the state."[64]

Prior to the standpipe's erection, potable water had to be wagoned in from Newsome Springs, five miles south of Colorado City because the Colorado River was too salty for human use.[65] A second source was the natural springs at "Seven Wells," though as Baum correctly points out, there were but four actual springs before the entire area became the bottom of Champion Reservoir.[66] Price per barrel for such water was 25 to 35 cents. In any event, a lasting testament to the Colorado City Standpipe is the May 1886 Sanborn map which features the object front and center on plot #1 of 3, next to Lone Wolf Creek. Supplemental to the map is an engineer's drawing and statistics regarding the standpipe's dimensions, storage wells, pipe pressure and pipe dimensions. The Sanborn maps reveal water lines on Main Street, 2nd Street, and all the numbered, tree-named side streets: Locust, Chestnut, Elm, Walnut, Oak, Pine, and Cypress. How the pipes fed into individual buildings (if indeed they ever did) is nowhere mentioned in the Colorado City histories. One can only assume that water was available at pumps and/or hydrants within the confines of 1886 Colorado City.[67]

Unfortunately for Mitchell County and Colorado City, the artificial production of water from below ground was in stark contrast to the usual and natural production from the skies of Mother Nature. Mary C. Jones refers to the "Lucifer-like fall in 1885-86"[68] while another historian notes that a record kept by John Haley, a barber in the city, mentions that "not a single drop of rain fell" in the 13 months from mid-1885 until mid-1886.[69] A modern history of the same time period establishes that Abilene had its own meteorological station staring in early 1885 and that the rainfall in West Texas was sporadic at best and that a "severe blight of drought" blanketed most areas.[70] The fat years of the early 1880s now yielded nary a stick of fresh grass which, coupled with exceptionally harsh and bitter winters, led to wholesale death of cattle on the plains of West Texas.

Although James Lowry Smith was now an accountant by profession, he still had a farmer's heart and he did keep a close eye on the weather because he knew the stockmen depended on water for survival and sales and the resultant dollars to purchase supplies at Burns, Walker. Three times in his 1885 correspondence, he refers specifically to rain or its absence. On April 21, he wrote to Marie: "We had a heavy rain last night which makes stock men wear smiling faces today." On June 9 he stated: "The weather has been very warm for the past three days, until this evening a cool rain fell and it is now raining as I write (little past ten)." Smith's infectious sense of humor then spilled over—almost literally—as he revealed in the same letter that several of the boys from the office, in search of young ladies, had to negotiate mud puddles and doubtless, "I'll see their foot impressions there in the morning; suffice it to say their toilets had to be rearranged." Ominous, however, of worse things to come are the lines he penned to Marie on October 4: "Wish we could have a little of the rain you are having in Miss. 'Tis dry and dusty—the dust interfering materially with Major Penn's [revival] meetings."

One additional factor that would spell eventual economic doom for Colorado City was a mechanical one: the failure to supplement the T &

P RR with a southern route. On April 4 Smith commented: "Mr. Dunn returned yesterday, but is off today with the Railroad delegation from Galveston. Colorado is making a desperate effort to secure the Gulf, Colorado & Santa Fe Road." In early spring of 1885 the weather was on its final cusp of providing abundant water, but Smith did not know that. He concluded the same letter on an optimistic note: "No better time could have been selected for the railroad delegation to visit this country; everything is fresh and green, and people generally in good spirits. T'would be a great thing for Colorado if it could get the Road." Alas, this road never came to Colorado City. Making the future of Colorado City transportation even bleaker was the planned alternate western route of the Fort Worth & Denver City RR, scheduled to be built through the Texas Panhandle, thus bypassing Colorado City entirely.

As the summer and fall brought baking heat and the beginnings of the great plains drought, daily life at Burns, Walker witnessed the advent of physical maladies. John Walker suffered a relapse of his vision problems during a fishing outing and had to journey to Cuba, Missouri for a prolonged series of ocular treatments (Aug 22). Dunn himself, who had been beset by "inflammatory rheumatism" in the Spring had been forced to cut back his work schedule then and for the next six months (Apr 18). In October, Colorado City was hit by the onslaught of Dengue Fever that reached almost epidemic proportions. The outbreak had begun in Austin earlier in the year and rapidly spread westward. Although physicians at the time were unaware that Dengue was caused by a virus carried by mosquitoes, they were able to provide a few potions to help sick people cope with the so-called "break-bone" fever that caused painful joint and muscle swelling, but was usually not fatal.[71] On October 17, Smith summarized the outbreak: "The Dengue is doing the town at present. John has had it for several days. A great many cases in town. Sam Henderson [former Burns, Walker clerk, now a furniture store owner] was delirious this evening: he has had it for two or three days." A week later he noted that four more Burns, Walker clerks were "down with it now" and added, "Those who have had it give an awful description of it, though one gets over it in about 10 days" (Oct 24).

On the brighter side, the parade of marriage proposals and actual weddings was itself almost contagious. C. H. Earnest, stalwart cashier at the Dunn bank and inscriber of Marie's autograph album on January 11, 1885, switched his heart from possible pursuit of Marie to a Miss Fannie Craig whom he eventually married on April 28, 1886.[72] John Walker continued his ongoing courtship of Bessie Peacock who showed up at the office frequently in the Fall of 1885 singing the praises of Marie Bynum who was working on Bessie's bridal trousseau. Bessie was preparing for her own wedding date set for mid January. Ivy Burney, absent from Colorado City at several junctures during 1885 to visit his out-of-town girl, sadly broke off with her over New Year's and had to bury himself in legal matters at the District Court (Jan 2, 1886). The most durable liaison belonged to Dr. Coleman and his wife of less than a year, the former Miss Lucy Hamm. Together they would heal the wounds, aches, and illnesses of Colorado City residents for the next 35 years. In the meantime, Smith, still uncertain of an exact wedding date of his own, fell victim to illness. The 25-year-old Smith finally admitted to Marie that he had been diagnosed with a kidney problem and had been directed to Hot Springs, AR, for a two-to-three week treatment. He announced that he would be departing Colorado City on November 4, but that his acquaintances were speculating about the real reason for his trip: "In fact, a great many will be ready to believe I'm going off to marry, but they can't just exactly decide who the party is" (Nov 1).

Smith's lengthy visit to Hot Springs, which one can imagine might be fraught with uncertainty, was actually a humorous chronicle of sorts as Smith had to parade back and forth to the baths. He had to wait up to an hour and a half for his turn inside the bath house, return after each treatment to his boarding house which he summarily categorized as the "gas factory" (Nov 13). The very same week his doctor advised that Smith may need to stay for two or three more weeks, so Smith wrote to Marie, "I went into hysterics immediately" (Nov 20). Apparently he was granted redemption because he posted a quick note on November 24 stating he would be in Horn Lake by the 26th.

His brief visit with Marie and her family was followed by a detour to Salado en route back to West Texas. His younger siblings, Forrest, Roxalee, Hattie, and Julia entertained him with piano music and Smith added that, by the way, "Mother likes your picture" (Dec 1). He did take time for a nostalgic visit to Salado College but wrote in a droll tone: "Went to the college and found ever so many girls who would come and speak to me that I did not recognize." Then, out of the blue, two surprises occurred: one a train wreck and one a life-changing economic opportunity. In his own words, he described the train accident in a December 6 letter to Marie:

On my way from Fort Worth here made a narrow escape from

being caught in a wreck. Was fortunate enough to be in the sleeper which was not thrown from the track. The two coaches   just   in front were derailed and demolished. By the merest accident no one was killed, but some twenty or more wounded. Was delayed twelve hours. When I had reached Fort Worth all the berths were taken, but Providence smiled on me when I met Clay Mann there and he gave me his; so that is all that saved me.

Finally settled back into his routine, Jimmie contemplated—once again—his financial future, admitting to Marie that he doesn't want "to sever my connections at Burns, Walker & Co and that, hopefully a salary raise might be in the offing come the first of the year, to say, $1,500" (Dec 6). A train may have derailed but, to the absolute consternation of Bookkeeper Smith, his economic future was right on track. Incredulous, he wrote to Marie on December 13 that he had suddenly been taken in as a 10% partner in Burns, Walker, to the tune of roughly $9,000 since the "total assets of the business is about $97,000," though his own immediate audit soon revised the actual worth at $82,536 (Dec 13 and Dec 14). Fortuitously, one of the 13 surviving letters from the new partner's fiancée is dated December 17: "I feel quite rich since <u>we</u> have been taken in as partners—though the firm didn't know they were taking <u>two</u> instead of one; there's nothing wrong about it, however, as it will soon be just <u>one</u>. I'll be very silent." Marie may have humbly assumed a taciturn demeanor, but the headstrong woman of Mary Sharp College was far from ever being reticent. In fact, her above written lines lend credence to the most oft-repeated anecdote handed down by her eventual niece, Katherine Bynum Cobb Baker. Allegedly, Marie communicated to her father and to Uncle Dunn that 'It would be satisfactory to marry a bookkeeper, but oh so much better to wed a partner.' Unbeknownst to her fiancé, Marie arranged the loan through her father knowing that the new partner could pay off the loan and its interest within four years.

No celebration of financial security and impending marital happiness would be complete for Jimmie and Marie without the unsolicited interference of the irrepressible George M. Bailey. Excerpts from several sample sentences of his December 11, 1885 letter to Miss Bynum will have to suffice: "Memory, on airy wings, floats back only one year" and hangs on the "dome of my thought" about your visit here and now your upcoming marriage to James L. Smith. He wishes her happiness in her future years "whether the skies be unbroken blue or mantled with the somberness of cloud and mist." He then thanks her for "Your own high opinion of my talent and your friendship" as his endearing thoughts for her future happiness "are wafted from the Texas plains." Little wonder that Bailey's existence was continually ignored by Bessie Peacock who refused to speak to the man and by Smith who strongly objected to Bailey's premature announcement of their impending nuptials.[73] The unabashed sentiments expressed by Bailey were made even more preposterous by the fact that he himself had hastily wed a wife of his own the month before!

Early 1886, one might surmise, would be filled with wedding plans for the finally agreed to March 3 date in Marie's hometown. However, Marie had first to superintend aspects of the Walker-Peacock nuptial scheduled for January 13, 1886 even though she would not be in attendance. A dedicated program of selfless stitching, hemming, and embroidering was the order of the day as Marie reported to Jimmie on January 6: "I sent Bess' dresses off yesterday and I am so glad they are gone, for I have been in more trouble about them than if they were my own." She asked also if, after seeing Bessie in her resplendent bridal gown, Jimmie would still be happy with Marie's own marital preference, a simple traveling dress rather than a Memphis-bought bridal array. Unaware of Marie's package being in the mail, Jimmie fretted in his January 5 letter that Bessie is "put out about things not having reached her yet," but he is cheered by the fact that Bessie's intended, now his business partner, has "had a long chat with me about our mercantile business" and that Walker has been "very free and open" in his discussions about the future of their joint endeavors (Jan 7).

Never one to miss the humor found in impending serious events, Smith penned a series of observations about the majority partner's upcoming wedding: "Told Bessie the other day we are going to close up on the wedding day and drape the store in mourning" (Dec 29). On January 7 he apprised Marie that all the attendants "will meet at the church Tuesday night and rehearse the modus operandi. Dick Boren calls it a funeral procession. Somebody ought to make John a bridal present of a copy of *Paradise Lost*." As John and Bessie prepared to depart on a T & P train for an eastern honeymoon, Smith highlighted Walker's first formal introduction of his new wife: "John so forgot the situation as to introduce his bride as 'Miss Peacock'" (Jan 15).

However, Smith has laughed a bit too soon because his own wedding plans underwent changes that would have taxed even the most patient bride and groom. At first, things seemed to unfold in an orderly fashion.

Colorado, Texas, Jany 5 1886

My Own Darling Marie;

To an observer, I would appear very inconsiderate towards you by donating such short time and unseemly hours to our correspondence. Here it is ten oclock now, and I am just beginning to write; and cant help myself either. What are you going to do with me?

It seems to me I've had more to do in the

First page of letter, Jimmie to Marie, January 5, 1886

The Walkers were off on a prolonged honeymoon and there was a promise of a much better income in the near future for Jimmie and Marie. He had even printed 600 new business cards that were set for distribution. The room at the St. James Hotel had been reserved for their first few months in Colorado City (Feb 16). Confident that everything was set, he had written Marie in January about the planned wedding date being locked and ready:

> The cattlemen's convention opens here on March 10th, so Dr. Tolar informed me today. I think it very important that John and I should both be here at that time, and so wrote him today—Mr. Burns is of the same opinion. In order for us to be here, our marriage would have to take place on the 3rd; that would allow us two and a half days at home, and we would arrive here on the 9th. (Jan 21)

When he expressed concern about obtaining the required marriage license (Jan 25), Marie reassured him that she would help arrange for it. He even received reassurance from John Walker that he and Bessie would be present in Horn Lake on March 3 (Feb 1). Three days later Smith confidently predicted that "I will leave here on the 27th," a newly tailored New York suit in hand, and with "cravat and gloves" to match Marie's own wedding dress (Feb 4). His sole concern was that his own singing voice not be put to the test on the wedding day because, for the moment, "I have discontinued to sing almost entirely."

Smith was even able to defuse what was a harbinger of twentieth-century civilization to come—a visit at Burns, Walker from a labor union, specifically the Knights of Labor: "The Knights of Labor waited on us yesterday evening. We told them that when we were unable to attend to our own business (or words to that effect), we would have guardians appointed. Of course that means that we will be boycotted" (Feb 7). Whether such a boycott ever occurred (the Knights of Labor favored boycotts over strikes) is not mentioned in the sparse business communication from 1886. In any event, the Knights were active, but subsequent history shows that their power was beginning to fade.

However, on February 8, the March 3 wedding date disappeared in a puff of smoke. A harried Smith had to inform his bride-to-be that "The Stock Journal comes out and says the convention opens here on March 2nd. Will it be <u>possible</u> for you to be ready by the 25th?" Then he pleads for her to leave off any further sewing of wedding garments and to "do it after you come here—you know you'll have me to <u>assist</u> you." He then requests her to employ the only electronic means of communication available: "Wire me and sign the telegram "John," so no one will suspect anything." Secretive to the last, Smith guarded his change of plans from unwary eyes. She did telegram him on February 12 agreeing to the changed date, but one only knows this from his brief follow-on letter of February 12 where he acknowledged the telegram's receipt. Ironically, in a letter dated Valentine's Day, he admits knowing she is "worrying" herself "to death" and probably regrets every promise she ever made to him: "Aren't you sorry now that you ever promised to come to Texas?" He also states that the letter of the 14th is "I suppose…the last letter I'll write you."

It wasn't. Evidently her own letter follow-up to her telegram—which has not survived—probably hit him like an iceberg because his February 15 letter began: "Your letter of the 12th has a coldness about it which seems prominent to me." He then apologizes profusely for the already-printed wedding invitations to her relatives and his and expresses remorse for having "angered you." At least their wedding, he notes, will be a small one compared to the Walker-Peacock affair. Evidently softened by the chance to contemplate their courtship on a larger scale, she reiterated in her own letter of the 17th that the "present date change excepted, the days of our betrothal have been very happy days for me" and she signs off by resorting to some cooing love talk that has dominated the avowals of love in so many of their letters: "Now, I must say "goo-night" to my "boy," and "may the God of Love watch over and protect you, and bring you in safely to me."[74]

One final letter was sent from Colorado City to Horn Lake a bare five days before the blessed event and it opens with a chastisement—*not* against Marie but against the obnoxious George Bailey who had, somehow, ferreted out news of Smith's departure date and published it in his newspaper on February 19. Rarely given to expressing any personal form of venom, James wrote to Marie the following day: "Yours of the 17th just to hand. Will leave tomorrow evening as I expected. Mr. Bailey was officious enough to make mention of the fact in his paper yesterday, though I had never spoken of it to him. Have already expressed to him my disapproval."

Things happened quickly: a night at the Peabody Hotel in Memphis; a short train ride south to Horn Lake; a wedding day; a traveling dress, and a departure for Colorado City with a stop in Salado en route. James Lowry Smith, now three times a visitor to Horn Lake, fulfilled his wedding promise to Marie Motheral Bynum Smith, by taking her, for the first time, to his home town where—as he had put it in his February 20th letter—"Ma says she awaits you and that I will find the old house just as it used to be." Preserved in Marie's scrapbook is the following undated two-paragraph newspaper account of that visit:

> J. L. Smith, of Colorado City, formerly of this place arrived here a few days since from Mississippi with his charming bride. The Brass Band, in connection with a score or more of Jimmie's old, tried and true friends met them on the threshold of the maternal roof and greeted them with music's sweetest charms and words of earnest welcome.
>
> Jimmie Smith says he couldn't marry all of his schoolmates and to keep any of them from feeling slighted he went off to another state and got a wife.

Where the Smiths settled down in Colorado City for the next two years or so is unknown, except for Jimmie's reference to an initial planned stay at the St. James Hotel. Only two bare artifacts survive from those years, both of them blank envelopes. One bears a Horn Lake stamp cancellation of June 5, 1887 and an arrival date to the hands of Mr. James L. Smith of June 7. Obviously, then, as in the years to come, Marie would make frequent trips to Horn Lake to look in on her aging parents. The second envelope bears a November 11, 1887 stamp cancellation from the Miss. & Tenn. R.R., Horn Lake, and is addressed to "Mr. J. L. Smith" in "Hot Springs, Ark." Possibly Smith had returned there for further medical treatment of his kidney problem (though there is no reference to this problem in any of his future correspondence).

What is known is the next chapter in the Smiths' history. John Walker and his partner James Lowry Smith, noted that the Fort Worth & Denver City RR was being rapidly built through the Panhandle east to west and that the Santa Fe RR was being built north to south into the same area. After surveying the territory in late 1887, Smith and Walker figured the freight wagons and cattle drives from the south would have to head the Palo Duro Canyon and so would the Fort Worth & Denver City. Everyone would head for the nearest main railroad point, a place they determined to be a small town that had just been given the name, Amarillo. It would be the perfect place for another Burns, Walker & Co. store. They were right on the money!

Chapter 4

Amarillo and Temple
1888-1902

Unlike Salado with its cisterns, telegraph poles, and violins and unlike Colorado City with its standpipe, telephone exchange, and church organ, Old Amarillo was water by the barrel, communication by word of mouth, and James Lowry Smith with his trusty (but seldom played) cornet. A civilized existence was absent in Berry's cluttered Old Town near the newly laid tracks of the Fort Worth and Denver City RR. It would be up to Jimmie and his Marie and other hearty pioneers to bring technology and culture to the primitive town of less than 200 inhabitants.

According to Smith's nephew, James S. Bynum, Smith and his partner, John Walker, weighed the location of towns such as Tascosa, Panhandle City, Washburn, and Amarillo as possible railroad centers.[1] As Smith and Walker surveyed the whole territory, both figured that an urban hub would have to be north—but not too far north—of Palo Duro Canyon, at a crucial central Panhandle point, and at a precise spot along the Fort Worth & Denver City and with, at the very least, access to the Santa Fe RR which was slicing at an angle through the Panhandle from the northeast to the southwest. That spot was Amarillo. Historian John Crudgington credits J. L. Smith with making the initial trip and that Walker then visited and "confirmed Smith's judgment" about Amarillo. Whatever the actual case, Smith was alone in Old Town when he paid the "occupation tax of $6.24 for six months operation of Burns, Walker and Company on May 7th 1888" and advertised in the first issue of Amarillo's first newspaper that the company would be "headquarters for ranch supplies, dry goods, clothing, hats, boots and shoes. Grain and rock salt. See them or write for prices."[2]

Where the exact location of the store was in Old Amarillo is unknown and Smith had yet to find a place for him and Marie to live in. According to Della Tyler Key, Smith eventually secured the so-called "Amarillo House," a former 'hotel' of sorts that had given way to Colonel Berry's Tremont

Hotel.[3] The Smith house seemed spacious with its dining room, kitchen, and bedroom, the latter formerly filled with cots for the all-male clientele. However, the Smith bedroom had a thin ceiling and wallboards that had shrunk creating cracks.[4] Marie's niece later confirmed that knocked-out knot holes created a peephole effect that caused her aunt to hang draperies to secure a modicum of privacy.[5]

In any event, Marie arrived a month or two after her husband with a wagonload of household goods, and accidentally started the first spa in Amarillo! While her goods were being unloaded, accommodating cowboys grabbed her old tin bathtub (which Jimmie had ordered left behind), and it was soon donated to a local tonsorial parlor.[6] The Smiths' stay in Old Town lasted barely a year because the well-documented torrential Spring rains of 1889 turned the low-lying area into a vast muddy lake. Perhaps it was prophetic that Smith, as early as November 3, 1888, had obtained lots in the new Sanborn addition where he erected an adobe building at 208-210 Polk Street to accommodate his burgeoning ranch supply business.[7]

Recounted in legend is the actual move of the Smith's "Amarillo House" to a new location at nearby 211 Pierce Street. The intrepid Marie continued to cook meals in the house and tended to the nesting hen on the front porch even as the house was being rolled to its new locale.[8] In the meantime, entrepreneur James Lowry Smith became what Della Key cites as the "popular and efficient manager" of the Burns, Walker branch, so much so that by June 1889 the store was doing a remarkable annual business of $100,000.[9] Smith's Salado educational experiences were foremost in his mind when it came to Amarillo's first school which was established in 1889. The school's initial furniture came from Burns, Walker and Company.[10]

Actually, the business of Burns, Walker was a two-fold one: banking and mercantile. A case can be made that though J. C. Paul opened the first public bank in Amarillo in the Amarillo Hotel Annex in 1889, Smith was the first actual banker, running a private concern out of Burns, Walker both in Old Town and on Polk Street.[11] So accommodating was Smith that he allowed customers to spend the night in his store—with his bank safe closed, of course. As G. A. F. Parker, a renowned Amarillo banker in his own right, would later recount it was Smith's pervasive good humor that always won the day. To an old ranch man, Smith said one day very early on, "That old man has six wagons to load with ranch supplies. He only

Mr. and Mrs. James Lowry Smith soon after they moved to Amarillo

comes to town once in six months, and he always stays a week to get his talk out. He will sleep here in the store every night, and we will load his wagons in a few days."[12] In early 1889, Smith's newspaper ads also highlighted his banking interests: "We Make a Specialty of Receiving and Dispersing Deposits!"[13]

As for the principle business, mercantile sales, only one five-inch-thick business ledger, the Burns, Walker & Co. one from Jul-Dec 1889, survives from the first 10 years of Smith's business operations.[14] The volume is a first-class indicator of how Smith helped civilize the early Panhandle by meeting a host of customer needs. The shear variety of goods carried surpasses the imagination and indicates what the railroads brought in by the carload.

As far as groceries were concerned, the list was seemingly endless. A sampling of some actual sales entries includes:

- one five-gallon keg of pickles: $2.75
- 50 lbs. of lard: $5.00
- 21 lbs. of potatoes: .63
- 1 doz. canned tomatoes: $1.40
- 4 lbs. bacon: .40

- 100 lbs. DC Flour: $3.25
- 1 lb. chocolate: .40
- 1 can sardines: .10
- 14 lbs. rolled oats: $1.00
- half gallon honey: .85
- 1 lb. Arbuckle Coffee: .30
- 20 lbs. YC Sugar: $2.00
- 4 lbs. salt: .10
- 2 cans peaches: .40
- 2 cans oysters: .34

Male customers could purchase a saddle for $47; 100 Grand Republic Cigars for $3.50; 10 lbs. of fine quality rope for $1.67; one box of axle grease for .15; a monkey wrench for .75; undershirt for .40; pair jean pants for $1.50; pitch fork for .75; but, alas, a top-of-the-line Stetson Hat cost $6.00. For women, silk gloves went for .75; 6 yds. calico for .50; 22 yds. gingham for $2.75; half dozen coat buttons for .10; a pair of hose for .35; shoes for $2.00-4.50 per pair; three-and-a-half yds. linen for .88. As early as late 1889 and early 1890, the list of in-stock items included: wagons & plows; crockery; cedar posts; grains and seeds; tarpaulins; and women's straw hats. Newspaper ads highlighted "everything from a spool of thread to a McCormick Mowing Machine."[15]

What are even more revealing are the orders from the nearby ranches that surrounded Amarillo. All ranch orders recorded in the 1889 ledger are by ranch owner name—*not* by the name of the ranch or the ranch brand— as a few examples will illustrate. To the immediate north of Amarillo was Glidden and Sanborn (Frying Pan Ranch) which purchased $82.97 worth of goods on July 5; Mrs. C. Adair (JA Ranch) placed an order on October 4 for $109.29 and another on November 9 for $170.28—including sarsaparilla soda for $4.00. To the southeast, the Matador Land and Cattle Company ordered $153.96 worth of men's work clothes on November 18 for their own store. To the immediate south of Amarillo, the Cedar Valley Cattle Company (successor to the T-Anchor Ranch) placed a small order on September 16. However, by far and away, the largest ranch order in the ledger from 1889 is a simple one-line entry from September 21 to the Running Water Land and Cattle Company (Circle C Ranch) for 19,983 lbs. of barbed wire for $664.38. This ranch, southwest of Amarillo in the four corners area of Hale, Lamb, Swisher, and Castro Counties, was run jointly by the Morrison Brothers (Tom W. and James Newton) and W. D. "Ramrod" Johnson.[16] If the Frying Pan was the first ranch to be completely enclosed by barbed wire in 1882, the Circle C may have been one of the last.

By the end of 1889, Smith supervised a staff of six employees, including future Amarillo banking magnate, B. T. Ware, and Marie's younger brother, Wade Bynum. Their salaries were $100 or less per month; the following year they were joined by another Bynum brother, Benjamin Chapman Dupree, aged 21, who would become Smith's closest Amarillo business associate for the remainder of Smith's life. Throughout the entire organizational process of Burns, Walker in the late 1880s, Smith was a role model of civility and integrity leading at least one banking customer to observe: "Burns, Walker had a strong safe and honest employees."[17]

In the meantime, Smith's wife, just entering her late 20s, was heavily involved in her own work on the Texas frontier. In three successive years and in three completely different involvements, Mrs. James Lowry Smith put her imprint on the map of Amarillo as its most forward-looking woman. First, following what Marie later termed a "red-hot town fight, the promising city moved one mile east" and in the autumn she established the Chautauqua Club, probably the first woman's club in Amarillo, but certainly its first literary club.[18] Marie led a group of college-educated women in discussions of such topics as political economy of the nineteenth century, Van Dyke's art achievements, the history of Rome, and, yes, even some physics and Latin. The club flourished for more than a decade.

Second, Della Key highlights Mrs. Smith's establishment of the First Baptist Church's Ladies Aid Society in 1890 as being the most significant money-raiser for the fledgling church.[19] But that is an understatement to say the least. The First Baptist Church minutes reveal that this woman's religious society set up the Buckner Orphans Home in Dallas as the primary recipient of church charitable funds for the next 40 years. In addition, the Ladies Aid Society is credited with presenting the first-ever pageant ("Pageant of Nations") in Amarillo history to raise money for the church seating and furnishings at the Church's location at Fifth and Pierce.[20]

Third, on July 10, 1891, Mrs. J. L. Smith received a letter from Thomas J. Hurley, President of the Texas World's Fair Exhibit Association that begins: "The County Judge of your County has appointed you as one of the seven Commissioners to represent your county…at the World's Columbian Exposition to be held in Chicago in 1893." Marie and her cohorts were tasked with organizing a patriotic and county activities' overview for what has become commonly known as the Chicago World's Fair. Marie readily agreed and received a sealed Certificate to that effect dated August 10, 1891. Whether Marie actually attended the Fair is doubtful because in the summer and fall of 1893 she was helping her aging parents in Horn Lake. Jimmie's five letters—all from that 1893 summer—represent the only correspondence between husband and wife that has survived their first 25 years in Amarillo.[21] In a July 30, 1893 letter to Marie, he states: "I will go via Memphis in going to Chicago or not. In fact will not go to the Fair at all if my business interests seem to require my presence here." Smith went on to state a week later that sales and bank deposits at Smith & Walker were lighter than they have been since the firm (a successor to Burns, Walker & Co. since 1891) began its operation.[22] This Smith letter was written in the midst of what has become known as the Money Panic of 1893 where the failure of eastern railroads and an overabundance of silver and lack of gold taxed the nation's banks resulting in many foreclosures. Fortunately, Smith had built up the cash reserve fund for his small private bank and had on hand in excess of $9,000. A few days later, Smith's ever-present humor reasserted itself when he inquired of Marie: "I notice in our room a new pair of Zeiglee La. Shoes. Are they yours, or do they belong in stock?"[23]

Besides his skilled business acumen, Smith was at the forefront in helping establish, almost single-handedly at its inception, the First Baptist Church, destined to go from its initial cadre of 16 charter members (of which the Smiths were two) to a Church of over 11,000 by 1989. Unfortunately, the actual church records for the first 10 years have been lost,[24] but there is testimony on Smith's steadfast exploits in the 1890s. J. S. Calloway, an Amarillo visitor in 1889, wrote of being "invited to attend a meeting one night for the organization of the Baptist Church. There were seven or eight other men besides Smith and myself. The meeting was held on the prairie just north of Amarillo."[25] Elder Thomas H. Storts reported that Mr. and Mrs. J. L. Smith "donated the organ and he was organist."[26] Smith, a versatile musician, "did play the cornet and trombone at many of the church services."[27] By modern standards the original wooden church structure was somewhat primitive with a metal tank baptistery and water hauled in by barrels from nearby windmill pumping areas. The church's damp underground meant hogs, chickens, and consequent fleas in summer, but a single stove provided some heat in the dead of winter.

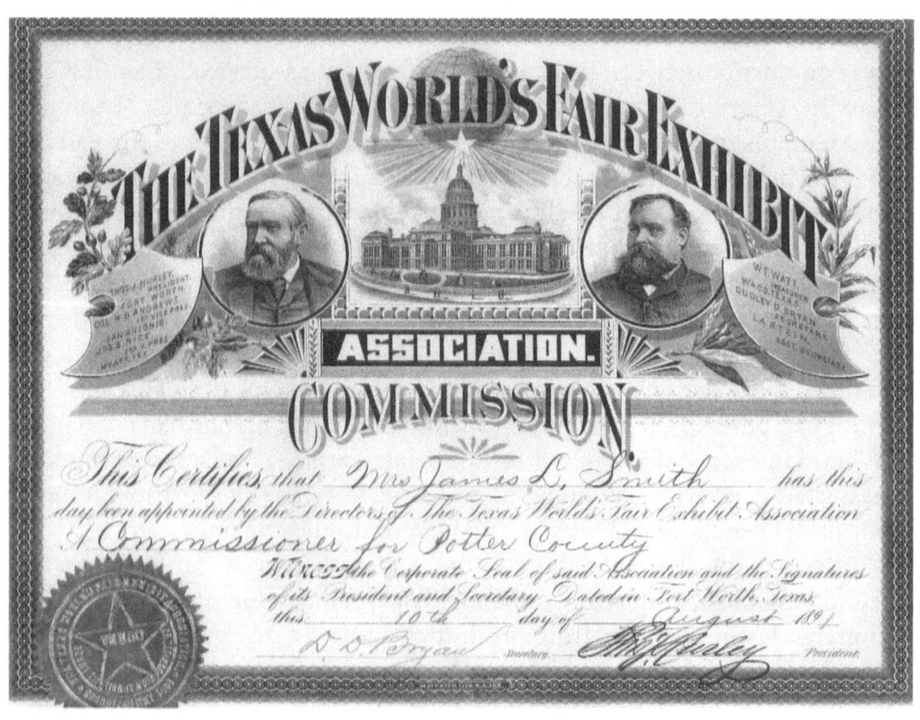

Mrs. James L. Smith, Texas Commissioner for Potter County for World's Fair Exhibit

Smith also served as Sunday School Superintendent and even taught bible classes along with Marie.[28] The Smiths were likewise present, along with representatives from eight other Panhandle Baptist Churches, at the inaugural meeting of the Palo Duro Baptist Association on September 21, 1891 in Claude.[29] From the beginning of extant First Baptist Church records, Smith is listed as nearly always attending this annual meeting. Smith, along with two others, formed the finance committee responsible for raising funds for First Baptist's initial building. As a perennial deacon, Smith was inevitably leading the way in church events. On at least three occasions, he chaired the Pulpit Selection Committee tasked with finding new pastors when a vacancy had occurred.[30] He was also the leading force in financing a parish-owned residence for ministers of First Baptist.

Even though Amarillo was not a "particularly attractive place in the 1890s" with its streets of mud in spring rains, dust bowl appearance in summer, and slush and chuckholes of winter,[31] social life did begin to emerge. Once again, the Smiths were providing leadership. On December 1, 1889, Smith played Lohengrin's Wedding March at the society marriage of Cora Brooks, daughter of Amarillo's first newspaperman, and John Wilson Wisner.[32] At the end of the same month, the Smiths opened their newly refurbished "parlors" in their Pierce Street home for a New Year's Eve party.[33] In yet another civilizing move, Smith staked Jack Floyd's new restaurant in 1895, a chophouse that featured fine cuisine for years.[34] In the meantime, the profits of Smith & Walker, jobbers and retailers of general merchandise from dry goods to groceries by car lots on the railroads, increased steadily reaching $71,500 for the last six months of 1893. Banking was also flourishing with deposits alone at $18,000.[35] From his wholesale suppliers in St. Louis, Smith secured new lines of goods: 13,000 lbs. of corn meal and five cases of mince meat sent via the Atchison, Topeka, and the Santa Fe.[36] "Ladies Fur Capes, Bust 33" were ordered from Chicago[37] and "four dozen of the $2.62 pants, waist 31-36, leg 30-35" from New York.[38] An added venture was the wholesale buying and selling of wool produced by Panhandle sheep. Smith & Walker received 213, 400 lbs. in August 1894[39] and sold 477 bags in St. Louis in late December.[40]

Such seemingly deliberate and calculated business transactions were a far cry from the man who actually performed them. Smith, an impeccably slim man of six feet in stature, was preeminently kind, honest, and completely trustworthy—something that cannot be said for many of his peers. He has been praised as a "Born Leader."[41] He was once singled

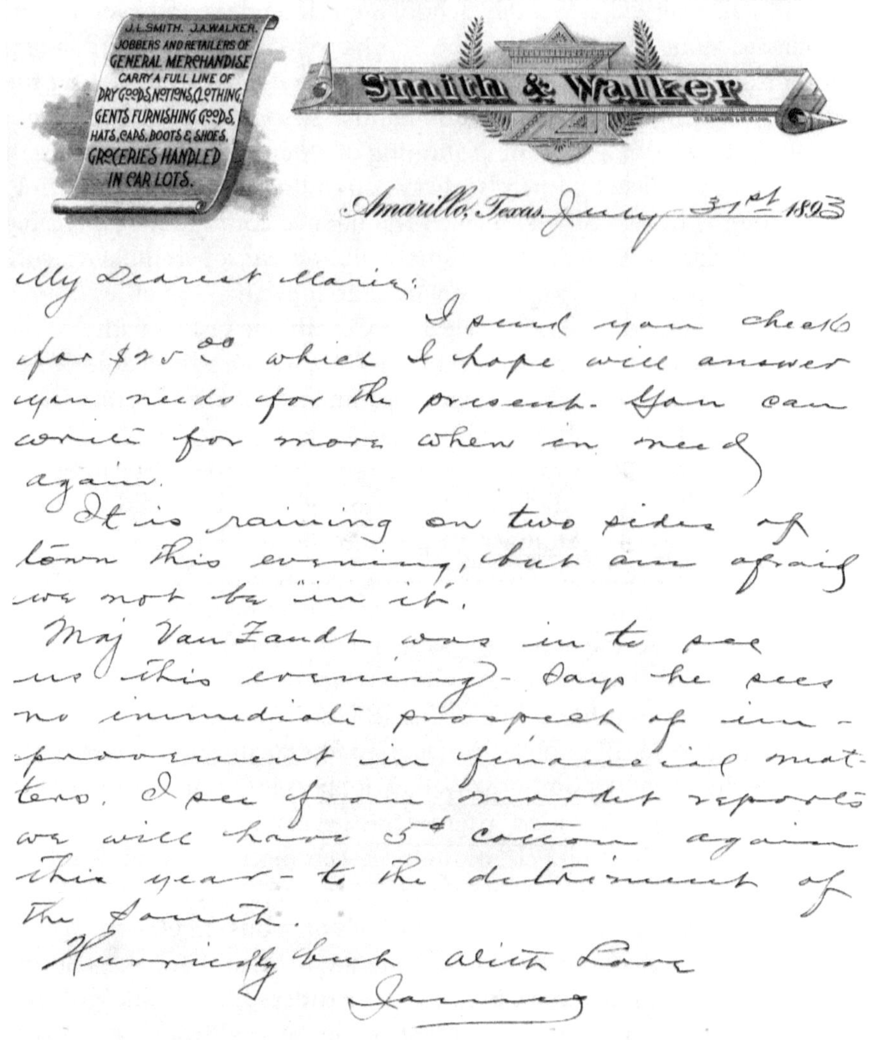

Letter James to Marie on Smith and Walker letterhead

out by an about-to-retire rancher in 1894 as "Friend Jim,…you have always been kind and considerate toward me."[42] In an interview late in life, Miss Addie Whitcomb recalled being invited by Smith not to leave the premises before coming back to visit with him; she saluted Smith as the business man who impressed her the most in her younger days.[43] Such civility also carried over to family members. When Marie's 21-year-old brother Ben came to Amarillo to work for Smith in the store in 1890, he was initially depressed by the flat and forlorn Amarillo landscape. Young Ben Bynum would go to the railroad depot and look in the direction from which he had come. He wondered what would happen to him if this "ribbon of steel track" were cut and severed him from civilization. He asked Mr. Smith why there were no trees. Smith shrugged his shoulders and replied that 'Trees just will not grow in this country, Ben.'[44] With one great exception and that exception was the green thumb of Marie. She has been given credit as the woman who planted the first tree in Amarillo, a locust sapling in 1889 that grew to a mighty bulk.[45] This initial horticultural success would pave the way for her much larger future landscape endeavors at Amarillo's principle city park the following decade.

By 1895 Smith & Walker had occupied the ground floor of the Opera House, though it was sometimes called the Smith House because of the name emblazoned across the portals and the goods advertised on the windows. In fact, 1895 was a significant year for James Lowry Smith in several crucial regards. Smith and his partner joined forces with their chief competitor, Wooten-Nobles Grocery Company, and Jimmie and Marie moved to Temple to supervise the beginning of one of the largest grocery chains in Texas at the time, Temple Grocer Company, which by the early 1900s would become Walker-Smith Wholesale Grocery Company which would grow to 20 houses (distribution points) in its heyday from Galveston to Pecos. It is important to note that between 1895 and 1902, Smith and his partner operated two separate enterprises: one, Smith & Walker, the original successor to Burns, Walker Co. in Amarillo—a strictly *retail* business; and, two, the new undertaking in Temple and Brownwood—a strictly *wholesale* business.

It was commonplace in early Amarillo for, say, a banker to be placed on the board of directors for a new hardware company or for a prominent merchant to be listed as a stockholder in a new bank. What was highly unusual was a joint association between two companies engaged in the exact same business; such was the deal reached in late 1894, a deal that bore all the earmarks of Smith's innovative business acumen. The most famous grocery firm in Amarillo history was originally established in 1892 by M. C. and H. A. Nobles. In a December 31, 1894 letter to John Walker, now in Temple, Smith acknowledged: "...it is now pretty generally understood here we will consolidate with Mess. W. N. & Co. on the 1ˢᵗ" and that we have "admitted Wooten and Nobles to membership in our firm." Less than two weeks later Smith provided Walker with detailed accounting, indicating a "W. N. & Co. Branch with $25,000 and the stock holdings at $12,500 each for J. L. Smith and J. A. Walker and $6,250 each for W. H. Wooten, M. C. Nobles, and H. A. Nobles."[46] So concerned was M. C. Nobles with the success of their joint enterprise that he forewarned Walker himself about a new grocery interloper in Amarillo, Mr. J. A. Kemp, and presumed a war would erupt if Smith & Walker and Wooten & Nobles did not protect their mutual investment.[47] Walker agreed and Kemp eventually became satisfied with a moderate slice of Amarillo business. As Della Key points out, somewhat summarily and incompletely insofar as finances are concerned and without reference to their allied interests, the Nobles, Wooten, and a man named G. S. Howard bought a half-interest in the Smith & Walker store in 1895 for $1,600 and moved into the former Smith & Walker quarters in the 200-block of Polk.[48] However, such a correct geographic observation only confirms the close business dealings between the two former competing retail grocery companies. In the meantime, Smith—once again most astute about emerging opportunities—wrote Walker that the Pecos Valley Railway was extending and predicted that a new, important town would appear where the rail tracks "cross the Terra Blanco Creek 35 miles SW of Amarillo."[49] That town did emerge and was christened Hereford and became a site for a branch of Smith & Walker and, eventually, a Smith & Walker private bank.

Smith was also successful in dissuading his wholesale grocery partner, John Walker, from investing in Memphis or Houston as an eventual company headquarters, opting instead to remain in Temple and extend to Brownwood. Temporarily, Smith and his partner named their Yancey & Branch Co. acquisition the Temple Grocer Company and then negotiated a buy-out of Ramey, Garnett & Co. Wholesale Grocers in Brownwood.[50] As to the actual acquisitions themselves, Smith had made sure that both Yancey & Branch and Ramey, Garnett were on solid financial footing before their actual purchase. Three extant financial documents attest to Smith's bookkeeper instincts about the eventual profitability of both firms. First, Smith's notations on a Yancey & Branch sales sheet reveal that company's sales for April through July, 1893. The total credit sales for the quarter stood at $54,051.74. The cash sales matched the credit sales almost dollar for dollar with $54,710.06 recorded. Second, a Ramey, Garnett & Co. sales sheet listed the by-month sales for the first 11 months of 1894 and a projected estimate for December. The total was $270,928.49. Third, another Ramey, Garnett sheet showed the value of products manufactured at their in-house candy factory as $6,607.82.[51] To guarantee a smooth transition and to provide day-to-day leadership along the way, Smith and Walker concurred in appointing J. B. Garnett as their company's first Vice-President and General Manager, a capacity Garnett filled for 15 years until his retirement in 1910.[52] Smith's accounting verve led him to predict that a well-set-up wholesale grocery company could "sell $600,000 at least at a net profit of 4%."[53]

If John Walker was far and away the principle stockholder in the fledgling Temple Grocer Company, Smith managed a $30,000 investment for himself and $3,000 for Marie, realized from the sale of her own hardware stock in 1894.[54] In the meantime, Smith had promised to keep Smith & Walker/Wooten & Nobles up and running in Amarillo, but by mid-1895 it was evident his skilled services were needed to carry the new and much larger wholesale enterprise forward in Temple and that he planned to move there in May. However, not before undertaking a two-week trip to New York City and St. Louis for two crucial purposes: to buy spring stock for the Amarillo retail business but, even more importantly, to visit several bankers in both cities to establish lines of credit for the new Temple and Brownwood venture.

Following up on his numerous business dealings with manufacturers and bankers in St. Louis, Smith engineered much-needed loans from that city's Fourth National Bank[55] and urged Walker to send completed stock certificates to each investor in the Temple Grocer business.[56] Clearly, the broadminded Smith always had an honest eye for protecting the rights and privileges of all the new firm's stockholders and eventual employees. Always the voice of caution and sanity in all his business undertakings, Smith early on advised the always eager John Walker that any eventual expansion of Temple Grocers into new areas such as Ballinger, San Angelo, or Cameron be placed on hold for a couple of years and only then based on inputs of a reliable "business man (not a grocer man)."[57]

Smith, Walker & Co, Bankers Letterhead

Although it is only an adjunct concern of this history, a case can be made that John A. Walker was the John D. Rockefeller of Central Texas. He owned a gold mining company in Mexico and was on the board of directors for three other New Mexico and West Texas businesses. He formed a very successful bank of his own in Brownwood and owned interests in a telephone company in San Angelo. With either Wade or B. C. D. Bynum, he financed the New Walker Hotel, Bynum & Walker, Proprietors, in Brownwood, plus early on purchased a huge portfolio of the American car company he knew would outstrip all the competition, namely General Motors. Likely, too, he bankrolled his stepfather and the two Bynum brothers in an allied retail grocery concern in nearby Killeen. Records also indicate he retained huge ranch land and other real estate interests near Colorado City.[58] What is patently clear from the outset is that Walker was the money man and Smith the details man for the new joint operation that would revolutionize the rural-area Texas food industry. Smith's allegiance to Walker would prove remarkable and extend far beyond the terms of his original small-investment partnership with Walker begun in 1885 in Colorado City.

How long Jimmie and Marie would be in Temple was anyone's guess. In a March 11, 1895 business letter to a customer and close friend, Smith mentioned, "I expect to move to Temple next month and make that my home" and, later that month, he notified Walker, "I expect to get a car in moving my HH goods to Temple and think we had better box and ship all our old account books."[59] Despite the latter indication, Smith & Walker of Amarillo remained open and flourished for the next seven years with Smith keeping in daily contact with his Amarillo business manager.

Not a great deal is known about the Temple hiatus in the Smiths' lives because business and family interests were joined together in one town and there is little discussion in any of the Smith business letters about daily life in Temple. However, the Temple Grocer enterprise operated differently from the one Walker conducted on his own in Roswell, New Mexico, the Joyce, Pruit & Co., run on a daily basis by Drew Pruit, Walker's cousin and a veteran of Burns, Walker & Company's Colorado City days. In a widely distributed July 31, 1895 circular, Joyce, Pruit boasted: "Our facilities for buying are the very best…our Mr. J. A. Walker being a member of the firm of Smith & Walker of Amarillo, Texas, and also President of The Temple Grocer[y] Co., of Temple, Texas, making four large concerns which buy together. This fact alone proves conclusively that we get lower prices than we could possibly do had we not those large connections." On receipt of his copy, Smith penned across the bottom: "We don't charge you anything for blowing your horn." Just such a gesture is characteristic of the humble Smith: he never felt it necessary to toot his own cornet about any of his business or civic successes and he made sure that the Joyce, Pruit grocery enterprises of Walker and Pruit remained financially separate from Temple Grocer Company except for very occasional oversized purchases.

Alas, John Walker and his wife Bessie did acquire a reputation for flaunting their wealth, including an October 31, 1895 receipt for a new top buggy, complete with leather boot, panel guards, and dust cover for which Walker insisted on a 4% cash discount.[60] Likewise, the general tenor of correspondence reaching Walker in Temple during the late 1890s showed his inordinate concern with receiving immediate added interest payments on loans he had made to other business and to real estate brokers. In addition both John and Bessie began to manifest what would soon become a lifelong self-accommodation: they loved to take expensive and prolonged vacations. For example, to the Walkers, vacationing at a seaside resort in Corpus Christi, Smith reported that the May 1896 receipts from their joint Smith & Walker/Wooten & Nobles operation in Amarillo totaled $25,092 and that, as a result of the high level of profits, new branches were being developed in Hereford and Canyon.[61] At the dawn of the new century, Walker sold his 1895 carriage and updated to a fancy new phaeton, complete with one-inch rubber tires, oil lamps, and seat panels with linen biscuit stuffing.[62]

At this juncture, a pause seems reasonable in order to examine the largest unsolved mystery in the marriage of Jimmie and his beloved "Sissie," as she was now known to a few relatives and close friends. The question is: did they or did they not ever have children of their own? In his brief history of his uncle, James Bynum states bluntly: "Mr. and Mrs. James L.

Smith had no children."[63] There are, however, two accounts of the Smith struggles to have children that share a common theme. First, Katherine Bynum Cobb Baker (b. Amarillo, May 14, 1912, d. Tucson, AZ, October 5, 1999) steadfastly maintained all her life that "Sissie's two babies died in infancy."[64] She even avowed that they were twin boys who died because of a blood incompatibility and that the Smiths' close physician and friend, Dr. White of Scott and White in Temple, paid a personal visit to Amarillo to try to save the infants. A second and more plausible account of the Smith 'children' comes from Sissie's two great nieces (and granddaughters of Marie's brother, Wade Bynum), Kay Coleman and LeBecca Paddock, who spent time in Amarillo with their great aunt very late in her life.[65] In an interview, LeBecca stated that on one visit, "Great Aunt Sissie told me she had suffered three miscarriages." Such unfortunate events have recently been verified by her cousin Kay Coleman who also heard Sissie speak about her miscarriages, the last one of which occurred just before a visit from Dr. White in Amarillo. He had come specifically to speak to Mrs. Smith about dangers to her own future health, strictly warning her, "No more pregnancies, Mrs. Smith." Kay also added that her grandmother, Lena Hildebrand Bynum who had married Wade Bynum in September 1892, was living in Amarillo at the time of the last miscarriage and told Kay the very same story about Dr. White's visit and caution to her sister-in-law. One might also add that either Dr. White or Dr. Scott was James Lowry's personal physician while he and Marie were in Temple, a relationship that continued into Smith's final years where he mentions visits from Amarillo to Temple to have complete physical examinations by Dr. Scott.

One undertaking, coincident with the Smiths' stay in Temple, was the founding of the King's Daughters Hospital, first located in a vacated church and finally in a newly constructed and dedicated facility. Jimmie and Sissie donated complete furnishings for one of the rooms at the new hospital.[66] Perhaps their charitable gift was in memory of the children they never had or in recognition of Jimmie's closest male friend from Salado days, Dr. Bob Barton, who was the oldest charter physician at the hospital and a long-time Temple resident.[67]

Unfortunately, few personal communiqués survive from the Smiths' four-year stay in Central Texas. One such is a touching letter written to her cousin, Walker Peebles, in Lake Cove, MS while she was visiting her parents in Horn Lake in spring 1896. She asks if there is some family member besides herself who could help take charge of her parents' needs because they are both "feeble" and no longer able "to take care of things" on their own. Marie does admit that, whatever happens, William and Kate Bynum will eventually "go to Texas" and live with her and Jimmie.[68] Scattered references indicate that Marie indeed made numerous trips over to Horn Lake to see to her parents all through their Temple stay. The only additional extant personal letter is one to Marie from her 22-year-old sister, Sally, in Horn Lake seeking advice from "Sissie" about Sally's taking a teaching position for "$30 a month including board and washing."[69] Sally did take the position but only on a temporary basis because her future lay in Amarillo.

While his wife catered to her immediate and extended family, Smith continued his work with the newly formed wholesale grocery firm in Temple *and*, via a constant flow of letters, with the now 10-year-old Smith & Walker mercantile operation in Amarillo.[70] The preserved letters illustrate the vast responsibilities involved in running a business at a distance and most of the correspondence is signed simply "Smith & Walker." What follows is a tip-of-the-iceberg overview of the Amarillo store and its demands. Three February 1897 letters indicate ordering canned goods of "good standard grade" by the carload and the recovery of an overdue loan note and its method of payment.[71] Two April letters reveal Smith's expertise at negotiating a temporary loan from his St. Louis bank and an order for "soft, felt hats for men, wholesale price $12 to $24 per dozen."[72] A year later Smith & Walker had opened branches at Canyon and Hereford and ordered a "safe" for Canyon to be delivered "immediately" because "believe we will do quite a banking business there."[73]

The shear variety of an expanding product line carried in Smith's Panhandle trade illustrates how diverse and widespread merchandising had become since the primitive wooden shop and tent-roofed business in Old Town a decade before. Orders were placed in the Oklahoma Territory for 100 lbs. of assorted size Navajo saddle blankets; in Missouri for orange velvet millinery; and in Illinois for Ivory soap by the box.[74] That bicycles—even automobiles--were supplementing horses as a means of transportation was shown by a May invoice for "inner tubes."[75] In the same month, Smith & Walker shipped off "3 sacks wool , 395 lbs. and 1 bundle sheep pelts, 150 lbs." to a manufacturer in Missouri and requested new pricing for bulk orders of White Loaf Flour from a firm in Colorado.[76]

In the meantime, the Temple Grocer Company and its Brownwood Branch in 1895 "enjoyed a volume of $689,000, bringing in a satisfactory net profit."[77] After four years of operation in Temple, assets at that location were sold off and Temple Grocer Company headquarters were moved to Brownwood in 1899; the name would be officially changed to Walker-Smith Wholesale Grocery Company in 1903 and this firm would continue to operate by that name for the next 40 years. Ever-increasing sales and the acquisition of a candy and coffee manufacturing facility in Brownwood led to expansion to the first of an eventual 20 regional grocery houses in San Angelo in 1898. Smith, seeing that the new enterprise was flourishing, returned to Amarillo in March 1899—but not before making yet another trip to New York City to visit bankers, letting them know that "J. L. Smith and J. A. Walker are the owners of good securities outside of Temple Grocer Company to the amount of $50,000 and $150,000 respectively."[78]

If John Walker was the financial guru intrigued by rapid increases in population and business in West Texas, James Lowry Smith provided a tempering and civilized balance to his partner's visions. He watched two Amarillo businesses flounder from excessive risk-taking while "undertaking to do a credit business with their limited investment," the result being "impaired capital."[79] Hence, Smith advised that any large business undertaken by Walker-Smith Co. always include held collateral to secure open accounts. For similar reasons, he also suggested that a new "iron clad building" for the newly opened San Angelo house was impractical from both a financial and cosmetic standpoint. Ceilings, walls, and disposable capital were, Smith felt, absolutely essential for a successful grocery house in a new location.[80] So astute was Smith's insight about operating a new business that he had previously insisted his partner's staff survey "both Temple and Brownwood territory and make a list of customers and also a list of those who are not customers but whom we would like to have."[81]

As far as the return to Amarillo was concerned, in one of the few times he ever vented about the *llano estacado*, Smith wrote his partner:

> Lots of disagreeable weather—high winds and cold nights. I would not undertake to make this my home for all the cattle lands in the Panhandle. The truth of the business is I don't want money bad enough to stay *here* to make it. Of course, I shall stay, however, so long as the conditions of our affairs require it.[82]

Evidently their home, now on the corner of 4th and Johnson, with its unpaved streets, rickety sidewalks, and windswept front yard, was a far cry from Temple's hills, nearby hospitals, and green landscape. Never one to complain for more than a fretful moment, Jimmie plunged back into church and community affairs with unabated energy. He joined Judge Veale and prominent banker W. H. Fuqua in canvassing the church members who had fallen by the wayside. Marie and her husband were immediately elected to represent First Baptist as delegates to the Texas Baptist Convention. Marie's imitation stained-glass windows in the small church had helped attract a total of 119 members while Smith was added to the deacon rolls. Primarily through Smith's diligent efforts the church was soon on a better financial footing or "comparatively out of debt" as he put it. During the next three years Smith and his wife were again chosen as church delegates to the state convention and to the Palo Duro Baptist Association. They pledged money to repair the parsonage and saw to it that the church had new electric lighting. Both Smiths served on a committee to raise the pastor's salary $200 to an annual one of $1,200. By mid 1901, membership stood at 154 and plans were being discussed for a newer and larger church.[83]

To boost Amarillo's stock as the premier town in the Panhandle, Fuqua, Smith, Nobles, and others formed the Amarillo-Panhandle Fair and Live Stock Association on August 25, 1899. Smith was elected as the organization's first vice-president, and the charter and immediate stock subscriptions heralded the upcoming event as "the greatest Fair and Live Stock Show in the West."[84] The first show took place on November 23 and was accompanied by full-page newspaper ads in the weeks preceding which showed committees for receptions, entertainment, boarding house, hall/light/badges, and transportation. The committee members included R. L. Stringfellow, Lon D. Marss, D. R. Fly, J. P. Floyd, and a host of other Amarillo notables.[85] Although this initial effort at a Panhandle-wide event gradually faded away, the initiative taken paved the way for Amarillo's eventual annual hosting of the Tri-State Fair.

To close out the nineteenth century in grand fashion, the two firms of Smith & Walker and Stringfellow & Hume Hardware established a long-distance telephone service to their branch stores in Hereford, thus marking a fundamental step forward in communications.[86] As Smith & Walker Co. entered their final two years of operation, the sales ledgers and newspaper ads began to reveal a distinctly different clientele from 10 years previous. For example, a half-ton of coal cost $3.75 and men's suits could be bought off the rack. Dress suits could be special ordered for the bargain price of $3.50.[87] Newspaper ads heralded "a complete line of Ladies' dress skirts, undershirts, jackets, and cloaks." Full-page ads for women's apparel included a high-fashion line of "cheviot skirts in black and blue with welt seams" on sale for $2.25 to $6.55 and the hiring of a woman's trimmer and millinery expert. Lace curtains could be purchased along with silk "Shirt Waist Patterns in silk that cannot be surpassed for beauty."[88]

Apples now arrived by the carload along with "Fresh candles, Nuts and Fruit Cake Ingredients for the holidays."[89] Of course, staple items continued to sell, but now there was a new emphasis on fresh vegetables such as "New potatoes and onions at proper prices."[90] Canned goods also witnessed increased sales with shoppers purchasing canned coffee, oysters, peaches, corn, and tomatoes by the case. Alas, so brisk were sales and so unavailable was trash pick-up that domesticated areas adjacent to Amarillo had "heaps of containers so high that the Panhandle was called 'Tin Can Land.'"[91]

The final ledger entries for Smith & Walker sales end abruptly in July 1902. However, because their wholesale grocery business was growing at a phenomenal rate in Brownwood, Jimmie Smith and John Walker had discussed terminating their retail businesses in the Amarillo area as early as 1901 with Smith advocating sales of the branch houses in Canyon and Hereford while continuing the private banking facilities they had established at both locations.[92] It took some doing, but Smith convinced his brother-in-law, Ben, to superintend all the details for the Hereford branch for the remainder of its tenure.[93] Ben could see that an end to the Smith & Walker retail business was in the offing. Indeed, he wrote to his father in Mississippi that he had just sent the firm's bookkeeper on a collection trip to New Mexico and that he hoped to get the Hereford matters in shape in the next several months so he "would no longer be compelled to stay in this place."[94] Bynum also knew that his brother-in-law had already secured lots on the southwest corner of 5th and Polk and was soon planning to build a new public bank.[95] Bynum wanted and would soon find a piece of that more fulfilling action. It is clear that Smith had good premonitions about the banking industry in the Panhandle, but that he wanted to solidify Hereford and Canyon as banking enterprises before carrying the banking to its next phase. In fact, Smith had made an alliance with a very knowledgeable Amarillo banker, G. A. F. Parker, to broaden his financial base and, of course, had also included John Walker in his plans: "New people are coming into the country who do not know Smith, Walker

& Co and we will have to do all we can at all times to patronize a National Bank as against a private institution."[96]

With a wholesale grocery concern with statewide distribution ambitions and expanded banking interests in three Panhandle communities, one would surmise that Smith's plate was full. True, demands of business, church, and the civic advancement of Amarillo were ever present, but one more opportunity beckoned. As the new century entered its second year, James Lowry Smith was about to become one of the Panhandle's first experts in oil well drilling and production.

James Christopher Paul was between Amarillo bank ownerships of his own in early 1901 so he partnered with Smith and opened Buffalo Oil Company located in the Beaumont field and near Spindletop, the first great Texas oilfield. J. L. Smith was president and Paul treasurer and, apparently, the on-site financial expert because Paul complained about the "uncomfortable living" along the humid Gulf Coast and longed for "the breezy plains" of the Panhandle.[97] In any event, Buffalo Oil Company letterhead advertised the capital stock at $300,000 full paid and non-assessable, while offering the public at large shares at 10 cents each.[98] Paul owned $25,000 worth of stock and Smith $4,307.50.[99] Never one to pass up a good deal, John Walker had purchased $3,196 worth of stock in May 1901 and, judging by the personal correspondence from Treasurer Paul, increased his holdings considerably over the next few months.[100]

The operations of an oil company in a rich production field are always complicated and Buffalo Oil Company was no exception. In addition to its Spindletop holdings, the company owned a 560-acre interest at nearby Vinton, LA, and a controlling interest in 8,000 acres within Jack County, TX. Even though located northwest of Fort Worth, Jack County land was listed as follows: "Not in very high demand now, but a splendid reserve, as it is a good oil property and worth several times what has been spent on it."[101] Buffalo owned its Beaumont acreage and other Jefferson County land "in fee simple." Indeed, early on the company drilled at least one large hole near but not on Spindletop, but on one acre of "Douthit land" valued at the incredible price of $15,000.[102] However, this well, dug to 1,500 feet, yielded only sandy mud and was written off as a duster.[103] Nothing ever remains stable in rich oil country and on September 2, 1901 J. L. Smith telegrammed Walker in Brownwood that "Buffalo has a first-class six-inch gusher. Came in yesterday." Apparently, a series of complex lease negotiations near "Spindletop Heights" meant a leap in earnings for Buffalo.[104]

What is patently obvious from all the extant Buffalo Oil Company correspondence is that it was not a wildcatter operation. Far from it. For example, lest stock shares proliferate beyond expected earnings, the company cut off all public offerings in late October 1901 because of what it termed the "lightning-like rapidity of change" ever since the discovery of oil on Spindletop.[105] In addition, when a contractor failed to deliver promised railroad oil cars to market the petroleum, Buffalo promptly increased its on-site storage facilities to include four 1,200-barrel wooden tanks "used for oil to flow into" and a 37,500-barrel steel storage tank equipped with all the latest valves, fittings, and fire safety features.[106] The end product of all the drilling—simply termed "fuel oil"—was used as a heating product and to fire industrial boilers and Buffalo advertised this product in all of its solicitations for sales of this end product.[107]

Buffalo Oil Company owned fully-paid-for equipment such as power boilers, a "first-class water well which does not lime boilers," two large oil pumps and three air compressors, plus two miles of 4 and 6-inch pipeline. They even owned a "$10,000 interest on a big refinery and pipeline project." In short, they could drill, agitate the flow, and get the black gold to several state-of-the-art storage facilities. At the April 10, 1902 Stockholder's Meeting, the company announced reserve funds of $23,000 in the treasury, but declined to pay dividends because new purchases of pipeline and "first-class oil pumps" were in the offing. The somewhat chagrined stockholders were rewarded, however, with a large dividend payment at the September 24, 1902 meeting.

The entire operation of Buffalo Oil Company in 1901, 1902, and for the next four years of existence is a testament to the forthright honesty of its president. Never one to hide a setback—there were several other dry holes early on—Smith even invited an outside inspector to attend the April 1902 Stockholder's Meeting where the directors and principle stockholders and the proxies of the remaining holders of 1,325,897 shares were fully represented. The inspector concluded: "I was shown the holdings of the company and from what I have seen and heard, believe the property to be progressively and honestly managed."[108] Just before Christmas of 1902, J. L. Smith wrote from Amarillo and apologized to John Walker for not updating him on end-of-the-year doings for Buffalo Oil because "[I] have been on the Grand Jury constantly for two weeks." Buffalo Oil had just sold 11,838 barrels for $3,056.55 and would have no problems delivering on another shipment to reach the 21,081 barrels promised in one of Buffalo's contracts.[109] The slightly more than 25 cents per barrel oil had exceeded the company's price expectations.

In his recent study of Amarillo, Paul Carlson expertly centers on Amarillo's cattle, farming, and oil and gas industries.[110] At the risk of oversimplification, one might extend Carlson's observation and argue that the Panhandle's development was divided into three 20-year periods where one industry dominated the economy. From 1880-1900 it was cattle; from 1900-1920 it was agriculture; from 1920-1940 it was oil and gas. Given James Lowry Smith's farming background in Salado, his expertise as a stockmen's outfitter in Colorado City, and his first-hand knowledge of Texas' first big oilfield, it is clear that he was very well equipped to absorb the business implications of the ranches that were beginning to be cut up or sold off. He was equally well prepared to meet the wheat farming boom already beginning in the Panhandle and the petroleum boom that would subsequently follow at the end of World War I.

Chapter 5

Amarillo
1903-1914

Between 1900 and 1910 Amarillo's population swelled from just below 1,500 to nearly 10,000, making Amarillo—percentage wise—the fastest growing city in the world during the first decade of the twentieth century.[1] If the population increased rapidly, so did the breadth of Jimmie and Marie's commitments to each other and to Amarillo: his to business and civic activities; hers to two major civic and social projects; and both to their beloved First Baptist Church soon to be one of the largest churches in the Panhandle.

Based on an 1875 statute, Texas laws prohibited the formation of state banks, so in late May 1903 the Controller of Currency approved the application of J. L. Smith and others to organize the National Bank of Commerce in a newly constructed two-story brick building on the southwest corner of 5th and Polk.[2] Even though Texas banking laws only required $25,000 to capitalize a national bank, Smith and his directors initially capitalized at triple that amount.[3] In fact, said bank was advertised on the first page of the first extant Amarillo telephone directory of September 1903. The ad stated that the new National Bank of Commerce was "successors to Smith-Walker & Company, Bankers" [private bank] and that the new bank would feature "Interest Paid on Time Deposits."[4] All new banks undergo a settling in process, but the three principle financial officers turned out to be: J. L. Smith, President; M. C. Nobles, Vice-President; and B. C. D. Bynum, Cashier. Obviously, from the outset, Smith turned to trusted business associates from earlier enterprises to form the core structure of his bank. In the early twentieth century, national banks were permitted to issue their own currency as a negotiable instrument. In fact, a signed $5 bill bearing Benjamin Harrison's engraved portrait and the original signatures of Smith and Bynum still survives and bears a June 26, 1903 issue date.[5] Theoretically, banks can still issue their own currency, but the 10% tax on non-Federal Reserve Notes makes such an undertaking cost prohibitive.[6]

Smith also ventured outside Amarillo with his changes in banking procedures. In late 1903, the former Smith & Walker Bankers in Hereford became Western National Bank, headed by veteran financial expert G. A. F. Parker but with John Walker participating and Smith serving as vice-president.[7] As early as March 28, 1904, assets were listed at $130,048.88.[8] Smith was also present at the organizational meeting of the Panhandle Bankers Association on June 6, 1904 and presented a paper on "Collateral" which was "of sufficiently high quality to be printed in its entirety in a special publication sponsored by the group."[9]

M. C. NOBLES, VICE PRES'T
B. C. D. BYNUM, CASHIER

J. L. SMITH, PRESIDENT
Nº 6865

R. A. DAVIS, ASST. CASHIER
C. C. CHENOWETH, ASST. CASHIER

National Bank of Commerce

Capital $ 75,000.00   Surplus $ 75,000.00

Amarillo, Texas

Early National Bank of Commerce letterhead

No sooner had Smith and Walker closed their own retail business in Amarillo, Canyon, and Hereford then another retail enterprise presented itself in a city northwest of Amarillo. One of the oldest clothing firms in the Panhandle was Haynie Mercantile Company in Channing, TX. A clearance sales flyer from July 25, 1903 gives a fine indication of the goods they carried as Jimmie and John prepared to invest in the company:

Our Stock of Summer Goods Must Go
- We will sell all summer Lawns, Dimities, Ginghams, Ducks, Piqués at 25% discount
- 1/3 off on all Ladies and Misses Low Cut Shoes
- ¼ off on all Ladies muslin underwear
- Men's $2.00 Hats go at $1.35
- Men's Suits, formerly $7.00, go at $4.25
- All 75-cent Shirts at 45 cents[10]

At the very same time of the advertised sale, Haynie Mercantile was undergoing financial difficulties. The source of the difficulty was that Haynie's assets had been greatly over-evaluated by a rival bank in Amarillo owned by W. H. Fuqua and had led Haynie himself to make a series of untimely and unsecured loans.[11] Jimmie and John immediately bought in and became shareholders and, with the help of Ben Bynum and others, they resurrected the business and put it on a much more solid foundation. However, no business transformation is ever as immediate as it first seems. In early 1904, Smith wrote to Walker in Brownwood: "We had to take charge of the Haynie business again." To cover the Haynie indebtedness, Walker pledged $11,000 in new stock and Smith $6,000.[12] From then on Haynie Mercantile prospered and its two financial saviors were able to take profitable dividends over the next 15 years.

But James Lowry Smith was not always restructuring businesses and counting bank deposits. The best indicator of a man's love for his wife is what he does for her family. Starting in the early1890s and extending into the second decade of the twentieth century, Smith opened his house as living quarters for four members of Marie's immediate family. Bachelor Ben Bynum was a household member for 20 years until his marriage to Bertha Kate Nunn on November 10, 1909. Marie's younger sister by 12 years, Sally Bynum, lived with the Smiths from the late 1890s until her marriage on September 14, 1909. The real story, however, was the arrival of Marie's parents in 1903. The aging Civil War veteran, William Joseph Bynum, lived there until his death on December 10, 1907 and his wife, Katherine Walker Bynum, until her passing on October 18, 1916.

To handle the influx of Marie's family, the Smiths built a large-frame house of some two-and-a-half stories at 1101 Taylor Street. It was completed in late 1904 at the cost of $10,000, and the family moved in during February 1905. The modest Smith was not trying to compete with his wealthy peers such as Lee Bivins, Henry Sanborn, W. H. Fuqua, or Albert Boyce who erected lavish homes along the silk-stocking rows of Amarillo's presidentially named streets. The Smith home featured a wooden foyer and staircase leading to upper bedrooms as well as a wrap-around porch to accommodate chairs for all his kin. All lighting fixtures, plumbing, and heating devices were purchased from local merchants under Jimmie's careful supervision. He did accede, however, to his wife's wishes for leaded glass windows on the front of the home and a stained glass window at the head of the stairs.[13]

Smith Home at 1101 Taylor Street

Despite having to care for her parents, Marie was at the forefront of Amarillo's becoming a first-rate civilized western city. Her being a charter member of the Social Dames Club in 1903 prepared her for her leadership role in the assault on Ellwood City Park.[14] 'Assault' is perhaps a strong word, but it required strong directional leadership to save the largest piece of undeveloped land in downtown Amarillo. Henry Sanborn had donated 20+ acres for a park in honor of his deceased son, Ellwood. For some years, Amarillo's citizenry had paid only token attention to the park's development until Sanborn wanted it back for real estate expansion. A lengthy series of legal battles ensued from 1903 until 1906 with Sanborn finally losing his suit against the city, provided Amarillo acted quickly to preserve the land for public use.[15]

Printed accounts highlight Mrs. Smith's fight for the right kinds of trees for the park area even to the point of Marie corralling her husband to take a yardstick and measure tree heights to assure that the billing costs matched the planted trees.[16] There were oyster suppers, ice cream socials, even Mrs. Smith's recruiting of Amarillo's young bachelors to each contribute a tree,

119

stand before it, and be admired by eligible young Amarillo women. Credit for the tree plantings is bestowed exclusively on a Clarendon Nursery at a cost of $164.85.[17]

However, Mrs. Smith's extant original notebook on the charter members of the Amarillo Civic League and their contributions reveals an Amarillo nursery connection made either shortly before or after the tree imports from Clarendon. Although an exact date is missing from the printed 190_ bill statement found tucked inside the membership notebook, 196 maples, 213 elms, and 28 ash trees were planted during March and April at the City Park by one C. C. Cunningham, a well-known Amarillo nursery man. The total cost, including nursery fees, was $393.30 with all monies paid by "Ladies of the Civic League."[18] According to the reprinted newspaper account, J. L. Smith had urged Marie and her group to work on the Ellwood Park project exclusively because "We men are too busy making a living to have time to make parks."[19] But Marie's Civic League notebook lists J. L. Smith as a member along with Mayor W. A. Miller whose wife was the treasurer for the Civic League in 1906. Some 72 names appear on the membership roster, including those of the town's leading physician, Dr. D. R. Fly; Jeff D. Bartlett of the Amarillo Board of Trade; Judge J. N. Donaldson; and even Frank Anderson, a saloon man. Prominent Amarillo women included the wives of two church ministers; Mrs. M. C. Nobles; Mrs. A. McKnight, Jr. whose husband was a prominent livery man; and Mrs. O. G. Roquemore whose husband built the Amarillo Court House and one of its schools. Clearly, Marie Bynum Smith knew who to recruit for one of the new century's most compelling civic tasks in Amarillo.

Even though she was one of the most highly respected women in Amarillo, Marie maintained an independent spirit and did not always kowtow to her husband. Family lore has emphasized Marie of the old Midland cowgirl fame who purportedly bested Sam Houston's youngest son, Temple (a nearby Panhandle lawyer), in a shooting match. Marie also supposedly wielded a pistol while answering the door of 1101 Taylor one moonless night only to nearly scare off a telegraph delivery boy. "My husband is out of town. I'm putting away the pistol. Please come back," she shouted at the retreating delivery agent.

Like wife, like husband as events soon proved in the life of Jimmie Smith. His calm demeanor was tested during a several months' battle with none other than his fellow Baptist deacon and competing bank president, W. H. Fuqua. Two years previous, Smith had accused Fuqua of duplicity during a joint attempt of Smith/Walker and Fuqua to buy the Hereford National Bank in nearby Hereford, TX. In a June, 1902 letter to Walker Smith had noted: "We figured for two days last week on getting control of Hereford Nat Bk in connection with Mr. Fuqua, but he betrayed us and took it in himself. We now know where to place him."[20] Adding to the fire was hankering over an original and extended note John Walker and James L. Smith had inherited early on from Haynie Mercantile. Fuqua's First National Bank held a 10% note payable by Smith and Walker and he willingly granted them a short extension of the note when it came due. When payment time arrived Fuqua claimed the note had been extended at an 18% rate of interest. Smith claimed it had not and that an 18% rate represented usury on Fuqua's part. Amarillo's premier banker, his feathers now ruffled beyond repair, called Smith's partner "a mere plunger and speculator in mining stocks" and insisted Walker appear before him in person to discuss the matter. Smith took umbrage and accused Fuqua of never having written to Walker as Fuqua had promised to do. "You are filled with venom, sir," Fuqua accosted Smith. Smith stuck a finger in Fuqua's chest and told him to write Walker and not make Smith the messenger. It took several more months but Smith, Walker, and Fuqua eventually resolved their business disagreement at an unspecified compromise rate of interest. Both Smith and Fuqua, even though not yet fully reconciled, agreed not to let their differences interfere with their joint work in putting into motions plans for constructing a new and more modern First Baptist Church complex.[21]

In strong contrast to Smith and Fuqua's civilized resolution of their argument is one that occurred the following year of 1905 between Amarillo's literal first resident ever, H. T. "Tuck" Cornelius, and his business partner, George Highfill. Tuck Cornelius and his wife were parents of the first child ever born in Amarillo and Tuck's mother is listed as the town's first recorded death. Like Jimmie and Marie, Tuck and Sarah Cornelius were pillars of the First Baptist Church, and Tuck has been described as the "beloved friend of the cowboys and ranchers in the early days."[22] Until recently, Tuck Cornelius' bitter feud with his partner in the wholesale butcher and market business has gone practically unnoticed. The circumstances are complicated but the upshot is that Cornelius went to their place of business and accused his partner of skimming money off the top. Highfill retorted, calling his partner an "old bald-headed son of a bitch" while holding a knife he was fond of whittling with when he was nervous.[23] Cornelius exited the store, returned to his home, grabbed his pistol, and reappeared at the back door of their establishment. When Highfill advanced toward him while still whittling, Cornelius discharged his pistol mortally wounding his partner who died later that day, November 2, 1905. Cornelius was promptly arrested and charged with murder. After two trials in Amarillo failed to reach a conclusive verdict (the first because of a hung jury and the second a set-aside conviction based on unspecified legal grounds), the venue was changed to Clarendon where Cornelius was found guilty of manslaughter in July 1907 and sentenced to five years in the penitentiary. However, a group of Amarillo townspeople circulated a petition for Cornelius' pardon, and Texas Governor Campbell pardoned "old Tuck" in November 1908, a few weeks after he began serving his sentence and three years after the killing.[24]

As was far more often the case, Jimmie Smith went far out of his way to help others with their pursuits. One such case is that of Dr. J. E. Nunn, the so-called "Battling Baptist" and an Amarillo newcomer, who purchased the fledgling Amarillo Telephone Company for $12,000 in late 1903 and refurbished it. But not without difficulties. He had to make a mad dash back to his native Kentucky to secure $6,000 to put with his Amarillo bank loan for the same amount. In his haste to return before midnight New Year's Eve 1903 when the buy-out was scheduled to fall through without the added funding, he boarded the wrong train at Little Rock; it was bound for Hot Springs, not Texas. Informed of his mistake, he had the train flagged down at the next junction and the distraught Nunn was conveyed the few miles back to Little Rock where he boarded the correct train and arrived in Amarillo only an hour before an impending forfeiture of his investment capital. Seven years later, Nunn would sell his company for an astounding $225,000. The profit was due in no small part to Jimmie Smith who had staked the initial bank loan, helped calm anxious creditors, and then agreed to serve as secretary-treasurer to the phone company spread across the second floor of Smith's National Bank of Commerce.[25]

Equally impressive was Smith's advice to his soon-to-be brother-in-law, Earl Cobb. As early as 1901, Smith had written to Walker about the then 24-year-old Cobb "being an extraordinary young man" who had worked in Canyon and Hereford for Smith & Walker.[26] Walker concurred wholeheartedly, even trusting Cobb with his power of attorney while Cobb served a short stint with Walker's own Bowen-Joyce Company (later Joyce-Pruit Company) in Pecos, TX, in 1904.[27] Anxious to make his own mark,

Cobb had gone to work as secretary and treasurer of Morrow-Thomas Hardware Company in late 1906. To his chagrin, Cobb had quickly discovered that as the junior officer on the board of directors, he frequently had to work long shifts, even far into the night, because his partners were either out of town or pursuing side business interests. To his fiancée, Sally Bynum, who was back visiting Horn Lake, Cobb wrote, "I am feeling like a dog…and I don't like the hardware business to save my life."[28] Cobb, who had no fixed residence and alternated stays at the Elmhurst and Amarillo Hotels, did note that all of Amarillo's vacant lots were quickly "filling in" and that increased pumping of the water supply meant more baths were readily available. With such modernization in mind, he had a prolonged talk with his mentor, J. L. Smith, in mid April, calling him one of his "few real friends" and decided to abandon the hardware business and, instead, go to Chicago to buy a machine and enter the ice business in Amarillo. By October he had arranged shipment of a $2,000, 40-ton York machine to the end of Cleveland Street near the railroad tracks. His partners in Crystal Ice Company were the ever-present M. C. Nobles as vice-president and H. P. Canode, proprietor of the Amarillo Hotel, as secretary and treasurer.[29]

Smith's sage advice not only boosted the confidence of his protégés but also carried over to First Baptist. On July 24, 1904, Treasurer Smith certified an annual financial statement of $2,597.57 which included the pastor's salary and another significant contribution to Marie's favorite charity, the Buckner Orphanage in Dallas. In October Smith, cognizant that the growing congregation was rapidly outstripping the 200-seat accommodations of the original wooden church, led initial discussion for erecting a new church which the deacons estimated "might cost $10-15 thousand" to build, but Smith knew the eventual price tag would far exceed the conservative estimates of his peers. Smith also chaired the pulpit committee in 1904 and early 1905 to select a new pastor, the Rev. Dr. Eugene Perry Alldredge, a Baylor graduate who, unknown to Smith, cherished grandiose ideas for a vast new stone church.[30]

Almost immediately, Smith's deliberate approach about bringing the new church's location "before the house" aroused Alldredge's ire about procrastination. Smith, perturbed but resolute in his step-by-step approach to committing substantial funds, offered to resign as treasurer, but the deacons refused to accept his resignation.[31] A location of 9th and Polk was agreed on, fittingly on land donated by J. L. Smith's fellow building committee member, W. H. Fuqua. For almost a year, no new minutes were written in the church ledger, in all probability because a firestorm broke wide open with Alldredge evidently chiding his deacons for their unhurried pace. On September 2, 1906, Smith stated he hoped "all ill will and hard feelings would be driven out and that fellowship would be restored." Smith again offered to resign from the building committee and as deacon, but the church committee again refused to accept Smith's offer.

Chastened by his deacons' backing of Smith, Alldredge resigned on October 1, 1906. The new pastor, Rev Robert Francis Jenkins, came in early 1907 and, already experienced in building other churches in Daingerfield and Greenville, readily acceded to Smith and Fuqua's plans. True to his giving nature, Smith credited Fuqua and the other building committee members (O. M. Eakle, G.E. Oates, T. J. Warren, and B. T. Ware) for the successful work in completing the new edifice. Not until every bill was paid in full—from electric light fixtures ($403.50) to heating plant ($1,050) to art glass ($1,047.85) to pipe organ ($2,950) and even a 60-cent thank-you telegram to the organ's builder—did Smith present a final accounting for the magnificent new church. The total inclusive cost was $44,306.98.[32] Truly, in the 20 years since the ramshackle Burns, Walker Co. building in Old Town, Smith and his civilizing influence had come a long way.

Lest Marie be left out of the Baptist Church equation, all one has to do is read the numerous published accounts of her driving her horse-drawn carriage around the difficult-to-navigate streets of Amarillo nearly every Sunday morning. She offered rides to and from church for those who wanted transportation. The cowgirl cutting horse rider from Midland had swapped her side saddle for a more modern and civilized rig. In the meantime, Jimmie himself, according to family stories, stood outside the new church on several occasions, pinning boutonnieres and corsages on many of the faithful attendees that his wife dropped off at the main entrance.

Although there are undoubtedly numerous instances of the Smiths' generosity that have been lost along the way, one singular example from the same time period survives. The occasion is only documented in one letter and on scraps of paper from December 10-21, 1906. When Smith learned that his mother-in-law needed immediate surgery, he personally arranged the trip from Amarillo to Galveston for himself, Mrs. Bynum, and Marie. To John Walker he wrote from Galveston's Tremont Hotel: "Mrs. Bynum was operated on by Dr. Thompson. The relief so far is complete and, I trust, will prove permanent." True to his bookkeeper instincts, Smith kept a running tab of expenses on the reverse side of two deposit slips from his own bank account: "3 to Ft. Worth, 30.15, plus 2 sleepers 4.00" and "3 to Galveston, 28.95, plus two berths 4.00." A pants pressing cost a quarter; a shoe shine a dime; the street car 20 cents each. While his mother-in-law was recouping, Jimmie took Marie to the "theatre, 4.00" and gave her $10 for miscellaneous expenses. The only item Smith purchased for himself as a 75-cent pocket knife.[33]

Of far greater financial significance was the rapid growth of Walker-Smith Company during the first decade of the twentieth century. At a January 23, 1903 meeting in Brownwood, the Board of Directors officially changed the company's name from "Temple Grocer Company" to "Walker-Smith Company."[34] John Walker was designated President, J. B. Garnett Vice-President, and J. L. Smith Secretary-Treasurer. From then until his death, Smith would have one foot anchored in Amarillo and the other firmly placed in Brownwood. Although the humble Smith would have been the first to deny the Colossus of Rhodes image conjured up by such an allusion, he was, nonetheless, the backbone of Walker-Smith. Perhaps a letter written from Smith & Walker in Amarillo the month after that first directors' meeting gave a firm indication of what was to be the chief concern for a corporation desiring to spread its distribution of wholesale groceries across almost all of Texas: the crucial item of railroad access for all the branch houses. In almost casual fashion, Smith wrote: "I spent Monday & Tuesday of this week at Beaumont, Wednesday in Houston, Thursday in Galveston and home last night."[35]

In addition to its headquarters in Brownwood and its first branch in San Angelo (1898), during its first 10 years the company opened branch "houses" [warehouse distribution points] in Brady (1903), Ballinger (1905), Abilene (1907), Sweetwater (1910), and Galveston (1913). An ever-expanding rail system meant that new and previously unavailable products could be shipped in by the carload. Fresh produce, for example, entered the wholesale marketplace—not without sometimes humorous results for neophyte retail grocers. One purchaser complained bitterly about 'these rough new banana things' until being instructed they needed to be peeled before being eaten. Another grocer said his customers were dissatisfied with the wilted green leaves before being told that one ate only the celery stalks, not the leafage at the end. Yet another intrepid grocer was advised *not* to try to sell cranberries as 'miniature apples' because the cranberries required cooking before consumption. From the small to the very large,

Walker-Smith Company offered a wide variety of standard goods and even appliances: lye, lard, canned goods, ham and bacon, sacked oats and flour, chewing tobacco, plus a carload of new commercial glass-paneled refrigerators and ice cream freezers.[36]

For the first 10 years of operation in Brownwood and the other houses, the primary means of distributing goods to retailers was by mule or horse-drawn freight wagons. Salesmen, or "drummers" as they were called, slowly made their way across newly fenced-in ranches to distribute goods and take new orders. To answer the demands of customers who wanted the most up-to-date grocery products, John Walker and James Lowry Smith added a coffee-processing facility to the candy factory next to their Brownwood headquarters. Green coffee beans gave way to fresh-roasted beans in buckets or bags. Cocoanut bars and stick candy and even peanut butter bore the Walker-Smith Pecan Valley label and were shipped along with a growing line of new cereal products including Cream of Wheat, shredded wheat, corn flakes, and oatmeal. The company also manufactured its own vinegar and grape juice, initially sold by the keg but later in gallon cans.

Capitalization of Walker-Smith was a subject of discussion in letters between Walker and Smith dating as far back as the Temple days. Walker's initial investment was $50,000 and Smith's $25,000, thus guaranteeing them as the primary stockholders. Smith even acceded to Marie's desire to invest some of her own stock dividends in her husband's enterprise.[37] Many times in his letters Smith acknowledged thanks for his partner's financial contributions to him in salary and added stock. In any event, by 1907 the capitalization was raised from 250 to 500 thousand dollars.[38] The volume of business soared in the century's first decade. For example, Treasurer Smith informed Walker that the company's gross for March 1906 was $115,842 with a net profit of $8,671, and a month later the company's vice-president gladly acknowledged that "We're selling more goods on time and have more collateral than we have ever had before."[39]

It would seem from such favorable profit reports that C. Y. Early's cheerful assessment of his company's history was fully justified. However, below the surface trouble was brewing, due in large part to Walker himself. First, the wealthy Walker was notoriously tight with money and stubborn to boot. For example, Buffalo Oil Company was still showing a profit in early 1904 but Smith disagreed with Walker about restricted dividend distributions because "I believe a majority of our stockholders would not agree to a dividend not participated in by all."[40] Likewise, when it came to new banking facilities for their grocery company Smith battled Walker about where to obtain more credit; Smith advocated St. Louis where he knew the lay of the land rather than opening new and untested New York City accounts.[41] Nonetheless, by mid 1907 Walker-Smith Company was on a roll and Smith successfully urged the reluctant majority stockholder to accept "the idea that our company can afford to pay more liberal salaries."[42] Second, a series of 1906 letters to Smith reveal, unpredictably and unexpectedly, that Walker was beginning to suffer from depression, an affliction that would follow him for the next 20 years. The first indication of Walker's physical maladies surfaced in early 1906 when Walker, hospitalized in Galveston, wrote of his impending return to Brownwood:

> It is now my intention to leave here on the night of the 30th and reach home the following morning. Don't want to stay in Brownwood more than three or four days and must be careful about remaining in the office. Have tried too early to control my hours by remaining there too long. Slept well last night and think my treatment will be of great benefit.[43]

Whether Walker ever made it back to Brownwood as indicated is unknown, but by late February he was again hospitalized in Galveston for "nervous prostration and my treatment is so severe that I do not as a rule rest very well."[44] Always the encouraging confidant, Smith wrote soon afterwards expressing concern that his partner "was not getting along better."[45] By April, presumably on doctor's orders, Walker was recouping for several months in Liverpool, England! In the interim, Smith had to stop his own Amarillo plans and make business trips for Walker to Kansas City, St. Louis, and New York City.[46]

What is remarkable about J. L. Smith is that only on the very rarest of occasions in a lifetime of correspondence with J. A. Walker did Smith ever complain about the excessive workload Walker's absence placed on him and his associates. Walker was for the most part an absentee landlord with subsequent ongoing hospitalizations in San Antonio, Johns Hopkins in Baltimore, and Battle Creek in Michigan. When Walker was not hospitalized he took up spring and summer residence in the upscale resort town of Chautauqua, NY, and fall and winter residence in Daytona Beach, FL. It was left to J. B. Garnett and Smith (1906-1910), then J. Blackwell and Smith (1910-1924), and then Smith and D. Coalson in the late 1920s to run Walker-Smith Company. By far, Walker's business correspondence for those years consists largely of weekly business summaries sent to Walker from Brownwood and weekly investment strategies and personal demands sent by Walker to Smith and Walker's succession of vice-presidents. At one point, the patient and enduring J. Blackwell purchased a personal vehicle, a new Dodge, for Walker and had it prepped and ready in Walker's Brownwood driveway awaiting one of Walker's infrequent visits to his company.[47] Nearly every letter written over the course of years from Garnett and Blackwell contains a report on some personal task performed for their boss—from hiring a new gardener to searching the Walker residence to retrieve some gewgaw to sending off mail to upstate New York or downstate Florida. Another glaring example occurred when Blackwell had to drop everything and package up and send off another set of items Walker needed in Chautauqua. To Walker's credit, he did write back to his Vice-President: "My golf sticks and shoes were received yesterday morning and I very much appreciate your kindness in this matter."[48]

Whether or not it was a requirement that members of the Board of Directors of Walker-Smith make an annual report of their assets is unknown. James Lowry Smith, however, dutifully reported his financial status to his superior stockholder and partner on several occasions. At the end of January 1906, Smith listed his total assets (aside from his share in Walker-Smith) as $116,709 with the majority derived from National Bank of Commerce stock ($27,700), the building itself ($22,500), investments ($36,320), and, of course, his paid-up residence at 1101 Taylor ($10,000).[49] Two years later Smith reported his net value at $147,430, with the majority again coming from National Bank of Commerce, but also new property investments ($11,000) and cash in bank ($19,000).[50] By contrast, among the John Walker papers is one of the few documents indicating his financial status, his federal income tax return in 1917 (first year Americans were required to pay annual income tax) where he showed a gross income of $211,000 for 1916.[51]

The intent of such a financial comparison is not to illustrate the triumph of the almighty dollar as much as it is to show how Smith kept his investments close to his Amarillo home. Without a doubt, the cost of running a household with four relatives as live-ins was taxing. Equally taxing was the incalculable number of trips Smith made on the Santa Fe to and from Brownwood, where each way was nearly 12 hours in the century's first decade. Smith frequently referred to 'grabbing his grip and dashing to the station,' but in character with his humility, he deferred being picked up or delivered by his employees, insisting instead on hoofing it or taking available public transportation. If he arrived at night, it was to the hotel and to Walker-Smith early the next morning; if following an all-night trip, he grabbed breakfast before appearing in the company's main office. In fact, so resourceful was Smith that in mid-February 1908 on a return train trip from a Director's meeting in Brownwood he ran smack into a Panhandle snowstorm but was not disheartened. He merely dryly observed: "My train was snowed under 3 miles from Amarillo and I walked in."[52]

To Smith and the company's vice-presidents go accolades for quickly applying modern technology to business. Smith insisted on long-distance phone service to interconnect all the scattered wholesale houses and he instructed that copies of all written sales orders be sent to the Brownwood headquarters so that an efficient centralized accounting system would allow orders and payments to be tracked daily.[53]

New modes of transportation also emerged. The company purchased its first salesman's automobile, a two-cylinder Buick purchased at $1,325 in August 1907, and others soon followed.[54] For the next half dozen years, however, such a seemingly civilized means of transportation was fraught with problems. Pneumatic tires were thin and inner tubes susceptible to constant piercing from an array of needles and brambles along bare wagon roads. Salesmen measured distances between flats and overheated radiators in the baking Texas heat. Service stations were few and far between so company vehicles had to carry five-gallon containers of gasoline tied to the running boards. The assistant salesman, equipped with a large toolkit and riding shotgun with the head drummer, had to be a good amateur auto mechanic because breakdowns were frequent. The biggest breakthrough in reliable transportation came in February 1913 when Walker-Smith purchased its first chain-drive truck manufactured by a Texas firm, the Wichita Falls Motor Company, which during their 20-year history from 1911-1932 established a reputation for trucks of "rugged strength."[55]

Two fires in 1913 marked the need for improved buildings. The candy and coffee-roasting facility, an adapted hangover from pre-Walker-Smith days, was ploughed under and, thanks to Smith's comprehensive insurance policy purchases, was soon rebuilt. A similar building project occurred in Abilene after a fire consumed its warehouse. As J. Blackwell wrote to Walker in Florida, "Mr. Smith went home Saturday night and will go to Abilene from Amarillo during the latter part of this week for the purposes of constructing our building there…at a cost of six or seven thousand dollars, mostly allowed by insurance."[56] Nonetheless, business sales continued to exceed expectations and by 1914 Walker-Smith was doing $3.5 million for the year. The number of employees passed 50 and was headed for the century mark. The always efficient secretary-treasurer always detected a cost-saving measure and by 1911 had traded the company's three Cadillacs for a fleet of Henry Ford's more efficient models.[57]

Smith's personal kindnesses to his partner continued as Walker's illness bouts increased. Smith personally handled the insurance on a number of Walker's properties even though such real estate holdings had nothing to do with Walker-Smith. He even had a policy written on Bessie Walker's first car in early 1911 writing her that "your car is insured for $1,600 good anywhere within the bounds of the United States."[58] Smith likewise successfully urged Bessie to follow up on the Temple Sanitarium's recommendation a year later that John Walker go to Johns Hopkins because the staff of doctors there "especially devote their time to nervous cases."[59] In the meantime, Smith took the entire matter of running Walker-Smith into his own hands, writing in early 1913 to Walker: "I may not have told you, but I think it is our intention to pay a 10% dividend at our February meeting. We expect our earnings to enable us to do this, and leave our surplus over $250,000. This is really all the capital we will need."[60]

In addition to attending personally to Walker-Smith Company business in Brownwood on dozens of occasions each year, Smith sometimes continued on a train to Houston to visit maiden sister, Julia, who lived with her sister, Roxalee, who in 1891 had married Frank Andrews, a noted railroad attorney and assistant attorney general for the state of Texas. Smith would even return to Amarillo via Cameron, TX, where another married sister, Hattie Ralston, alternated care of their mother, Julia McDowell Smith, with Roxalee.

One would think that while serving as treasurer for a church, as—in effect--chief financial officer for a burgeoning wholesale grocery firm, and as president of a growing bank that Smith would have little or no time left for civic affairs. Such was not the case as Smith undertook a variety of Amarillo activities that helped spur on the city's civilized growth during the century's opening decade. True to his Colorado City days, Jimmie helped with a large cattleman's convention in 1905 and he humorously described Amarillo's being in an "uproar on account of the vast number of visitors and auxiliary meetings thereto." Noisy cattle moved down Polk Street, even climbing over the steps fronting the National Bank of Commerce. Smith took the mild stampede in stride, though finally admitted that the sudden influx of "1,500 visitors taxed the town to its limits to care for them."[61] In 1907 Smith accompanied 10 Amarillo businessmen to Austin to argue for a direct Santa Fe RR route into Amarillo, an issue that had festered for years. As Smith put it succinctly to Walker: "There is an effort being made by Amarillo citizens to have the legislature authorize the Santa Fe Ry to take up its track between Panhandle & Washburn and lay it direct from Panhandle to Amarillo."[62] It took another year to overcome the pro-Washburn lobbyists, but the new line, crucial to Amarillo's trade and giving access to the Pecan Valley line, was completed in April 1908.[63]

Although he never ran for an elected office, Smith served Amarillo in another important capacity. He became a director of the Amarillo Chamber of Commerce when it was organized on August 8, 1907. With Smith's help, all of Amarillo's streets were graded and new cement crossings added at key points. By 1912 Smith was co-vice-president of the Chamber along with his close friend and former Burns, Walker employee, B. T. Ware. Sewers were extended, sidewalks and curbing added, and a new high school building approved to the tune of $65,000.[64] Reaching beyond Amarillo's immediate confines, Smith offered his financial skills as President of the Panhandle Bankers Association for 1910-1911.[65]

Well-earned were two 'luxury' items dating from 1909. The first was a 10-day vacation in the Caribbean in the spring where Jimmie and Marie visited Puerto Rico, Jamaica, and Cuba. Smith had even invited John and Bessie Walker to join them on the outing, but they declined.[66] In the summer the Smiths acquired their first automobile, a 1909 Cadillac touring car purchased on August 24 with Amarillo tag #145. Jimmie promptly modified the vehicle slightly by having the front headlights raised well above the fenders to make the lights less susceptible to stones and road debris in the mostly unpaved roads of the Llano Estacado.[67]   The carriage house behind their 1101 Taylor Street address now became classified in the succeeding Sanborn maps as simply a garage.

If foreign travel and motor cars represented the best in civilized life, three other events tangentially related to the Smiths revealed some of the less-than-exemplary sides of emerging modern life. The first involved a letter about substance abuse; the second a medical conference paper about the previously taboo subject of public school sex education; the third a sensational series of crimes centering on adultery and multiple murders.

James Lowry Smith, ca. 1910

While escorting her mother on a visit to Horn Lake and Memphis in the spring of 1908, Sally Bynum wrote a letter to Marie about one of their mutual acquaintances who had a life-threatening drug and alcohol abuse problem: "Oh, yes, Mrs. Will _________ is in a private asylum in a straight jacket, with guards day & night, all brought on by constant and excessive use of drink and sniffing cocaine."[68] Three years later, Marie's Civic League helped plan several events for doctors' spouses attending the Forty-Third Annual Meeting of the State Medical Association of Texas held in Amarillo, May 9-11, 1911. One highlight was an automobile ride across the Staked Plains and a barbeque of buffalo, Persian sheep, and longhorns in the Palo Duro Canyon. The menu is not nearly as surprising as the keynote address topic of the Medical Association's opening session on Public Hygiene held in the hall of the First Baptist Church. One Dr. Charles A. Pfender of Washington, DC, spoke on "Prophylactic Value of Instruction of Children in the Elements of the Physiology of Sex."[69] As a side note, Marie's interest in medicine extended beyond conventions. A surviving piece of letterhead from the Texas Anti-Tuberculosis Association reveals she served as secretary for a statewide committee on legislation and municipal regulation chaired by prominent Amarillo physician, Dr. D. R. Fly.

When he was asked to be a pallbearer at the funeral of his friend and neighbor, Colonel A. G. Boyce, on January 16, 1912, James Lowry Smith had no idea that Boyce's tragic murder in Fort Worth's Metropolitan Hotel lobby three days before would touch off one of the most widely publicized series of criminal events in Texas history.[70] The so-called Boyce-Sneed Feud has been well documented, so only the crucial aspects are given here. Boyce's fellow Amarillo banker, John Beal Sneed, shot Boyce because he thought Colonel Boyce was complicit in allowing his son, A. G. Boyce, Jr., to free Sneed's wife from a Fort Worth sanitarium and run off with her to Winnipeg, Manitoba. A lengthy trial ensued and, much to the dissatisfaction of many American and Canadian newspaper readers, a hung jury resulted and Sneed was ordered to await a retrial later in the year. In the meantime, the resourceful Sneed then snuck back to Amarillo and emptied a double-barreled shotgun into Boyce, Jr. in the middle of Polk Street and promptly turned himself in to the Potter County sheriff. Despite facing two murder charges, Sneed was eventually acquitted of killing father and son because Texas jurors in Fort Worth and then the change-of-venue trial on Boyce, Jr. in Vernon considered both deliberate shootings to be 'crimes of passion.'[71]

No such negative thoughts occupied Marie's mind in the century's first decade as she devoted herself to genealogy. Meticulous handwritten records reveal she examined documents from North Carolina, Virginia, and Washington, DC, as she traced her Bynum and Walker lineages. She was not merely interested in constructing a family tree, but wanted to become a full-fledge member of the Daughters of the American Revolution. In the process, she traced a direct line back to her maternal great grandmother, Esther McCrory, the daughter of Captain Thomas McCrory, the commander of the 9th Regiment of North Carolina Continental troops.[72] Marie determined that Esther, though only a girl at the time, served as a covert messenger for her father while also doing seamstress work for her father's soldiers. Marie even managed to get the endorsement of Louise McCrory Spencer in 1909 when she was the Tennessee State Regent for the DAR.[73] However, before Marie could begin her Founding Regent activities, she needed to join a DAR Chapter. On March 2, 1910, she became a member of the Mary Garland DAR Chapter in Brownwood, TX.[74] Such a move was very reasonable since her first cousin's wife, Bessie Peacock Walker (Mrs. John A. Walker), was a member of that Chapter. To gain further background, Marie began attending Texas DAR state conferences, including the one in Waco in November 1910.[75]

Equipped with a wealth of information and having canvassed Amarillo's rapidly expanding female population base, Marie Motheral Bynum Smith submitted a series of documents to DAR Headquarters in Washington, DC. In her own handwriting, she submitted an announcement eventually placed in Amarillo newspapers:

> The Esther McCrory Chapter D.A.R of Amarillo Texas was organized April 11th 1911 at the home of the organizing Regent, Mrs. James Lowry Smith, who was appointed April 25th 1910 to accomplish this work. All, except two who came by transfers, were new members of the society.

The original charter application contains 21 names, with Mrs. James Lowry Smith as Regent, Mrs. William Boyce as Vice-Regent, and Mrs. Samuel Lefter Seay as Recording Secretary.[76]

The stereotype of a DAR chapter is one of upper-crust women flaunting their ancestry, sipping tea from china cups, and pecking at cucumber sandwiches. The Esther McCrory Chapter, one of West Texas' first chapters, adhered more to the founding principles of the DAR when it was first

Marie Lowry Smith, ca. 1911

established in 1890. It was a chapter dedicated to community service first and social events second.

In the first recorded meeting the following month, the historical theme focused on "Girls of the Revolution," including presentations on "The Courtship of Miles Standish" by Mrs. Emma Stockman Hendricks and Miss Frances Lide, plus a concluding reminiscence on Esther McCrory presented by Marie's own mother, Mrs. Katherine Walker Bynum.[77] And, true enough, succeeding Amarillo newspaper accounts highlight regular monthly DAR meetings, almost always accompanied by a listing of one or two new chapter members. But, in the meantime, Marie was not resting on her organizational laurels. She attended a lengthy meeting of the annual DAR Continental Congress in Washington, DC, in April 1912,[78] followed by the state DAR convention in Dallas that November. As chair of the DAR State Conservation Committee, Mrs. Smith endorsed a U.S. Congressional bill authorizing the federal government's purchase of "certain lands located in the Texas Panhandle," hopefully for establishing a national park.[79] The national park designation never did reach fruition, but the Panhandle's most significant geological formation, the Palo Duro Canyon, did become a state park. A large part of the groundwork for this most civilized recognition of a Panhandle landmark is due to Marie and the McCrory Chapter.

In the meantime, Amarillo's Washington's Birthday, Flag Day, and Independence Day celebrations were fully supported by the chapter, along with Mrs. Smith's own contributions toward furthering state DAR communications by her work on the magazine committee. Thus, in the long run, the seemingly complacent work of a group of dedicated Amarillo women was far more enduring and productive than the momentary personal scandals that captured newspaper headlines.

A familiar aspect of the Smith love story repeated orally over the years has it that in recognition of his wife's DAR achievements, Jimmie bestowed on his wife a diamond lavaliere necklace valued conservatively at $3,000. When Marie chided him about such a lavish gift that she knew he could not really afford, Jimmie admitted that he had accepted the necklace as payment for a $6,000 loan default at the National Bank of Commerce. 'You see, Marie, I seized the opportunity to become a jeweler, not a banker, and you, my dear, are the beneficiary.' She withdrew her objections and insisted her husband place the lavaliere around her neck for the first time.

Jimmie and Marie had three nieces and three nephews to spoil on their frequent visits to 1101 Taylor Street. The first two were Wade and

CHARTER NUMBER

APPLICATION FOR CHARTER.

National Society Daughters of the American Revolution

Please Read Carefully the Following Notes to Chapter Regents,

Your attention is respectfully called to the importance of having the names and data written very carefully, or printed. Each letter should be unmistakably plain. More than thirty-eight names is not advisable, as the size of lettering is thereby affected.

REMITTANCES should be made by cheque or money order (never by cash), payable to the Treasurer-General. The required fee is $5,00.

City *Amarillo*

State *Texas*

Date

TO THE V. P. G. IN CHARGE OF ORGANIZATION OF CHAPTERS :

The undersigned Chapter Regent hereby makes application for a charter, to be engrossed and issued as follows:

Name of Chapter *Esther McCrory*

Date of Organization *April 11th 1941*

Where Located *Amarillo Texas*

Date when Fee is received by Treas.-Gen'l _______ 19___

NAMES OF CHARTER MEMBERS.

(These names, in all cases, must have been accepted by the Board of Management, prior to the date of organization.)

Nat. No.	
83429	1. Mrs. Katherine Pannehill Boyce
84956	2. " Clarissa May Martin Broadwell
84957	3. " Katherine Walker Bynum
84958	4. " Sarah Bynum Cobb
84959	5. " Daisy Martin Currie
85681	6. " Ida Jones Elliott
87342	7. Mrs. Ethelia Rush Harrell
24982	8. " Emma Stockmon Hendricks
85682	9. " Willie Elliott Kirk
85683	10. Miss Harriet Witherspoon Kritser
86972	11. Mrs. Ada Dunlap Lumpkin
85684	12. " Corinne Taylor Mathews
86954	13. " Mattie Jackson Rush
86955	14. Miss Mamie Louise Rush
86142	15. Mrs. George Katherine Mathes Seay
78250	16. " Marie Bynum Smith
85685	17. " Mary Honeyman Turner
85686	18. " Willie Alberta Lockett Turner
85839	19. " Miss Lilian L. Whitman
72716	20. " Frances A. Lide
86953	21. Mrs. Jessie Naomi Ross
	22.
	23.
	24.
	25.
	26.
	27.
	28.
	29.

Fair Copy Esther McCrory DAR Chapter application

Lena Bynum's two daughters, Mary (b. Nov 6, 1892) and Emma (b. Feb 28, 1895), who lived in Memphis where Wade was a partner in a cotton broker firm. Uncle Jimmie bestowed a prize ring and bracelet on Emma for Christmas 1906, and she wrote him that both were "just as pretty as could be" and "fit me to the dot."[80] Shortly before Mary's nineteenth birthday, Marie invited over 40 of her own friends to meet her niece in the parlor and living rooms amid pink carnations and a buffet luncheon. The guest list read like an Amarillo 'Who's Who' and included Mrs. Lee Bivins, Mrs. C. T. Herring, Mrs. B. T. Ware, and Miss Lillian Eakle.[81]

Ben Bynum loved fast horses, new cars, and younger women. He was the businessman extrovert who complimented Jimmie's more reserved nature. His prize horse, Grover, once outpaced Judge Paul's stud through the streets of Amarillo before B. C. D. upgraded to one of Amarillo's first horseless carriages, a silent Northern in 1907.[82]

Fortunately, the sweet but firm Bertha Kate Nunn Bynum tempered her new husband's passion for the open road and settled him into their new home at 1500 Monroe Street. Son William Joseph Bynum was born November 10, 1910, followed by James Smith Bynum on February 25, 1913. Earl and Sally Bynum Cobb also contributed to Amarillo's population boom when daughter Katherine Bynum Cobb was born in a bedroom at 1101 Taylor on May 14, 1912. Following his sister-in-law and wife's insistence, Earl purchased a small yellow home at nearby 1209 Polk Street where Bayless Earl Cobb III was born on December 14, 1914. Thus, the Bynum and Cobb children were tiny stair steps who would eventually make their upstairs playroom at 1101 Taylor their home away from home.

If the personal touch and social outreach characterized life at 1101 Taylor, the same atmosphere carried over to the frequent newspaper ads for the National Bank of Commerce—much more so than the depersonalized plea for funds at more staid Amarillo banks. "The most valuable asset any Bank can have is the confidence reposed in it" read one inviting ad; and "Many others have found an account at this bank very helpful in assisting them to get a start in the world," stated another ad, geared to Amarillo's younger generation.[83] "Your bank should be your friend" and "The officers of this bank give personal attention to the wants and needs of every customer" were no mere come-ons, but expressed sincere concerns for every Amarillo depositor.[84]

The financial condition of a bank is crucial to its success, of course. Smith's institution manifested steady growth from its inception, and the capitalization by 1909 had reached $130,000.[85] Resources and liabilities stood balanced at $549,066.31 in mid 1912 and had risen to $587,372.58 by early the following year.[86] The proof of the pudding is in the taste and by early 1912 the National Bank of Commerce was offering 5% interest on "timed deposits."[87]

Whether in Amarillo or elsewhere in the state, James Lowry Smith was always the perpetual optimist. The facing side of a postcard written from Abilene just after the Walker-Smith Company fire there in 1913 shows black smoke billowing from the building, but Jimmie penned, "Today I pass my 53rd milestone. We will rebuild. Love to everyone at home."[88] By year's end, Smith and Bynum were able to relish a bird hunting trip to South Texas. From Rockport on December 20, 1913, Jimmie displayed his always-present sense of good humor in a telegram to Marie: "Sixty-three ducks, one goose via Wells Fargo. Old *Gander* follows tonight." Little wonder is it that in a feature article on Amarillo banks, Smith was singled out for his astute business sense accompanied by his solid "premonitions of things to come."[89]

If any technology indicated an advance in civilized life it was transportation: the ability of a person to get from one place to another quickly and efficiently, for pleasure or for business. The first half of 1914 was the one time in their marriage where Jimmie and Marie were separated for a prolonged period. She took a last-minute trip to Europe, North Africa, and the Holy Land while he traveled throughout Texas on vital business pursuits. Fortunately, it is a period comparable to their courtship days in Colorado City and Horn Lake because numerous letters and Marie's own meticulous diary have survived.[90]

John and Bessie Walker had agreed to meet their daughter, Mary, who was studying in New York City, for a three-month long Spring Dunning Tour of the Mediterranean, Nile River, Holy Land, and the Greek islands. At Bessie's renewed urging, Marie took a train from Amarillo to New York and arrived several days before the sailing date. She had barely managed to obtain a last-minute passport which bears the date of January 28, 1914. Their ocean liner, R.M.S. Coronia, sailed January 31 carrying 400 passengers on a five-day Atlantic crossing where many passengers suffered seasickness because of rough seas—except for Marie who relished the bath steward's call at 6:15 am each day for a warm sea water bath followed by a cold shower while her room mate, Mary Walker, slept in.[91] Aboard the Coronia, the Dunning tourists criss-crossed the Mediterranean, stopping at Madeira, Gibraltar, Algiers, Monte Carlo, Nice, Capri, and finally Alexandria where they took a train to Cairo to begin a 15-day excursion up the Nile to the Aswan Dam.

Coincidentally, within the exact same time period, Jimmie had embarked on a similar voyage by train, in effect circumventing Texas in two weeks, with stops in Brownwood (Walker-Smith's annual directors meeting), Houston (visit with the Andrews, his sister Julia, and brother Forrest), Galveston (opening of a new Walker-Smith warehouse), Cameron (visit with Hattie and his mother), Greenville (check on land purchase), Fort Worth (physical exam), Mineral Wells (dentist), and back to Amarillo.[92]

Rather than summarize Marie's diary, a better approach is to continue to focus on transportation and the numerous modes—ancient

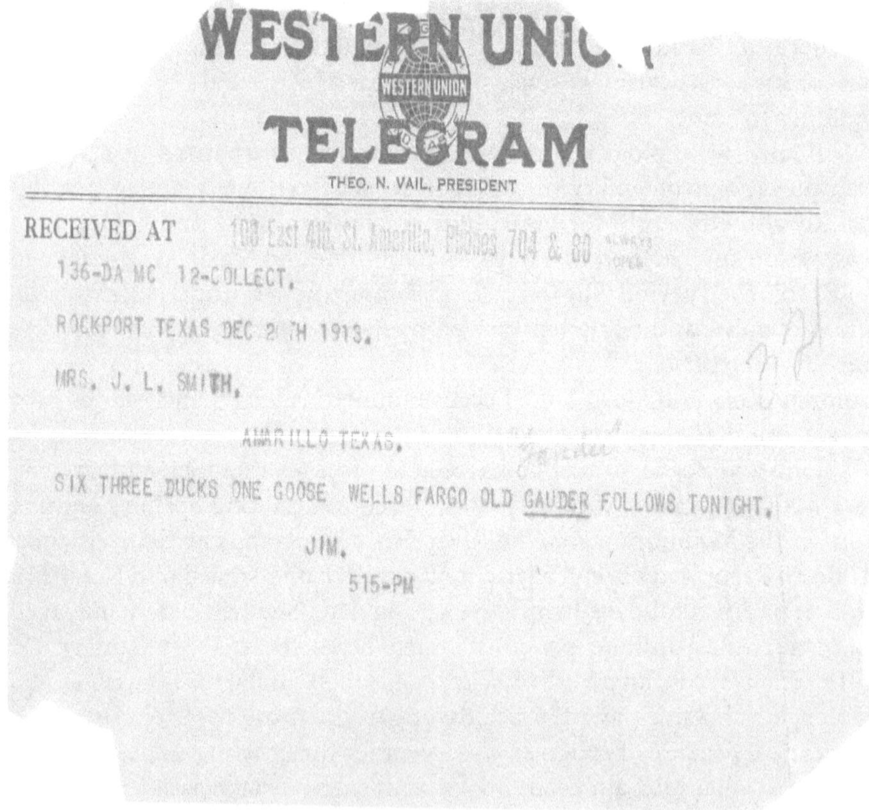

Telegram, Jim to Mrs. J. L. Smith, December 20, 1913

and modern—that she took in her travels. An added reason for such a choice is that much of the diary reads like an in-depth travel guide, with Marie's acute observations about the size and shape of artifacts and lecture summaries from Mr. Bailey, the ever-present tour conductor. Thus, only her key personal insights are occasionally interspersed. Marie's first extensive land tour was at Gibraltar where she and others were conveyed in "peculiar style carriages drawn by one horse only" (9, Feb 9). The only modern form of passenger transportation Marie did not take was an airplane. However, pausing in a carriage in Monaco, she looked down at the calm Mediterranean and "saw a hydro-aeroplane flying above the water and light on the water then skim along like a bird to land" (17, Feb 13).

A Baptist woman about to turn 50 would very naturally be shocked by a nighttime visit to a Monte Carlo casino. Marie remarked about a svelte European woman wearing a "split skirt above the knee" placing losing bet after losing bet at a roulette table whose wheel Marie refers to as a "terrible blight" with the appended note that she is pleased the U.S. government doesn't permit such gaming on American soil (16, Feb 12). After going ashore at Alexandria, the party boarded the first of many trains for railway side trips, this one to Cairo where they embarked on the steamer Germanica for their Nile cruise. At one stop, she noted Bedouins fighting each other for ship-supplied saddles for the donkeys the Bedouins used to convey passengers on Egyptology tours. Because it was the dry time of the year and the Nile banks were muddy, Marie went ashore like a rural Cleopatra "in a chair carried by six bedouins" (24, Feb 20). After visiting the splendors of ancient Luxor, she traveled across the Nile by sailboat and a short time later by rowboat "to the great dam of Assuan" (32, Mar 3). All her diary entries are written with a new state-of-the-art fountain pen bestowed on her by her brother-in-law, Earl Cobb, as a bon voyage present.[93]

The return trip from Luxor to Cairo was by "deluxe train with a small lav between adjoining compartments" (42, Mar 13). Once in Cairo the group went "via street cars" to their hotel (43, Mar 14). As one might suspect, disagreements did arise among the four traveling companions, though Marie only shared her critical observations with her husband. Unfortunately, the picture that emerges is only a confirmation of John Walker's self-centeredness: "He doesn't want to be crossed on anything and he makes sure he gets the lion's share of everything," she wrote from Denderah, Egypt. Then, in an inexcusable act 10 days later, Walker delayed 24 hours before finally handing Marie a packet of sought-after correspondence from Jimmie, her sister, and others. Marie also confided a few days later that Walker fretted over his Texas telephone stock and constantly reminded Bessie that he needed to get home before too long even though, as Marie puts it, "I frequently hear Bess say to others that Mr. Walker has not been able to attend to business of any kind for four years."[94]

The same day that Marie had a camel ride out in the desert (43, Mar 14), the foursome then embarked on a nighttime illuminated tour of the pyramids. Disaster struck swiftly as Bessie fell off of a wall and tumbled eight feet into a rocky crevice, shattering her arm (44, Mar 14). She was rushed to the English hospital in Cairo where she spent several weeks followed by a lengthy period of recuperation in a luxury hotel suite. Bessie did insist that Marie continue on with the tour to the Holy Land; Marie did so, not knowing that Bessie would undergo a complicated surgical procedure to reconstruct her elbow. Thus, following a trip by train and "donkey-drawn sand cart" (46, Mar 17), Marie reached Port Said but not before observing ships and boats transiting the Suez Canal and looking from a distance "as if they were sailing on an ocean of sand" (49, Mar 18).

At crucial junctures, including Bessie's emergency, the Smiths communicated with each other by the only e-mail means available at the time, cablegram. However, such electronic transmissions were not inexpensive, costing between 10 and 20 cents per word, depending on the place, time, and urgency required for delivery of the printed message. Judging from the letter exchanges between the two, the use of cable also required a code book to obtain the proper destination for communiqués. Marie, ever the affectionate wife, apparently sent cablegrams to her husband on his birthday noting that March 12, 1860 as "the most important thing to me" (41, Mar 12).

The vessel carrying Marie and other Dunning Tour passengers to the Holy Land had to anchor two miles offshore at Jaffa (near modern-day Tel Aviv) and the tourists and their luggage went ashore in "longboats" to the rocky shore (50, Mar 19). Traversing Palestine, Syria, and Lebanon, all still under the sway of the Ottoman Empire, involved unusual modes of travel: horse-drawn carriages near Jericho (55, Mar 23) and "three-seated hacks" north of Jerusalem (62, Mar 30). Up-to-date modern transportation was in store via a "train with an observation deck and equipped with strange wicker chairs" en route to Damascus.[95] The trip culminated with a brief rack-and-pinion cog railway journey near Beirut (74, Apr 9). Her asides about the actual physical constraints of the Holy Land are memorable: about Turkish soldiers required to separate Armenian and Latin chanters at the

Church of the Holy Sepulcher because each contesting group was "trying to drown out the other" (61, Mar 29) and the streets of Jerusalem "where I have never seen such filth in my life" (58, Mar 25). Side by side with her well-drawn spiritual comparison of the gnarled olives of Gethsemane with Christ's wounds and suffering (55, Mar 21) was her shock at the almost total lack of trees in Palestine because the "Turks taxed the people $3.00 for every tree whether it yielded anything or not" (56, Mar 24).

As Marie observed seascapes from Beirut to Constantinople, her husband wrote of Texas seascapes, particularly Corpus Christi where Wade Bynum had relocated for health reasons and new business opportunities. Twice in the space of six weeks Jimmie diverted from Brownwood to Corpus at Wade's request. In late March he encouraged Bynum's plan to place a cotton compress on a Corpus Christi pier, but only after asking him for a long-range business plan did Jimmie agree that Wade's intercoastal barge enterprise between Galveston and Corpus was a worthwhile endeavor. Emboldened, Wade asked Smith to join him in both undertakings but Smith declined, citing already excessive demands on his time in Amarillo and Brownwood.[96] One Amarillo undertaking, occupying nearly two weeks in late March and early April, was an extended church revival conducted by George W. Truitt, pastor of the First Baptist Church in Dallas. In one of the longest entries in the First Baptist Church, Amarillo minutes, both Smith and Truitt are lauded for recharging the entire pastoral and missionary movements of the Palo Duro Baptist Association.[97]

Smith and his sister-in-law, Sally Cobb, gave Marie constant updates on the nephews and niece situation: "Sissie done done far away" and "Sissie done way off on chu chu train," the two-year-old Katherine Cobb stated on several occasions while William seemed forlorn at his aunt's absence during several trips over from 1500 Monroe to 1101 Taylor.[98] Sally and Earl had also graciously agreed to let Marie's mother stay with them rather than have to endure lonely days in an empty house at 1101 Taylor. To help with maintenance, the furnace man from the Baptist Church kept the Smith home up to date as far as winter maintenance was concerned.

On the banking side, Smith had written to John Walker at the outset of 1914 that "I am on a deal to sell my stock in the bank [National Bank of Commerce] and if you will mail me your certificates they will be included."[99] The ambitious vice-president of the bank, S. F. Sullenberger, had come into an unexpected inheritance and had offered to buy out Smith. On February 9, Sullenberger was elected president of the institution, inspiring B. C. D.

Bynum to immediately write his sister in Europe that now that Jimmie had departed, "I cannot stay with him [Sullenberger] for long" because "he is dictatorial and never listens unlike your husband."[100] Even so, the capital stock of the National Bank of Commerce was at an exceptional $150,000 at the time Smith sold his bank.[101]

Smith was probably following his uncanny instincts in setting aside banking temporarily because, as events soon developed, one Amarillo bank, "The First State Bank here was closed today by the Commissioner of Banking" and less than a week later Brady-Neely Grocery Company was $7,000 overdrawn and had to sell out hastily to Nobles Brothers. Another business acquaintance, Z. Z. Savage, was convicted of bribery the following month and sent off to the penitentiary for two years.[102] Freed from the demands of running a bank and having just realized a profit from its sale, Smith readily acquiesced in Marie's wish to continue with her tour by adding Europe to her itinerary once the Dunning Tour of the eastern Mediterranean area was complete.

If ill winds were blowing in Amarillo, Marie's occasional diary entries displayed an unusually perceptive sense of foreboding for what was about to happen in Europe. In northern Palestine she noted passing by an "extensive Turkish barracks" (63, Mar 31) and on the island of Samos off the coast of Greece she saw "a company of young Greeks drilling" and then a "dark cloud came up from the mist" just after a young Greek lieutenant had spoken to her in precise English about "the people here getting ready for another war" (78-79, Apr 13). Up near the Bosporus she saw "dozens of newly erected barracks where they were drilling" (91, Apr 20). Near the island of Corfu, she mentioned seeing "two German men of war, the Goeben and the Breslau at anchor in the harbor" (102, Apr 28). (These two ships would soon be chased across the Mediterranean by the British Navy shortly after the start of World War I). Later in her travels outside Nuremberg, she observed German army units constructing a new pontoon bridge (137, Jun 8).

Perhaps Constantinople presented the most mesmerizing incidents of Marie's tour. "Bullock-drawn wagons" (82, Apr 16) hauled their luggage from the pier to the hotel, and she marveled at the spic and span streets, but was aghast that "There is not telephone or electric light plant" (91, Apr 20). The mosques and churches were spectacular, but the spinning religious ceremony of the "whirling Dervishes was something to make one's head stand on end." Intertwined with oriental mosques were the occidental Roberts College for

Boys and the American College for Girls (87-88, Apr 18).

After reaching Brindisi, Italy on April 29, Marie took a train across Italy (103, Apr 29) and toured the Amalfi Coast; she took an "elevator lift" from her cliff-side hotel down to the beach followed by a "ferryboat" to Naples (106, May 1). After seeing the sites of Naples, Marie boarded "a small electric railroad" and was later conveyed to Pompei and back (113, May 11). In any event, she had rejoined the Walkers in Naples just in time for a bombshell announcement from John Walker: he was booked on a steamship scheduled to depart Naples on May 5 and headed via Lisbon to New York. He had, he said, "business" to attend to in Texas; however, he promised to re-cross the Atlantic to Liverpool two months hence and make the return trip with his family.[103] Still under the weather, Bessie opted for rest in Naples and told Marie that she and Mary would join the Dunning Tour of Italy and Switzerland if she felt sufficiently recovered. Not one to sit around in Europe or any other place for that matter, Marie, despite Mary Walker's objection, arranged to join her veteran traveling companions of the past three months, Dr. and Mrs. Howard Paine, for a follow-on spring tour of Europe they were conducting for a small group. Only a dozen people were on the Paine Tour with its carefully pre-arranged itinerary for stops in northern Italy, Switzerland, Germany, Holland, Belgium, France, and finally England where the tour would conclude on July 4. At the price of $470 Marie had found herself a bargain.[104] She was glad to leave Naples with its street-side "public urinals for men with but <u>narrow</u> shields and exiting while buttoning or zipping their pants" (114, May 12).

In Rome she toured by foot and occasionally in an "automobile" before the Paine party tour headed for Pisa (119, May 15). En route to the Tuscany region, Marie mentioned they passed "the first wireless station which Maconi first used for experimenting" (121, May 18); in fact, the early radio station had been erected at Coltano the previous fall.[105] After a "gondola ride to our hotel in Venice" (124, May 21), Marie and two equally stalwart women visited Lido, termed by Marie as the "Atlantic City of Italy" (125, May 22), and swam in the Adriatic (126, May 24). Borders overlap in certain areas of Europe, and Marie enjoyed breakfast in Bueno Italy; lunch in Mortigny, Switzerland; and, after a brief "electric mountain train" journey, dinner in Chamonix, France (128, May 28). Thus, not five days after her dip in the Adriatic, Marie braved a spring snowstorm and, after a cog railway trip near Mt. Blanc, made an ascent by foot to the Mer de Glace glacier under the watchful eye of an Alpine guide (129, May 29). Not missing a beat, she arrived at Interlaken by "steamcar" and later caught a "cab" during a downpour (133, Jun 1).

Although Marie and her party spent nearly two weeks in Germany in mid June, the diary entries are almost exclusively devoted to in-depth descriptions of visits to art galleries and museums. Marie admired the "orderliness" in Germany, especially the well-conducted bus and street-car tours around Berlin (142-144, Jun 12-14). The diary ends abruptly with a June 20 entry on the Hague and the palace of the Queen Mother "where the Peace Conference was held in 1899" (147-148, Jun 19-20). In a June 18 letter to Jimmie, Marie appeared worn out by all the traveling: "We are moving so fast & seeing so much that I find it hard to get time to write about it." This comment is backed up by the only surviving letter she wrote from England, a series of observations, by date, and mailed to Sally.[106] She mentions a "bus coach trip" to Shakespeare country and several delightful London tours on their double-decker busses.

As early as May, Sally had written to her sister of Jim being "so good to Mama and all the rest of us, advising Wade and writing letters for him all the time."[107] One of Smith's younger associates, Chad Elliott, had also asked for financial advice prior to his impending marriage and Jim was more than willing to comply.[108] In the meantime, John Walker had been advised by his Johns Hopkins doctors "not to stay in too much heat."[109] So what did the impetuous Walker immediately do but 'turn on the heat' in two different ways: first, he pursued a law suit against Dunning accusing the tour company of being negligent in his wife's accident; second, he took off for Fort Worth to have dental work accomplished. So used was Walker to, in Marie's words, "having someone else work for him especially if it costs him nothing," that Walker avoided his pressing business in Brownwood entirely and never saw Jimmie at all. What is more, he adroitly side-stepped his commitment to see Wade Bynum and consider buying stock in his enterprise, a favor that Jim had asked of his partner.[110]

In a long-distance phone call from Vice-President Blackwell in Fort Worth, Smith had learned that Walker had collapsed and was under the care of a trained nurse. Smith quickly admitted to Marie that the news of John's relapse was "very distressing to me," one of the very few times Smith had ever complained in writing about his business partner. However, the situation was worse than at first imagined when Smith got the full story a few days later. As he wrote to Marie: "Dr. Ratliff told me he was only spraying John's mouth and had done no work on him at all when John had a fainting spell. He had to be carried to the hotel on a stretcher and was subsequently escorted to Baltimore by his relative, Mr. Peacock."[111]

Marie's prior assessment of Walker's being a "grasping and threatening man who changes his mind" was immediately borne out by Walker's incredulously rapid recovery at Johns Hopkins and his subsequent departure for New York City's Marseilles Hotel at Broadway and 113th Street where he wined and dined having informed his wife and daughter he would not undertake a voyage to Liverpool but would be prepared to greet all three returning passengers around July 10. Even more unbelievable was Walker's decision that his family and he himself would have a leisurely recuperation from all their stress at a summer-long rural retreat in New England. All the exasperated Smith could do was advise Walker in no uncertain terms that he should "drop his damage suit against Dunning." The adverse publicity from such a pursuit "would hurt him even if the suit was successful."[112]

The outspoken Sally also put her two cents worth in by expressing outrage at the way Walker "has always treated you, Jim." Walker had denied Smith a raise "early on" and another one year later. Asked face-to-face if Jimmie would ever have treated an employee that way, Smith admitted that both refusals still "rankled him" and that a fair man always anticipated his employees' needs: "No, it would not have been necessary in the first place for him to have made the request." Sally concluded the lengthy summary of her conversation with her brother-in-law with her own observation: "Jim was for the first time critical—that I ever saw of Cousin J."[113]

In the same letter to her sister, Sally hoped that Marie had enjoyed her ocean liner passage back to America because she likely would never "ride it again." The reference to "it" would nine months later acquire a profound irony because the name of the vessel was the Cunard R.M.S Lusitania. Thus, as the world stood on the brink of the Great War, Marie Bynum Lowry Smith returned to the Queen City of the Plains with up-to-date and first-hand knowledge of Europe that only a handful of Amarillo residents could ever claim. Such knowledge would stand her and her DAR in good stead when it came to aiding the war effort looming on the horizon.

Marie's letter to Jimmie written night before Lusitania docked in New York, July 9, 1914

Chapter 6

Amarillo
1915-1927

Was she to rest on her laurels after five years as Regent of her Amarillo DAR chapter or was she to pursue broader DAR goals on the state level? Fortuitously, she chose the latter course and with gusto. She knew that a woman in far West Texas could not go it alone when it came to aspirations for becoming State Regent, so she wisely spent a good part of 1915 in active preparation. Her first endorsement came from her sister-in-law, Roxalee Smith Andrews, a prominent Houston socialite. Even though Roxalee was *not* a DAR member herself, she spoke to several women "who are close personal friends of mine." Roxalee went on to add, "It looks like easy sailing for Sister Marie" and "I will make doubly sure of that in this area of Texas."[1] To her husband away on business, Marie wrote in late January that some "DAR friends in Dallas, Fort Worth, Waco, Galveston, and Austin" had readily offered to support her candidacy.[2] A week later Bessie Walker let Marie know that her Brownwood DAR chapter had written "to all the chapters in the state" to "ask them to endorse you."[3] Two additional letters of endorsement quickly followed, one from the Regent of the Paris chapter and another from the Regent of the Austin chapter—both glowing in their support of Mrs. James Lowry Smith.[4] The Esther McCrory Chapter was also delighted at the prospect and received a telegram of thanks from Marie who was in Corpus Christi at the Wade Bynums dealing with her mother's illness contracted during a visit with her son and daughter-in-law.[5]

The election as State Regent became a *fait accomplis* in early November at the Sixteenth State Conference in Texarkana. Even though she was not scheduled to take office until the following year, Mrs. Smith quickly stepped in and "assumed the duties of State Regent during the entire congress week as the Regent, Mrs. Andrew Rose, was too ill to attend."[6] When Marie formally assumed office at the State Conference in Fort Worth the following year, a special song, "Our State Regent," was sung, having been composed in Marie's honor by Miss Julia F. Lockett of Amarillo.[7] Unfortunately, Mrs. Smith was not in attendance because her mother had just passed and Marie was in Horn Lake arranging her mother's funeral and burial in the Bynum cemetery plot. However, Mrs. Rose stood in for Marie, thus repaying the favor of the year before. In the meantime, Marie never neglected the Amarillo chapter. For example, she arranged for Professor James A. Hill, later president of West Texas State College, to address the Esther McCrory Chapter in October 1917.[8]

Marie's take-charge attitude was most clearly manifest on the state and national levels with America's entry into World War I. The National DAR's largest effort was the War Relief Service Committee and Marie chaired the Western Division of that undertaking with nine states under her direction. She pledged that "Our Texas men and our Texas boys" would hold back the "hostile horde" in Europe.[9] The full extent of her contributions are detailed in the Texas DAR History, but crucial aspects included fostering a nationwide Liberty Loan and War Savings Certificates program; shipping foodstuffs and gifts to overseas military; and collecting pledges to foster training camps for young women. As the War began to wind down, she and her Texas cohorts redecorated the Texas Room at the DAR headquarters in Washington, DC. Ten organizing regents for new local chapters were appointed during Marie's two-year term and five new chapters were added to the Texas rolls.[10] So appreciated was her work that even unofficial accolades came her way, such as an impromptu luncheon given at Dallas' Adolphus Hotel in her honor as she was en route back to Amarillo from a National DAR meeting in Washington, DC.[11]

As for her husband, it is the unsung and unheralded work that marks a man of true humility and genuine worth. No man was more devoted to the expansion of membership in the First Baptist Church during the war years than Jimmie Smith. Early on in 1915 he pleaded successfully with certain recalcitrant members of the congregation to make good on pledges from the previous year.[12] A month later Smith was a stalwart member of the pulpit committee to seek a new pastor. Smith personally asked that the committee have eight members, "two of whom should be women."[13] Once Dr. Wallace Bassett had arrived, Smith advocated a $3,000 per year salary and a parsonage for the family; Smith himself made a "large financial contribution to this new undertaking."[14] Whether it was the Palo Duro Baptist Association or the Texas State Baptist Convention, Smith led the way as a representative nearly every year.

After Bassett had left in 1918 for a prestigious Baptist Church in Dallas, he wrote a personal letter to Smith thanking him for all he had done for Amarillo and congratulating the pulpit committee on gaining the services of Dr. I. E. Gates.[15] Gates, like Bassett, soon departed for another church in San Antonio. Unfazed, Smith worked for a third time in four years and recruited Dr. Herbert W. Virgin in 1919. In the same time period Smith supervised repairs to the dome of the Church building and saw to it that an updated heating plant was installed and that needed roof repairs were completed.[16] And, needless to say, the Church's financial records were always under Smith's careful scrutiny.

When the Baptist Church wasn't calling on his skills, the ever-expanding firm of Walker-Smith demanded his attention in capacities that would have overwhelmed a lesser man. As the waters receded from yet another Galveston storm in 1915, Smith waded in—literally—to determine which canned goods stored on upper shelves could be saved and he saw to it that the warehousemen ridded the place of moldy beans, melted sugar, and ruined sacks of green coffee beans. Insurance did not cover flood damage and Walker-Smith's Galveston house and railroad siding damages amounted to more than $35,000.[17] A new venture at Stamford in late 1915 also caused problems when a leased building's foundation gave way while several trucks were trying to load shipments. Fortunately, the loss was mostly in the pride category and Smith helped negotiate a new building enabling Stamford to proceed with business.[18]

On the positive side, the wholesale grocery enterprise was constantly expanding with new warehouses located in Houston (1915), Corpus Christi (1917), and Dublin (1919). When the Ranger oilfield boomed in 1919, Smith saw to it that Walker-Smith acquired the Ranger Wholesale Grocery Company and ordered grocery stocks that would appeal to roughnecks and business entrepreneurs alike.[19] Thus, perhaps the greatest civilizing influence of Smith's guidance was instilling in the company the ability to adapt to changing circumstances—even if those circumstances were generated by their sometimes adversarial boss, John A. Walker himself. Smith backed his friend Blackwell in successfully urging Walker not to withdraw unnecessary dollars from the expanding company.[20] By mid 1918 Smith had convinced Walker that Smith should have Walker's power of attorney, particularly if Walker's ongoing absence from Brownwood would continue to hamper day-to-day operations.[21] Up to his usual tricks, Walker sent a letter to Blackwell and Smith while en route to Los Angeles via a two-day stopover at the Grand Canyon. The contents read like a set of military orders as Walker demanded Smith convert some of his Liberty Loan Bonds and make a $20,000 deposit to Walker's Brownwood bank. Blackwell was commanded to look into better discount rates on loans at banks in Kansas City and Galveston. The only 'thank you' in the letter is directed at Smith for seeing that "my remittance for my income tax was sent to me by special delivery."[22]

One of Walker-Smith's newest ventures was the processing and packaging of its own brand of peanut butter. All went well until Blackwell received a notice "from the Department of Agriculture, United States' Southern Division advising me to appear on Monday the 5th [1918] for violating the Pure Food and Drug Act by making Peanut Butter Interstate without being properly labeled as to its net weights, all occasioned by the numerous changes in the shipping department of the Candy Factory." With Smith's concurrence, Blackwell successfully presented the Walker-Smith case that four of its shipping clerks had recently been drafted into military service and that a new clerk, working at the end of the manufacturing line, had inadvertently omitted the proper labels. Both Smith and Blackwell greatly appreciated the "cordial" treatment by the Justice Department in dismissing the case and, thus, thankfully avoided an escalation of what Smith humorously referred to as the peanut butter fiasco.[23]

Despite setbacks from a natural disaster, faulty building construction, and a continually absent CEO, Walker-Smith showed steady profits from their increasingly diversified line of products and widespread Texas distribution points. The World War I years were especially fruitful ones for the Company. For example, Blackwell informed his boss in mid-1914: "Mr. Smith probably told you that we had booked and sold a large amount of future goods. In fact, we have never sold as much as we have this year heretofore."[24] The following year, Walker wrote to Blackwell on The Men's Club, Chautauqua, New York letterhead: "Our liabilities as shown on the trial balance you sent are gratifying. You must be receiving good collections because of the grain crop in Texas. This is unusual in my experience. Our customers should be in a financial condition to enable us to push sales in the fall."[25] After finishing up with the business end of the same letter, Walker unleashed another personal request: "Will want another automobile when I return home." Walker wanted to replace the "wide tread 1914 model Cadillac touring car fully equipped" that he had purchased in fall 1913.[26] What the new car was is never revealed though

Brownwood, Texas, Oct. 30, 1915.

Mr. J. L. Smith,

% Walker-Smith Company,

Houston, Texas,

Dear Mr. Smith:-

Mr. Blackwell tells me that you wish to know the address of Ernest Garnett. I am informed through Garnett White that his address is, Encinitas, San Diego County, California.

Yours very truly,

JTH:GC

Sample Letter on Walker-Smith Company letterhead

extant sales contracts show that Walker purchased a 1914 Ford touring car for Bessie and a 1915 model of the same manufacture for his daughter.[27]

Whatever the case, part of Smith-Walker's increasing success came from diversification of goods sold. A case in point occurred in mid-1916 when Blackwell reported to his boss still living in self-imposed exile: "A large amount of ammunition is to go out during July but payment will not be made until December 1st. This will materially help our sales and profits. I understand from Mr. Coalson that he remitted $37,000 for the ammunition yesterday."[28] Innovative business practices also contributed to the Company's visibility and sales increases. Thanks to Smith and C. Y. Early, Walker-Smith had aligned themselves with the Southern Wholesale Grocers Association in 1915 and the following year began to hold annual sales meetings for all their drummers.[29] By 1917 the Board of Directors increased Walker-Smith's Capital Stock from $500,000 to $1,000,000. Some 80% of the increased value came from "surplus and undivided profits now accumulated by us," but John Walker did lead the way with $100,000 from his own pockets.[30] Thus, by the end of 1919, the Company could report a sales volume in excess of seven million dollars, a trend that would continue to expand for several more years.[31]

It is very important to note that nearly every piece of correspondence sent to John Walker by his series of vice presidents at Walker-Smith between Walker's first mental breakdown in 1906 and into the late 1920s contains some reference to Smith's extraordinary attentiveness to the immediate and future needs of Walker-Smith Company. The tenor runs as follows: 'Mr. Smith is in touch with us every day about the profit and loss columns of the business and not a single decision is made here in Brownwood without his experienced and valuable input.'

The only continual fly in the ointment at the outset of what would later be called the "Roaring Twenties" was the exasperating John Walker. Smith had to personally intervene to get Walker to abandon his penchant for always seeking the cheapest Texas banks to secure business loans. Smith wrote to Walker, once again camped out in upstate New York, a gracious admonition that Walker-Smith avoid loans from "Texas banks with which we do no business." Smith argued that money was readily available all over the state and cautioned that the firm's prestige would not be helped "by ignoring the banks who have greatly helped us in the past."[32] A year later Smith again expressed concern about Walker suddenly and inexplicably going incommunicado, particularly when Smith was awaiting word on a sensitive account statement he had sent relative to their business with Nobles Brothers.[33]

Perhaps as a sane counterpart to the seemingly always troublesome Walker-Smith Company, but certainly because of his own astute personal assessment of the banking world, Smith contemplated a new endeavor. James knew full well that Texas had reinstituted the State Banking system in 1905 and had permitted a State Guaranty Banking system in 1910. The latter was close to but slightly different from the FDIC system which was passed as part of the Federal Reserve Act of 1913. A state guaranty bank in Texas had two options: to post a substantial bond or to make an annual percentage contribution of the bank's deposits to a central state fund that could be tapped in the case of any guaranty bank's failure. Nearly every participating bank opted for the percentage choice since contributions to the central fund were spread over time. Smith also knew full well that such an institution was absent from the Amarillo financial scene.

With a flourish of ads in Amarillo newspapers, but with little other hoopla, the Guaranty State Bank opened its temporary doors on June 17, 1916 at the renovated Old Post Office at 111 East Fifth. This time around Smith listed himself as Chairman of the Board; the remaining officers were B. C. D. Bynum as President, C. M. McCullough as Vice-president, and C. P. Elliott as Cashier. Careful planning must have been paramount because the stockholders reflected Smith's savvy for gaining a cross-section of white and blue-collar investors. To name but a few of the over 40 initial investors: S. H. Madden, Attorney-at-Law; H. A. Nobles, Nobles Bros. Wholesale Grocers; G. D. Bowie, Manager, Amarillo Sash & Door Co.; Mrs. S. E. Putty, Investments; T. M. Caldwell, Indian Motorcycles; W. E. Danver, Master Mechanic, Rock Island RR; C. C. Cunningham, Nurseryman ; Wm. P. Hopkins, Stock Farmer; Mrs. E. S. Poage, Land and Investments; D. F. Cook, Painter; E. E. Pickerell, Jeweler; J. D. Cazzell, Upholstery; J. J. Petty, Panhandle Lumber Co.; and W. W. Hamilton, Plumber. On the first day alone, deposits came from 76 people and totaled $81,000.[34]

Under Texas law, a guaranty bank capitalized at $40 to $75,000 was restricted to deposits of eight times that amount.[35] Smith and his directors had capitalized at $75,000 and in just two months they had 493 accounts and $189,955.04 on deposit.[36] Two critical benchmarks of any bank are continuity and stability, and both were part of Smith's banking bible. By early the following year, the Guaranty Bank was operating in its own building at 407 Polk in the heart of Amarillo's business district. Modern teller cages, ceiling lighting, and brass spittoons lined the bank's spacious lobby.

Once again, the initial newspaper ads all contained a warm and inviting appeal: "Let this bank be your friend;" "We assure you fair treatment;" "Consider the crowd you are in. …The profligate big rich are the people who spend the most money foolishly and are really weaklings."[37] Less than six months after its opening, deposits stood at nearly $350,000 and the bank could proudly proclaim: "History of banking in this country is full of regrets. Our state government has recognized this and provided the law which enables us to assure you that we are protected."[38] Even the "COWMAN" was invited to join with the "time-honored hospitality of the plains" by "joining the unity of forty-five of Amarillo's oldest and best citizen stockholders."[39]

Not simply satisfied to maintain the status quo, Smith joined forces with Judge J. C. Paul, the dean of Panhandle bankers, and J. H. Paul, his son, and made them majority stockholders in 1920. By the following year, the resources and liabilities statement of Guaranty Bank showed a net of $1,535,111.42 with, of course, an increased capitalization.[40] Thus, in just over 30 years, Smith's latest bank had advanced another step beyond a clapboard Old Town building where depositors slept on sacked flour beside a large safe to a civilized state-of-the-art financial institution with insured and secured accounts for every depositor. Instead of mules attached to a wooden freight wagon on a rutted dirt road, Smith's 1915 Franklin automobile—and possibly by then even a new Essex--was parked on a paved parking spot on Amarillo's main thoroughfare.[41]

Always the thoughtful and loving husband, Jim sent Marie a telegram the day of their wedding anniversary while he was checking on the new Houston warehouse and visiting his sister: "I am thinking of thirty-three years ago today and of you. Pledging my love for another thirty-three. James" Like other prominent Amarillo families such as the Boyces, Sanborns, and Bivins, Jimmie and Marie hosted occasional dinner parties. Marie had chosen her own china pattern, an intertwined logo of their six initials on plain white place settings. Her silverware had a habit of disappearing when larger dinner parties were held and other guests brought supplemental ware. According to Ann Bynum Whittenburg, Marie finally decided to mark the backside of each of her pieces with a small "x" so that she would not loose any more silverware. However, foremost on the agenda at 1101 Taylor were not loud parties but quiet teas, occasional luncheons, and family dinners. B. C. D. and his wife, Bertha Kate, and their two boys and Earl and Sally Cobb and their two children frequently converged on the Smith home. Incredibly enough, the Bynum nephews and Cobb children each had different sets of names for the Smiths. For Bill and Jim they were Uncle Jimmie and Aunt Marie, but for the two Cobb children, possibly under the influence of their mother who was the youngest Bynum sibling, it was always Papa Jim and Sissie. From earliest days, Bill Bynum loved bouncing in Uncle Jimmie's lap and later sitting by his desk at the bank. Jim Bynum, fascinated like his father with any mechanized form of transportation, relished the former carriage shed and now garage behind the Smith home where he would pretend to drive the Walker-Smith Company Ford or the Franklin. Katherine always preferred the old cast-iron hitching post in front of the residence, either swinging from it or using it as a balance beam. Among Katherine's earliest recollections is an old sea shell that rested on an end table next to her grandmother's bed. 'Hold it to your ear Katherine,' Mrs. Kate Bynum said, 'because someday you will see the ocean.' The youngest, Earl, reportedly bolted from the dining table at age five when he learned that his favorite chicken, "Ol' Mrs. Red," was the Sunday dinner main course. "Not Ol' Mrs. Red, not Ol' Red! I can't eat her. I can't!" It took all Papa Jim's restorative powers to finally calm the boy although Earl refused from then on to eat chicken in any form at the Smiths.

The most sacred memory was the annual Christmas tree lighting in the large foyer of the Smith residence. Papa Jim mounted the stepladder and held Katherine while she placed an ancient cloth Santa Claus atop the tree. Then Papa Jim carefully lit the real candles on the tree to accentuate the garlands of cranberries and popcorn while all three families sang "Silent Night." Adjacent to the foyer was the library with its huge sliding oak doors. This was the domain for family business and the children were relegated to the upstairs playroom while the parents discussed family affairs.

One such meeting in the early 1920s had Earl Cobb front and center while he recounted a not very adept business decision he had made several years earlier when he was Vice-president of Texas Mercantile & Manufacturing Company in 1920, a confections and soft drink distributorship. Offered a contract by Coca-Cola to establish a bottling plant in Amarillo, Cobb had declared the soft drink 'but a passing fad' and had declined, leaving the go-ahead to J. B. Dickson, his business partner, so that Earl could concentrate on his modestly successful Southwest

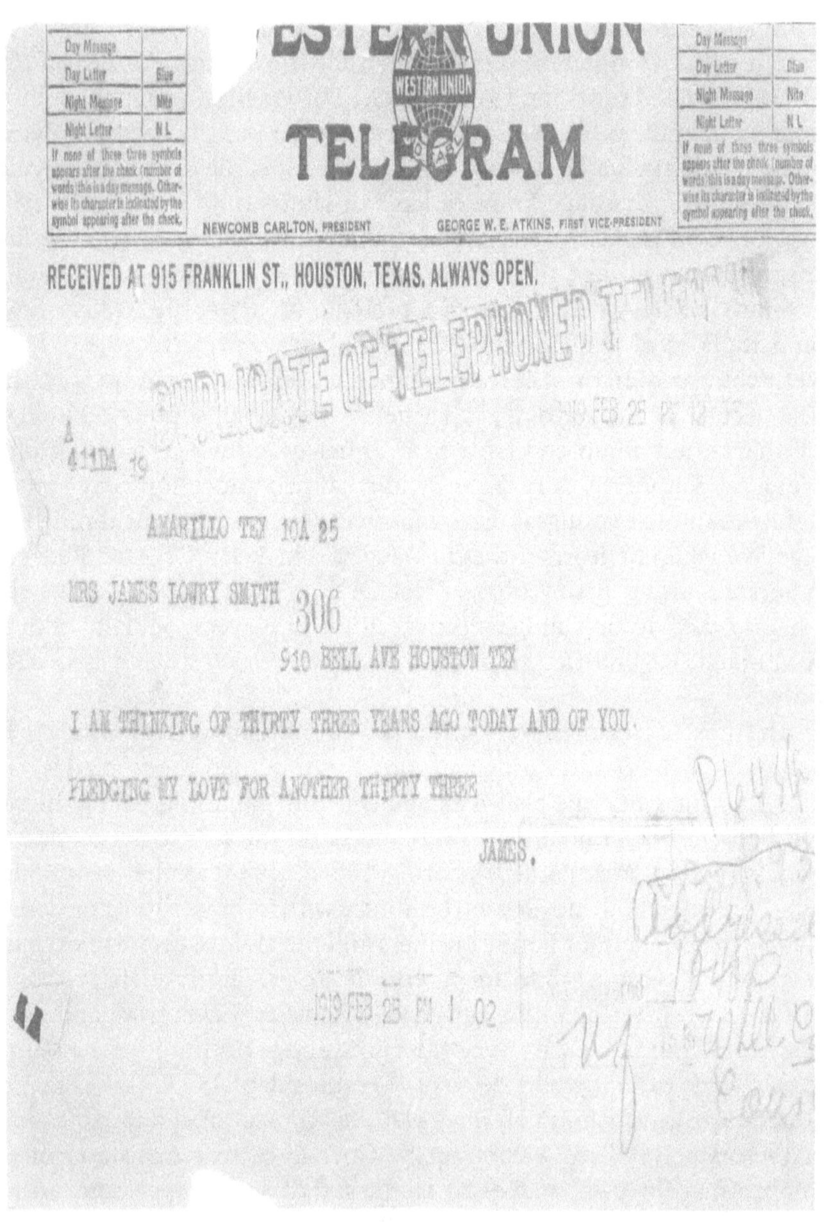

Telegram, James to Mrs. James Lowry Smith, Feb 25, 1919

Coal Company. "Alas," Cobb sadly related, "Coca-Cola thrived and the coal business nose-dived. To my everlasting discredit, I made the wrong choice."[42]

The summer of 1920 was a remarkable time for Papa Jim, Sissie, and their Cobb niece and nephew. While Earl Cobb was off on a lengthy business trip, Sally took her two children by train to Chicago where they would eventually meet up with the Smiths who had driven by car from Amarillo. In a cheerful letter to John Walker regarding their motor trip Smith reported: "We had a good trip and stood it well, though both of us find it will take a couple of days to recuperate fully. …Distance Amarillo to Chicago 1,223 miles; gasoline 75 gallons; lubricating oil about 2 gallons. And only two flats!"[43] The Cobbs and Smiths both stayed at the Shore Crest Hotel near Lincoln Park, and Katherine happily informed her father: "Papa Jim took us to the zoo in Lincoln Park where they were feeding a big cinnamon bear."[44]

That same summer witnessed the passage of the 19th Amendment granting women's suffrage. On Smith's personal stationery and in his own handwriting is the text of a speech about women being given the right to vote. Whatever the event was is unknown, but the invitation was last minute, issued on the morning of the evening's delivery. The contents are anything but last-minute reflections. The speech begins with a thoughtful and humble perspective on how he is not a very good public speaker. Nonetheless he proclaims: "The most that I can hope to do is to encourage you in going into this new field of activity. For some years I have had the strong conviction that women were entitled to the ballot, and that many of the present pernicious laws, and still worse conditions, would never be overcome until we could have the help of women with the ballot." After numerous reflections on the previous injustices of poll taxes and having to be a member of landed gentry to vote, Smith goes to the heart of the matter by citing the modern woman's entitlements in home ownership and in the marketplace:

> The right to the franchise is justly hers—she is a joint owner with the husband in all the property he possesses, and in many cases has her separate property in addition. The business world can hardly do without her now in the office.

Even as he spoke, Smith's remarks were being put into practice by his trusted wife who had assumed a national office in the DAR the previous year.

In 1919 Marie was elected a Vice-President General of the DAR where for the next three years of her term in office she was, in effect, a 'cabinet' member serving at the behest of the National President of the DAR. Marie soon found herself engaged in a bevy of activities, some of which included being a member of the "Memorial Fountain Committee" and on June 4, 1921 she attended the dedication of the fountain in honor of the Pilgrim Mothers at Plymouth, MA. A few days later she presented a maritime painting of WWI convoy ships which would be placed in the French National War Museum. Later the same year she arranged for the Texas Room at the Memorial Continental Hall to serve as a committee room for the U.S. government-sponsored Disarmament Conference.[45]

Her most conspicuous role, however, was as the Western Division's chief representative on a national DAR board for "Americanization and Patriotic Education," a successor endeavor to the War Relief Committee of previous years. In this capacity Mrs. Smith made major contributions to a Manual for Immigrants (chiefly immigrant women) of which 45,000 copies were published in 1921, printed in four languages: French, Italian, Spanish, and Polish.[46] By late 1923, the manual had been translated into Hungarian, Yiddish, Russian, and German.[47] This manual was the culmination of work that had begun two years previously by Marie's successor State Regent, Mrs. Lipscomb Norvell, who, at Marie's request, had issued a statewide proclamation in September 1919 to "make foreign-born women our special case."[48] At the same time, the state of Texas endorsed a richer and more elaborate Civics educational program for public school students. On the national level, Marie helped arrange a similar effort by dedicating a portion of an $80,000 grant to the cooperative efforts of the American Legion and National Education Association to promote such education in all public schools.[49] In view of the recent World War, Marie and her cohorts wanted international relations to be the focus for the next generation of American schoolchildren.[50]

Another civilizing and civic-minded kudo for Marie was her ability to secure Amarillo as the site for the 1922 State DAR Convention. As Marie put it in her welcoming address, "I have awaited eleven years for this eventful day when Amarillo could draw to her hearthstone this distinguished gathering."[51] Never before had such a large group of women converged on Amarillo. Business meetings were held in the Central Presbyterian Church.

The invocation was rendered by Dr. Herbert W. Virgin of First Baptist Church. Mrs. Ray Wheatley, Regent for the Esther McCrory Chapter, then introduced O. V. Vernon of the Amarillo Board of City Development, plus presidents of the Rotary, Kiwanis, and Lions Club. Mrs. G. T. Vineyard, president of the Potter County Federation of Women's Clubs, addressed the assembly with a brief overview of historic Panhandle women.

Then it was down to a full agenda of DAR business and historical presentations, including one by Mrs. L. L. Hunter, Treasurer General, and another by Mrs. G. W. Hanger, Organizing Secretary, who had made the trip from Washington, DC. There were tributes to cowboys and cowmen and numerous reports on the vast array of Texas DAR women involved in activities such as "New Movies," "Revolutions in Transportation," "Geological Conservation," "Welfare Reform," and "National Old Trail Roads," the latter of special interest to Marie and her chapter who had been instrumental in placing granite markers along a section of historic Texas trails. Marie hosted a large informal tea at her home as part of the festivities.

The only bump in the road for the Esther McCrory Chapter occurred in mid 1924 when former regent, Mrs. Avery Turner, withdrew and started the Llano Estacado Chapter of the DAR on May 4, 1925.[52] Allegedly, some Amarillo women who qualified for DAR membership felt excluded by the McCrory Chapter and its emphasis on lineage. The feeling was probably not without warrant because pedigree was often overemphasized in the DAR. However, a steadily growing Amarillo could certainly support a rival but compatible group who shared the same aims.

To a certain extent, a central Amarillo DAR event in 1926 marked the completion of a circle that had begun in 1889. Marie Bynum Smith has generally been given credit for planting the first tree in Amarillo.[53] It was a stately old mountain ash planted as a sapling when the original Smith home was transported from Old Amarillo. The tree and house had to go to make way for Colonel Herring's new multi-story hotel. Not wanting the sturdy tree to be cut up for firewood, Marie had souvenirs cut from its trunk, including a gavel which was made and subsequently donated to her DAR chapter.[54]

Despite its flappers, its jazz, its flashy motor cars, its speakeasies, and its bootleg whiskey, there were ominous clouds on the business horizon during the early and mid-1920s. The years 1919 and 1920 had been banner post-war years for most businesses and nearly all banks, but the next three years witnessed a steady decline in the prices of goods and services. Walker-

MRS. JAMES LOWRY SMITH
Amarillo
Vice President General 1919-1922
State Regent 1916-1918
Honorary State Regent

Marie's official DAR photo

Smith Company was no exception, though their problems stemmed not so much from lowered prices as much as competitive services offered by two 'new kids' on the block, namely the attempt of foodstuffs manufacturers to market directly to grocery stores and the sudden appearance of retail chain grocery stores.

It was almost as if Smith could see what was coming when he wrote metaphorically in the autumn of 1921:

> The good Book says there are some things no one can know:
> the course of an eagle in the air, the movement of a snake on
> a rock, and the ways of a man with a maid. Equally uncertain
> is the immediate future of wholesale grocery businesses.[55]

Walker-Smith and a host of other wholesale grocers were able to counter the threat of big packers who were sending route cars "directly to retail outlets by gaining a favorable verdict from the Federal Trade Commission that such practices constituted restraint of trade. Packers were ordered to be packers and wholesale grocers should continue as distributors."[56] What Company historian C. Y. Early termed the "dragon of the Piggly-Wiggly syndrome"[57] was a tougher rascal to handle. First, Smith combated the chain-store influx by proving through examples that the wholesale grocer could deliver goods more quickly and reliably than the chain-store headquarters with their inefficient bureaucracy. Second, he sent out skilled salesmen to show the retailer how to set up better store lighting, how to better organize displays of key products, and how to arrange products on lower shelves. The latter advice was crucial since, increasingly, shoppers were pushing carts through aisles rather than requesting clerks to reach up with hooked poles to grab cereal boxes and coffee cans. Retailers across the state appreciated the above-and-beyond recommendations, particularly when there was competition among chain stores to obtain supplies from a single and often unreliable central headquarters.

Nonetheless, Walker-Smith was face-to-face with shrinking profits ($4 million volume in 1921 vs. $6 million the year before) caused by peacetime overproduction of agricultural products (particularly wheat, cotton, and beef) and consequent price drops in the resultant finished goods for public consumption. In addition, in the midst of this temporary crisis, the attention of Vice-president Blackwell was continually diverted from righting the grocery business to meeting the demands of John Walker's personal pursuits in Central Texas. In early 1921, Blackwell spent considerable time obtaining a series of appraisal and repair estimates on Walker's vast real estate investments in Sagerton, Brownwood, San Angelo, and Colorado City, to name but a few. Furthermore, he had to file reports with Walker on the status of some of Walker's new investment banking pursuits in the Houston area. In spite of the decreased business volume, Smith knew his partner had to fulfill a promise Walker had made during the glory days of the previous year—a new recreational facility for Company employees, the so-called Pecan Valley Lodge, to be erected on a lakeside property in Brownwood. Walker's solution was to have employees contribute a portion of their paychecks to pay for the facility. Smith objected vehemently to Walker's Indian-giver attitude and stated that either the Board of Directors underwrite the project as originally planned or that the project be canceled entirely. There was some grumbling, but Walker finally gave in and the recreational area was developed.[58]

Due to Smith and Blackwell's dedicated efforts in diversifying product lines, Company profits improved significantly by late 1922. The steadfast Walker's response was not thanks and generosity, but just the opposite. On Johns Hopkins' stationery, Walker wrote that "it is to my interest for W-S Company to pay say five percent dividend this year,"[59] a much-reduced figure from previous years. Smith, who had himself handled some of Walker's personal business during the year and had pleaded for fairer treatment of their employees, had apparently already received advanced warning about what Walker might propose. He was—for once—infuriated. He wrote immediately to Walker, reminding about their discussion prior to Walker's departure for Baltimore and he re-emphasized that, given the present circumstances, "the business of Walker-Smith Co. should be liquidated" and "that we have nothing to gain by further postponing steps in that direction." If not an entire liquidation, Smith added, then at least a consolidation of resources since Walker's physical and mental "indisposition have been so prolonged." Smith concluded his letter to Walker by quoting Blackwell. In reply to Smith's verbal query, even Blackwell had admitted that, given everything James Smith had explained, "we should close it out."[60]

What transpired over the next year to cause both Smith and Blackwell to show a renewed interest in Walker-Smith is unknown and not documented in any of Walker's vast collection of business correspondence. A possible explanation may be that Walker, the man with the Midas touch, provided

Smith with a substantial sum of money to make profitable business loans—
"guilt-edged" loans as Smith called them—to a number of very reliable
Amarillo businesses in mid 1923. It is the one and only time that Smith
listed multiple loans (as distinct from numerous letters addressing singular
loans) in his correspondence with Walker. A partial list of the loans, all for
six months and at 8% went to:

Landergrin Bros.	$20,000
Earl Cobb	5,000
Green Bros. Co.	30,000
Texas M & M Co.	15,000
Amarillo Oil Co.	14,800
Panhandle Lbr Co.	15,000
Thompson Drug Co.	10,000
Roberts & Oliver	15,000
General Auto Supply Co.	10,000
Mission Oil Co.	10,000[61]

In spite of Walker's continued absence from Brownwood, Smith went
ahead with three vital Walker-Smith business pursuits in each of the next
three years. To begin with, Smith knew that a new university was about to
emerge in Lubbock despite its sparse population of just 4,000 and no paved
roads. According to C. Y. Early, "Mr. Smith planned the Lubbock House.
He selected the lot and employed a contractor at Amarillo to do the work."
The finished building had all the modern conveniences—elevator, cold
storage, loading wharves, and substantial office space.[62] The house opened
in early 1924 and by October Smith was proudly able to report to Walker
in Chautauqua, NY, that the September 1924 business receipts for all of
Walker-Smith were the second best of any September in the 30-year history
of the company. The new Lubbock House alone had $46,823 in sales for the
same month. The most enlightening lines of Smith's report occur at the end
of the letter: "I have purposely not heretofore made any reference to our
having entered that territory. I fancy, however, that in some way your eagle
eye has caught it that we are doing business there."[63]

By early 1925, Smith and Early had erected a new replacement house at
Stamford, built next to a switch of the Missouri, Kansas and Texas Railroad.
When a devastating fire destroyed the San Angelo House late the same
year, Smith made a personal trip to that city and told the local employees:

"We will build again!" Finally, a house was temporarily leased at Plainview in 1926, but Smith insisted on an eventual new building and "stayed out in the rain and drizzle most of an early January day" marking the corners of the lot.[64] Smith's forceful hand in all matters pertaining to the growth and stability of Walker-Smith were reflected in the bottom line of one monthly report from spring 1925. To Walker's Stafford Hotel in Baltimore, Smith reported a $404,617 revenue for March 1925 compared to $337,639 for the previous March.[65]

If, judging from the loans Smith negotiated for Walker, the business world of the Panhandle-Plains area was a bit unsettled, the banking institutions also felt the pinch. The ads for the Guaranty State Bank took on a patently honest but nonetheless bleak aspect. As the new year began in 1922, the Directors of Guaranty Bank revealed:

> During the year just past, we have had an entirely new business experience. The commodities produced by this country have uniformly shrunk in value at least 60 percent, and the values everywhere have been dissipated in like manner. In consequence of this unprecedented condition there have been many business and bank failures, both State and National. To pay the guaranteed deposits in the failed State banks dollar for dollar, this bank has paid out over $22,000.00 of its good assets through the Guaranty Loan Fund. Moreover, we have charged off some $12,000.00 of losses on loans.[66]

In late March of the same year, the ever-observant Smith wrote to Walker, temporarily established in a San Antonio hotel: "It looks like the Guaranty feature in Okla. banking may go on the rocks. It is getting to be very burdensome in Texas. Guaranty State Bank here shows debit on "Guaranty Fund" acct. $44,189.30."[67] Although a later ad in 1922 highlighted the bank's "safe and conservative business policies" and its basically "sound financial strength,"[68] the long-term handwriting was on the wall regarding guaranty banking in the Lone Star state. By early 1924, the assets at Guaranty State had shrunk by $400,000 to $1,116,337.92 on deposit.[69]

Because Smith and the bank's directors felt such a burden was too heavy and not consistent with good banking practices, Guaranty State Bank withdrew from the state system and converted to the American State Bank in mid 1924.[70] Although Bynum and other directors remained on the Board to provide a smooth transition, Jimmie decided to retire and C. M. McCullough became president, then, following McCullough's sudden death, Mr. Paul took over in 1926.

So, one might well ask, what was responsible for the collapse of the state guaranty banking system and its official demise under a new Texas repeal law in 1925? There is an obvious and easy answer as well as a deeper, more substantial one. The obvious one, particularly for the Panhandle, was a decline in cotton and beef prices. In 1919 beef cattle were priced at $7.90 per hundredweight, but by 1924 the price was $4.15. Cotton went from 35 cents per pound in 1919 to 23 cents in 1924.[71] Consequently, loans were put in jeopardy and frequently had to be written off. The harsher and more convincing truth lay in the original Texas banking laws which had permitted a person with as little as $10,000 to capitalize a bank, plus negligence on the part of state auditors to enforce strict banking regulation. However, the stunning statistical fact is that between 1920 and 1925 69 Texas banks failed mainly because of poor management practices and another 75 mainly because of "defalcation" (embezzlement on the part of one or more bank officers) and speculation.[72] In a retrospective study of Texas banking of this era, Avery Carlson cites the following largely ignored warning of the United States Controller of Currency in 1923: "The guaranty of bank deposits tends to make all guaranty banks look alike to the public, and to put the conservative banker who is unwilling to make large promises and to take chances at a disadvantage."[73] Thus, for Smith and many other men of integrity, the sin of greed was—and still is—the most uncivilized and hurtful sin of all.

Despite the demise of the guaranty banking system in the state, James L. Smith continued as Vice President of The Western National Bank in Hereford. Now in its twentieth year of operation with the steadfast G. A. F. Parker at the helm as the institution's President and with B. C. D. Bynum leading the way as one of the bank's Directors, Western National reported its Capital and Surplus at $125,000 on June 30, 1922. The resources and liabilities of the bank balanced at a modest but steady $362,312.44.[74] One can only conclude that one of the greatest commercial civilizing legacies Smith bestowed on the Panhandle was his stellar work in helping found three of its banks. He ran them with absolute honesty and integrity unlike so many of his banking peers.

Regrettably, little direct information has been uncovered about Smith's interests in the Panhandle oilfields of the 1920s, though doubtless he was an honest investor who brought his considerable Beaumont experience of two decades previous to bear on petroleum exploration. Several references from Smith's friends and family members do indicate, indirectly, the degree of Smith's involvement. David Warren, a reporter for the *Amarillo Daily News* from 1918-1926 mentions: "I became well acquainted with Mr. Smith and occasionally saw him in the Panhandle on his way to the oilfields."[75] B. C. D. Bynum's son, Jim, recalled simply: "When the Panhandle Oil Field was discovered, Mr. Smith drilled several successful wells east of Borger."[76] Jim's daughter, Ann Bynum Whittenburg, additionally mentions a story her grandfather told about the two veteran bankers staying up all night at a well site until, fortunately, a gusher came roaring in.[77] Coincidentally, B. C. D. Bynum, along with Sam L. Seay, Wales H. Madden, and R. Dean Kirk, formed Badger Oil Company in February 1926. In fact, Smith did participate in Badger Oil during what would have been the last full year of his life. Indeed, the move was an advantageous one for all concerned because "east of Borger" meant Hutchinson County where "production soared from a little more than one million barrels in 1925 to more than twenty-five million barrels the following year."[78] Even though this company was eventually dissolved in 1957, royalties on holdings are still paid out to original stockholders and/or their descendants. In addition to Hutchinson County, Badger Oil had extensive drilling operations in Lynn and Moore Counties as well, all of which stemmed from initial Smith and Bynum ventures.[79]

Despite the banking problems at Guaranty State Bank, the year 1924 encapsulates the civilized lives of Mr. and Mrs. James Lowry Smith in a wide variety of aspects. Thankfully, a number of extant documents have survived and bear witness to their lives during that year. Jimmie's New Year's resolution was to, once again, keep a diary and he wrote in a preface: "In my day this record will not attain the interest that comes of age, but none-the-less will afford some occasion for musing."[80] What Smith calls "the outstanding feature" of New Year's Day was a turkey dinner at the Bynums, attended by the four Cobbs and Earl Cobb's maiden sister, Nettie. The record zero temperatures moderated two days later to reveal a "busted hydrant" in the Smith backyard. In the company of Earl and Sally after supper on the 4th, Smith read aloud from an Amarillo newspaper including what he terms "a large amount of sensational and salacious stuff gathered by a detective agency" regarding a scandalous divorce suit.

About to enter his 64th year, Smith was experiencing physical problems including "discharging from my ears" and a sense that "my hearing is growing painfully dull." Nevertheless, Sunday School attendance at First Baptist had reached an astounding 842 students with Smith himself elected as President of the Sunday School. That same Sunday evening Marie and Bertha Kate accompanied Jimmie on a hasty motor trip to the South Santa Fe yards to track down Ben Bynum and deliver a message as he was about to depart with several carloads of cattle for Kansas City.

Another Walker-Smith Company 12-hour trip to Brownwood for the annual meeting followed on the 7th, but the sociable Smith chatted with fellow passenger, Dr. J. A. Hill of the Normal College, on the way to Canyon; with a Mr. Massey from there to Plainview; and with a Mr. Swinbeck as far as Slaton. The following day, "Mr. Blackwell tendered resignation as Vice Pres and Director on account of health conditions." Coincidentally, on the train to Temple, Blackwell was his companion though Blackwell was headed home eventually to his native Galveston.

The next three days document dreary weather and a series of prolonged medical appointments with Drs. Scott, Wilson, and Woodson. Plagued by headaches, Smith grudgingly agreed to fast for 48 hours at Dr. Scott's request and has his first meal the night of the 11th. The diary, alas, ends abruptly at this juncture. Perhaps that was for the best since, by his own admission, the abortive 1924 diary was a "decided contrast" to the cheerier ones "kept by me in my teens."

At 1101 Taylor, Marie hosted the year's first meeting of the "Women's Club" on January 17 with a series of presentations on the "Historical Marys" given by Mrs. Louis Anthony, one of Amarillo's first schoolteachers in 1892. Other presenters included three women whose husbands were among the most prominent oilmen of the Panhandle: Mrs. S. F. Sullenberger, Mrs. H. A. Nobles, and Mrs. R. B. Masterson.[81] Clearly, Marie's leadership in such literary and historical endeavors was a modern extension of the old Chautauqua Club from Amarillo's first days.

Perhaps the biggest item for discussion at First Baptist was establishing a mission church in the rapidly growing San Jacinto area of Amarillo, a project strongly urged by Pastor Virgin. However, when Virgin resigned in May to accept a position in Chicago, the congregation was chagrined. The Church minutes report that Smith rose to the occasion and "eased the tension" by explaining that an expanding Church did not depend solely on who was in charge at a particular time.[82] For his efforts, Smith was 'rewarded' by again being asked to chair the pulpit committee for selecting

Smith in office in mid-1920s

a new pastor. The seven men and two women found a veteran pastor who had served in Tyler and McKinney, Dr. G. L. Yates, who was willing to serve. Widely praised for his "unusual insight and vision," Yates superintended all church activities for the next 12 years until his untimely death in 1936.[83]

Yates and Smith bonded immediately and by November the two had helped secure the services of a much-needed Educational Director, Edgar Williamson, a 35-year-old energetic man who also became Church treasurer the following year.[84] Together, Yates and Smith made absolutely sure the San Jacinto Mission Church was on sound financial footing, including the building and property which, under Smith's guiding hand, became an independent operation on February 10, 1926 with a deeded value of $15,000.[85] Smith also was justifiably proud of his thriving Sunday

School and gave a pat on the head to his niece and nephew, Katherine and Earl Cobb, for attaining Honor Roll distinction in the summer of 1924.[86]

In fact, a very signature 12th birthday for young Katherine in May 1924 showed the resourceful and attentive Papa Jim in rare form. Her father was in Fort Smith, AR, and in the process of relocating Southwest Coal Company prior to the Cobb family move from Amarillo. On the very day of her 12th birthday, she began a letter to her father: "Just think. Earl and I went up in an airplane Monday." There were two planes and Katherine, followed by Earl, went up in Lieutenant Gray's for 12 minutes each at a cost of $2.50 per person. "Papa Jim wanted mother to go but she wouldn't." While Sally Cobb was at a tea with Mrs. William Boyce, the Cobb children had gone to Canyon with Papa Jim who then "let Earl and I ride all the way from Canyon to town on the runningboard!" At her actual birthday supper, Katherine recounted that "Papa Jim gave me three boxes of stationery and he paid for each of us to ride in the airplane. Wasn't that nice of him?"[87]

For two weeks in late June and early July, Smith devoted all his time to a task that was extremely beneficial to John Walker but of absolutely no personal benefit to Smith himself. The creditors for Walker's Joyce-Pruit Company in Roswell, NM, had besieged the directors to the point of the company going into bankruptcy. Smith personally interceded with trusted bankers at the National City Bank in New York City and negotiated a rescue package totaling over $40,000. Smith communicated directly: "Let it be understood I have no personal interest in JP Co. or the Joyces aside from friendship." National City Bank even sent one of their officers out to Roswell with instructions to cooperate with Smith to conserve the Company's assets. The bank's Vice-President, Wm. W. Woods, added that a telling point in his bank's decision to support Joyce-Pruit's bailout was a phone call from "Governor Hinkle of New Mexico who called in to us at your request."

Acting entirely in Walker's behalf, Smith pressed ahead to locate funds to accommodate the stalling tactics of another New York bank Smith had requested be added to the National City Bank rescue package. Smith's series of letters and telegrams fully admit some injudicious investments by Joyce-Pruit but argued that any "confiscation of their available cash" would "result in the company's further defaults" on existing loans and lead inevitably to "liquidation" and the loss of commercial paper already held in several New York banks. Finally, on July 9, Smith had a telegram from D. A. Forward, National Bank's chief negotiator in place at Roswell and then

Carlsbad that "I have released the balance" to allow "their continuation in business." Vice-president Woods, in turn, cabled a personal confirmation of just such a sum while Assistant Vice-president Forward laid out the exact nature of the sums loaned and the terms of renewal notes and repayments due to "Mr. J. L. Smith as attorney for J. A. Walker." Smith then had a legal document drawn up after having gotten Walker to supply additional funds to finally underwrite the "subordinating debt" of the Company in which he, Walker, owned a controlling interest.[88]

In effect, when all was said and done, what Smith got the New York banks to tender was a debt consolidation loan, a task difficult enough to arrange with a private creditor and almost impossible to obtain from a bank. Smith had put his reputation on the line--and on the dotted line as well. That Smith was able to achieve such a successful resolution was due to his years of experience working with banks outside of Texas. Moreover, such a free and open negotiation on Smith's part is a lasting testament to his unselfish devotion to John Walker and to business transactions that benefit others and not himself. If solving this lengthy problem in Walker's behalf were not enough, Smith had to remind his lifelong business partner two months later that "Mr. Coalson needs to receive compensation for arranging some of your personal papers and for doing your income tax work."[89]

As for the husband, so, too, for the wife. In late 1924, the *Amarillo Daily News* paid unasked-for accolades to Mrs. Smith at the Texas Federation of Women's Clubs convention in Amarillo in November. The article saluted her as the "woman [who] opened the way for clubs" in the Panhandle and the woman who has been identified "with many of the foremost club movements in Amarillo."[90] Over 225 women from across the state were in attendance at the convention with Mrs. Smith and other Amarillo women hosting them at social events in their homes. As in Midland some 40 years before when she had literally been singled out for her feats as a cowgirl on a quarter horse, now, at age 60 she was metaphorically named the "trailblazer" for women's civic advances in West Texas.

The first quarter century of the First Baptist Church's minutes conclude with a last handwritten entry from mid 1926 (all successive entries are in typed form and much briefer than the handwritten minutes from 1899-1926). Although the clerk, Frederick Kendall, entitled the entry as "A Brief Outline of Baptist History in Amarillo," in the main the piece is a miniature biography of the Smiths and their contributions to First Baptist

Church. Marie was, in effect, the interior decorator of the initial wooden Church; she coated the interior glass, thus giving the Church "the effect of Cathedral glass." Jimmie and Marie were given credit for forming the "team" around Dr. G. L. Yates in mid 1921 as earnest discussion began to emerge for building a new Baptist Church to accommodate the swelling congregation.[91]

The 'retirement' years of 1925 and 1926 showed Smith still keeping a hand in Amarillo business because he is listed in the phone directories as a dealer in "negotiable paper" at 26 Smith Building for 1925 and simply as "investments" for the following year.[92] He continued as the faithful and ever-available Secretary-Treasurer for Walker-Smith Company and was, doubtless, keeping John Walker fully aware of their joint Western National Bank interests in Hereford. If keeping John Walker informed was a daunting task, another thankless chore Smith accepted in 1925 was superintending Walker's J. L. Smith Trustee Account wherein Jimmie paid out most of Walker's charitable donations. By late 1926, said Trustee Account stood at $24,000.[93] One such donation the following year occurred when Walker was vacationing at San Antonio's Menger Hotel: "Mr. Smith handled wholly your contribution of $10,000 to the Howard Payne College endowment drive."[94] As for Marie, she continued with her ever-demanding DAR tasks. An extant 1926 Texas State DAR Convention ribbon is one example that shows Marie was present at state conventions whenever possible and at most national continental congresses as well.

Several additional documents from early 1927 reveal other aspects of the Smiths' later years together. In the initial issue of the *Panhandle-Plains Historical Review*, both Smiths are listed as charter life members of the Panhandle-Plains Historical Society (headquartered at West Texas State Teachers College in 1921).[95] At the annual meeting held in Canyon on February 18, 1927, Smith followed up his lifelong friend G. A. W. Parker's paper on "Texas' Debt to the Panhandle" with a motion "that a letter be sent at once to citizens of the Panhandle-Plains territory asking for financial assistance for the Society." The motion was readily complied with.[96] On the final day of February, Smith wrote to the Cobbs thanking them for remembering the Smiths' 41st wedding anniversary: "We were at the breakfast table on the morning of the 25th when the messenger boy brought your wire. How sweet for you to remember us. …We love our Cobbs and thank a kind Providence for every remembrance of them."[97]

On St. Patrick's Day, Marie wrote a lengthy letter to her sister in Fort

An old DAR Ribbon from 1926 State Convention

Smith thanking her for a recent update letter on Katherine and Earl because "as time goes on and our family circle becomes smaller, we learn to appreciate the importance of family." She added that she had paused in compiling her Patriotic Education report for the upcoming DAR Continental Congress to host a dinner for members of the Nunn, Freeman, and Bynum families that included "shrimp cocktail, two young hens with dressing, peas, fresh spinach with eggs, sweet potatoes with marshmallow, and a salad of fine whole stuffed tomatoes and a dessert of individual strawberry shortcakes." Marie concluded, "Everybody with one accord said the dinner only needed you and Earl to make it complete."[98] Certainly the civilized claims of such a fine dining experience was a far cry from Old Amarillo meals hastily put together on an old wooden stove.

No series of correspondences would be complete without yet another missive from John Walker, this time thanking Smith for yet another intervention in helping redirect Joyce-Pruit Company's assets on a more profitable investment path. Toward the conclusion of the letter, Walker added an ill-timed remark that must go down in the uncivilized annals of human compassion as an extreme instance of the pot calling the kettle black:

> Received a telegram from Mrs. Blackwell thus morning stating that Mr. Blackwell has had a stroke partially paralyzing him, and in a stupor. While the information is quite a shock to me there is rather a high percentage of long drawn out nervous cases which suffer from that experience.[99]

To Smith's everlasting credit, he wrote back to his business partner noting "my own appreciation of Blackwell's faithfulness. None of us is perfect but he never wavered in his job."[100]

On the night of April 29, 1927, having just returned from yet another trip to Brownwood, Smith raced home from the train station to keep a prearranged meeting time with his pastor and Mr. H. C. Pipkin of First Baptist Church; Pipkin was a key player on the Church building committee.[101] Undoubtedly, the main topic up for discussion that evening in the Smith library was the evolving plan of action for the new First Baptist Church to be located at 13th and Tyler. At about 10:30 pm, Smith's head slumped over to his chest and the revered deacon was dead from a heart attack. He was still sitting upright in his chair.

Marie was en route home from Washington, DC, having stayed

after the Continental Congress to work on other DAR projects. She was reached in Memphis and rushed home to take charge of Jimmie's funeral arrangements. Marie insisted that a visitation take place while Smith's body lay in state at 1101 Taylor Street. The actual funeral followed on the afternoon of May 3 with Howard Paul, J. L. Nunn, and H. C. Pipkin among the active pallbearers. The honorary pallbearers numbered more than 75 people whom Smith knew from every phase of his life.

Fittingly, the service itself was conducted by Dr. Yates, with Bishop E. Cecil Seaman of the Episcopal district and Dr. R. Thomsen of the Central Presbyterian Church assisting.[102] The Salado youth who had worshipped with Campbellites and Methodists would have relished the ecumenical spirit of his wife's arrangements. Although the verbal tributes were profuse, it was Pastor Yates who truly captured the essence of the man: "Brother Smith was one of the best men I ever knew. …He was as gentle as a woman and as brave as a lion. …He was transparently just in all his dealings with his fellow men."[103] Smith was interred in the family plot at Llano Cemetery. His epitaph reads:

James Lowry Smith
son of Prof James
Lowry and Julia McDowell
Smith, Born Independence
Texas March 12, 1860, Died
Amarillo, Texas April 29, 1927

Smith would also have relished the simplicity of the inscription and the touching references to both his parents.

Chapter 7

Amarillo
1927–1934

It became an oft-repeated family story that upon hearing of his partner's sudden death, the lethargic John Walker roused himself from his sickbed and took personal charge of Walker-Smith Company until his own demise in 1942. Douglas Coalson, a Walker-Smith employee since 1912, succeeded James Lowry Smith as Secretary-Treasurer and served in that capacity for the next 16 years.[1] Mrs. Smith did become a member of the Company's Board of Directors to fill the vacancy caused by her husband's death.[2] Her brother, Ben, was likewise elected to the Board to represent the Smith Estate as Trustee.[3] In fact, B. C. D. delayed his eventual re-entry into the Amarillo banking community in order to settle the estate of his late brother-in-law. For the next five years, 1927-1931, Bynum is listed in the Amarillo phone directories under "Smith & Bynum" and as manager for the J. L. Smith Estate.[4] Except for Marie herself, whom Bynum credited for being a very sensible business woman, no one knew more about Smith's real estate holdings, oil interests, leadership at Walker-Smith, and banking interests in Hereford than B. C. D. himself.

In the immediate months following her husband's death, Marie devoted even more time to her sister and brother's families. Katherine Cobb, age 15, came to Amarillo the summer of 1927 at Sissie's request and spent time studying in Canyon as well as taking part in near-by Methodist and Baptist encampments. She had evidently inherited some of Papa Jim's humor because she told Sissie that she got an A for content on an English theme, but a C+ in form "because honestly all I know about punctuation was to put a period at the end of the sentence."[5] Upon learning that Katherine had been elected class president for her upcoming senior year at Cotty Academy in Nevada, Missouri, Sissie wrote immediately: "I want to give you the class ring now so you can wear and enjoy it while you are in the class. Get a nice heavy one—Let me know how much it will cost and I will send you a check."[6] Indeed the 1928 Cotty Academy ring was in Katherine's jewelry box for the remainder of her own life and is now a treasured family heirloom.[7]

When her niece graduated from Cotty on May 29, 1928 Sissie made the trip to Fort Smith for two weeks to visit her returning niece and the Cobbs. It was a time for parties, bridge, and dining out as Katherine prepared for summer school Algebra class prior to enrolling at Sophie Newcomb College for Women in New Orleans that fall. Sissie insisted it was "young Earl time" and took Katherine's 13-year-old brother back to Amarillo for a long visit.[8] Earl shared his Amarillo visit with Wade Bynum's granddaughter, LeBecca Wills, herself just turning 12. Their visit included time at the Smith cottage in Canyon near the Palo Duro Canyon.[9]

Another oft-repeated story from Katherine concerns an event that occurred during the late 1920s, though the exact year is unknown. Katherine had gone to Amarillo and was tasked with driving Sissie back to Fort Smith for a visit. Part way across Oklahoma, they were passed by an Oklahoma driver in his big sedan and the two were left inhaling his swirling cloud of dust. At which point, Sissie reached into the glove compartment of her Hudson, hauled out a pistol, rolled down the window, and shouted at her niece: "Speed up, Katherine! I want to shoot out the tires of that Oklahoma road hog!" Fortunately, Katherine's cooler head prevailed and no shots were fired; the remainder of the trip was only accompanied by a few of Sissie's choice sputterings. Certainly, such an episode again illustrates that the spunky frontier woman side of Sissie was far from extinguished and only hibernating.

Following Katherine's first semester at Newcomb, the Cobb family, with Sissie in tow, drove from Fort Smith to New Orleans where, as Katherine wrote on December 23, "Sissie and I staid in bed most of the day." However, the family did enjoy Christmas Day in the French Quarter. The day after Christmas they all boarded a steamship for a week-long trip to Havana where Katherine and Sissie visited some of the same places Papa Jim and Marie had seen almost 20 years previously, including a New Year's Eve show at Cuba's National Theatre.[10]

Sissie herself wrote to her sister in November 1929, inviting all the Cobbs, "but especially my Katherine" for Christmas in Amarillo.[11] Both Christmas and New Year's were celebrated on the high plains, the Cobbs having driven the 541 miles from Fort Smith to the Panhandle. Uncle Ben Bynum had his niece as his guest at the Rotary Club's luncheon for Amarillo college women at the Herring Hotel on December 29. That same evening Katherine and Sissie attended "the last day of services in the old Baptist Church." Sissie even packed boxed lunches for the Cobbs on January 1, 1930 and they returned safely home "with only a little car trouble and one flat along the way."[12] Twice more in early 1930 Katherine heard from her favorite aunt and the woman she referred to as "my second mother." Sissie sent her a special-delivery cake to celebrate her initiation as a Kappa Alpha Theta and, fittingly, in her final diary entry Katherine mentions a surprise visit from Sissie and a special dinner at Antoine's on April 8.[13]

Even the usually irascible John Walker was more attentive to his cousin's needs in her widowhood as he helped her set up a $5,000 scholarship in the name of Mr. and Mrs. James Lowry Smith at Howard Payne University in Brownwood.[14] The Smiths were always unpretentious about their contributions to charity. Although Pastor G. L. Yates may have exaggerated a bit when he praised the Smiths' generous support of First Baptist and various charities "running into many thousands of dollars each year,"[15] they did support local and regional hospitals, including a significant contribution to Baylor University's Dallas facility.

Marie continued to reach outward to family in the early 1930s, knowing that her deceased husband would have encouraged such ventures. She made a trip to visit Roxalee Andrews in Houston in mid 1931.[16] Her niece, Mrs. Mary Bynum Owens, herself a recent widow, spent Thanksgiving of 1931 at 1101 Taylor Street. Knowing that Mary was struggling to make ends meet for herself and her daughter, Kay, Marie donated money to Mary for support and to pay delinquent taxes.[17]

The DAR, of course, continued to command considerable time and energy. Even at the November state convention immediately following her husband's death, she saw to it that two chairs were donated for Constitution Hall since she had recently been appointed to the Advisory Board for that Hall. In addition, largely through Marie's efforts a new $5,000 scholarship was obtained for West Texas State Teachers College.[18] The following year Marie was honored as a special guest at the Jane Douglas Chapter's meeting in Dallas.[19] She also received a lengthy personal letter from a prominent DAR member in Fort Worth thanking her for all she had done over the years on the national, regional, and state levels. If it weren't for Marie Smith, Ethel N. Nichols went on to elaborate, then some of the bickering about the etiquette of proper chapter recognitions would have burst into a major DAR controversy.[20]

At the state convention in Galveston in 1928, Mrs. Smith delivered a stirring talk on national defense, urging DAR members to "combat the forces of radicalism."[21] At the Waco state meeting in 1930, Marie accepted appointment to a state DAR committee tasked with "placing a bell for Texas in the Washington Memorial at Valley Forge."[22] She praised the conference in Houston in 1931 as one of the best she had ever attended, particularly because of its accurate presentations on Sam Houston as a Texas revolutionary.[23] Having received the title of Honorary Regent for her own chapter in 1921, Marie continued to host meetings at her Taylor Street home in October 1931 and again in October 1932. Likewise, she led the way in making a sizable contribution to the DAR national campaign for child education in 1932. Yet again in 1932, she represented her chapter at the state DAR meeting in Austin.[24] In short, Marie Bynum Smith would eventually be given the posthumous accolade of having attended "almost every state and national meeting of the society."[25]

As the new First Baptist Church at 1208 South Tyler was nearing completion, Marie followed through on a long-contemplated course of action to honor the memory of the closest and most cherished person she had ever known. Working with Pastor Yates and with Chester Meneely of the Meneely Bell Company, Troy, NY, she ordered a set of chimes consisting of 10 large specifically wrought bells which were soon located in the Campanile Tower of the Church. The largest bell weighed in at more than 3,000 pounds. The chimes are still today, as then, electronically operated from a keyboard at the organ console. On the evening of the Church's formal dedication on August 3, 1930, the chimes were dedicated in a separate ceremony at 6:30 pm.[26]

Four of the bells were engraved with messages, three of them citing, respectively, Smith's birth, charter membership in First Baptist, and contributions to business in the high plains. The so-called second bell[27] was personal and contains Marie's personal tribute to her late husband:

IN LOVING MEMORY OF
JAMES LOWRY SMITH
WHOSE LOVE AND COMPANIONSHIP
PUT A NEW SONG IN MY HEART

LET THE MEMORY OF THESE BELLS BE FOREVER THE VOICE OF
MY GRATITUDE
MARIE BYNUM SMITH
1930

**Cover of Dedication Program for James Lowry Smith Memorial
Chimes, August 3, 1930**

In her own twilight years, family continued to be at the forefront of Marie's life. She invited Mary Owens' daughter, Kay Owens, then just turning 17, to spend the summer of 1933 with her at 1101 Taylor Street. When asked about her impressions of her great aunt, Kay admitted she had been led to believe that Mrs. Smith was an "austere figure, the family dowager who always issued instructions." The actual person Kay met was anything but that. "She was gracious to me at all times and had a neat, whimsical sense of humor. One day she pointed to the grandfather clock on the first landing of the foyer staircase and told me the old clock was stiff and upright, but that we, Kay, must always have a spring in our step!" Kay spoke of trips in the venerable Hudson where Marie was the passenger and Kay the driver. "She praised my ability to parallel park the car because it was something Aunt Marie had never mastered. She let me do some of the grocery shopping and showed me how to test melons and peaches for ripeness." There were trips to Palo Duro Canyon, to a swimming pool, and, of course, First Baptist Church. "Yes, Aunt still had her occasional teas with other Amarillo ladies, but I remember that she also introduced me to a number of young women my age."

The only exclusion Kay experienced occurred at 10 am most mornings when B. C. D. Bynum arrived and brother and sister adjourned to the library to discuss the latest family business. "I shall never forget the feel of the wooden banister and the thick leaded glass windows at the front of the house that gave a slightly wavy appearance to the world outside." Kay's favorite times were the evenings at the kitchen table savoring chicken and ham and talking about Marie's years on the great plains. "The only unusual thing about the kitchen was that for reasons I never asked about she kept the canned goods under lock and key in the pantry. You know at the end of that summer she gave my mother the money to pay for my upcoming education at the University of Texas from 1934 through 1938. Now that was truly generous because I could never have gone to college without Aunt Marie's help."[28]

Family members began to gather round as Marie's health deteriorated in the spring of 1934. Her nephew, 18-year-old Earl Cobb, wrote to Sissie from the University of Texas in early March: "I got a special tonight from Dad. I certainly was very sorry to hear you are sick. Glad that Dad is in Amarillo now. I have phoned others and I am sure they will write to you."[29]

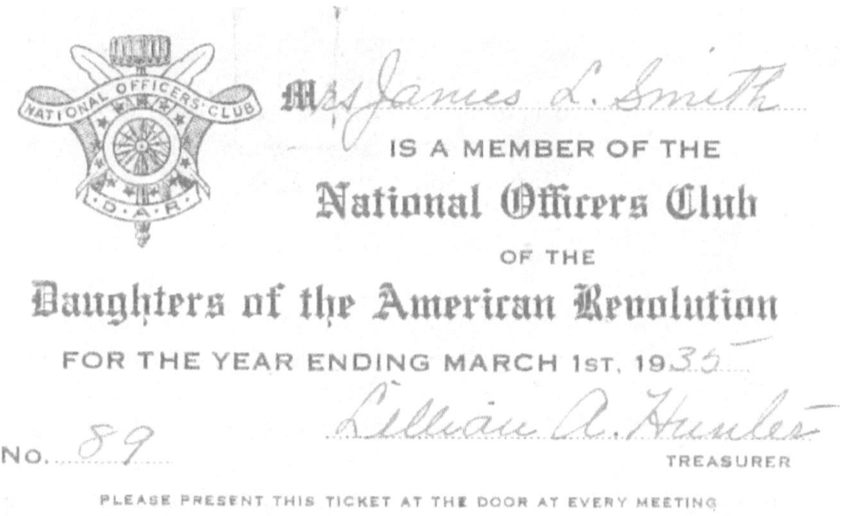

NATIONAL OFFICERS' CLUB

D.A.R.

Mrs James L. Smith

IS A MEMBER OF THE

National Officers Club

OF THE

Daughters of the American Revolution

FOR THE YEAR ENDING MARCH 1ST, 1935

No. 89

Lillian A. Hunter

TREASURER

PLEASE PRESENT THIS TICKET AT THE DOOR AT EVERY MEETING

Marie's final piece of DAR memorabillia

Her brother, Ben, had gone to Temple and had flown back to Amarillo with Dr. Arthur C. White of Scott and White Memorial Hospital. However, there was little he could do to rally Marie from her rapidly deteriorating health condition.[30]

Marie Motheral Bynum Lowry Smith died early in the morning of March 17, 1934. At her request, a simple funeral service was conducted at 1101 Taylor Street and she was buried beside her husband with the following epitaph added to their joint headstone:

Marie Bynum Smith
Wife of James Lowry Smith
Daughter of William Joseph
and Katherine Walker Bynum
Born DeSoto County Miss.,
March 7, 1864; Died
Amarillo Texas, March 17, 1934

In her simple two-page will she left a third of her estate to her brother, B. C. D. Bynum; a third to her sister, Sarah Bynum Cobb; and a third to the two daughters of Wade Bynum. She bequeathed the Smith lands in Bell County to her sisters-in-law, Mrs. Hattie Smith Ralston and Miss Julia Smith. Only the Walker-Smith Company interests were excluded: "I direct that the Walker-Smith Company, a wholesale Grocery Company with headquarters at Brownwood, Texas, shall continue in business as long as my Trustees [B. C. D. Bynum and Earl Cobb] consider it is profitable to continue the investment."[31]

The immediate possessions of china, silver, and jewelry were also excluded but were eventually awarded to her sister, Sally, and then to Katherine, and now to Katherine's three daughters. The cowgirl ring from 1884 is on a necklace one of those sisters, Sarah Cobb Baker, wears frequently. The diamond lavaliere rests on a velvet cushion in the family lockbox in Fort Smith, AR. These two pieces of jewelry—a plain gold ring and a diamond lavaliere—symbolize two conjoined aspects of Marie, the civilized cowgirl of the Queen City of the Great Plains.

Epilogue

Even with B. C. D. Bynum and Earl Cobb on the Board of Directors following John Walker's death in December 1942, the controlling interest in Walker-Smith Company lay with Walker's only child, Mary Walker Edwards. In 1945 she sold the Company to Fort Worth entrepreneur and philanthropist Kaye Kimball. The Guaranty State Bank went through several iterations but survives today as Chase Bank in downtown Amarillo. The Smith home was sold in 1944 for $17,500, but it still breathes today as a Texas Historical Site at 9th and Avondale where it was transported more than 50 years ago. In 1949 Earl Cobb donated $11,000 worth of prime stocks to the Panhandle-Plains Historical Museum with the stipulation that the money be invested and used to form the Smith Memorial Library. The greatly increased value of the original stocks has funded the purchase of numerous books over the years. The Smith Memorial Library continues to grow, a fitting tribute to these two civilizing people on the Texas frontier. The literal voices of Jimmie and Marie may be silent, but, in a sense, their voices ring out loud and clear each and every day from the bells in the Campanile Bell Tower atop the First Baptist Church.

Afterword
The James Lowry Smith House Today
by
Myrna Loy Smith

The James Lowry Smith home at 1101 South Taylor Street in Amarillo, Texas, was the third house of its class and size to be built in Amarillo. It was completed in late 1904 and the Smiths moved in it in early 1905. The legal description was Block 149, Lots 6 -10 in Plemons Addition. City records Volume #68, p.418 show that in 1918 streets were repaired for J. L. Smith for Lots 8, 9, & 10, Block 149 of Plemons Addition. An original photograph of the home as it sat at 1101 Taylor is shown in Ray Franks and Jay Ketelle, *Amarillo, Texas - The First Hundred Years 1887-1987*, plate #50.

Following the death of her husband in 1927, Mrs. Smith remained in the house until her own death in 1934. The home was subsequently rented for about 10 years before being sold by the heirs of the Smith estate. One family who lived in the home on Taylor Street was named Florry. He was in the grocery business and had several daughters. A Mrs. Greer, a friend of one of the Florry girls, was a friend of an acquaintance of Berry F. and Myrna Loy Smith. She had lived a short time with the Florry's.

The reason the house was moved from its central downtown location was that the purchaser, Jess Rogers, wanted to move his Chevrolet Automobile Dealership to a more 'suburban' location from 4th Street downtown. They thought the house much too lovely to be dismantled and decided to make their home out of it, so consequently they had the white-frame house cut in two and had it moved with much ado in 1945--as the local newspaper carried running articles about it, telling the progress it had made from day to day on its trek across town. Heavy I beams had to be brought up from Midland/Odessa area to move the big house on as there was nothing around here that could handle the load. A visitor to the house in recent years told us he was a welder who worked in the basement welding the steam pipes while the house was supported across the basement on these huge beams. He looked at the house in awe from the driveway and something akin to fear in his eyes. He said that he gave his soul to God the day when something cracked and gave way and he thought the house was going to fall in on him. The house was relocated to its present location at 9th and Avondale.

The Chevrolet Dealership was located at the corner of 11th and Taylor until several years ago when it was moved out on East Interstate 40, and the property owner built offices at the 11th and Taylor location. The Smith home is situated on three acres that were lovingly landscaped by Mrs. Rogers, an avid gardener who created a visual showplace of the home and its gardens. She kept a full-time gardener to care for the grounds. The Amarillo Country Club is directly across the street to the North. The Rogers originally had purchased Block 1 of Roberts Place Addition Country Club Terrace bounded by streets on three sides. Their home was situated on the Northwest corner and extra land was sold off in five small lots by later owners who only purchased the property for investment which included the disbursement of most land outside the chain link fence surrounding the home. The Rogers had horse stables across to the west across Avondale Lane, as it was called then, because it was a dirt road. Their two children would just run over across the street to ride their horses.

After Mr. Rogers died in March 1956, no one lived in the house after that who loved it. It began to fall into disrepair and neglect. However, from 1961 to 1964, a Dr. & Mrs. Hartfelder lived at the house and he operated a chiropractor practice in the house. Subsequently, some people named Dixon leased w/option to buy at $200 per month rent and a selling price of $52,000. They left and the house went back to a Daisy & Ely Bruce Estate, friends of the Hartfelders, who held the note and received the house back when the Hartfelders defaulted on the note; however, they never lived in the house. The executor of the Bruce Estate, Ruth Webster, a friend of Daisy & Eli Bruce, took over for Eli Bruce who was incapable. Daisy Bruce died October 29, 1968. Eli died November 14, 1969 at age 89. The house was then leased to a Sigma Nu Fraternity from West Texas State University in Canyon (now known as West Texas A & M University in Canyon) for 9 months at $300 a month.

In the summer of 1970, Berry F. and Myrna Loy Smith drove by and noticed a large moving truck in the driveway of the house. It was the first time they had ever noticed the house, even though they had been looking for a big old historical house for some time. This was when the Fraternity was moving out on a Sunday. After searching out the person in charge of the house the next day, and getting to see the house, it came about that Berry F. and Myrna Loy Smith were able to buy the house from Ruth Webster. It was never put on the real estate market. We started caring for the yard, etc. that summer and actually got to move in July, 1970.

We don't know the condition of the house when the Fraternity rented it but it had been badly damaged when they left. It was dirty, holes in doors and walls, broken windows and abandoned trash. The yard was a jungle and one of the first things we did was pull in trucks and use chain saws, clippers, etc. to try to tame the overgrowth of the yard. Since the soil is so fertile, everything just roots and grows--unwanted trees, weeds, etc. For the nine months the Fraternity was here they just mowed a couple of feet in front of front porch. The Fraternity had numerous bonfires out in the garden area so much work was needed to get the soil free of cans and litter and fertile enough to garden in.

Numerous changes were made in the original Smith home after its move. This Greek revival home was bricked, baths added, electricity and plumbing updated with landscaping and decorating at a cost of $100,000. The front porch was changed somewhat with four large round wood columns supporting the large front porch at the third floor level over the double front doors. The original inner double front doors are still the oak and leaded beveled glass as well as matching transom with the original house number '1101' built into the beveled glass above the solid oak inner double doors. The original matching leaded upper windows are still in the large front window casings of the living room and library/den on either side of front entry doors. Many of the original windows are in the home and show many bubbles, waves, and other characteristics evident of their age. The elegant oak staircase remains as was as well as the large stained glass window located on the turn of the stairs landing. Huge double pocket doors of oak are still in place between den/library and entry; entry and living room; living room and dining room.

A pair of the huge pocket doors separating the dining room from the front entry hall was removed after the house was moved to its 9th Street location in order to put an enclosed radiator in that wall. The change also afforded more wall space in the dining room. All door knobs and back plates are ornate antique copper and brass with the egg and dart design depicted on both. The anaglypta designs on ceilings were added by the Berry F. Smiths. Since the house was placed over a partial basement encased entirely beneath the house, access was created from the kitchen area; whereas, on Taylor Street, the basement was accessed from outside.

The house is plaster over wood lathe except in areas of remodeling after moving. The kitchen was slightly remodeled and enlarged and has metal lathe under the plaster. The outside wood walls were left on with a space between them, and the new brick was added all around the house making very thick outside walls. All the open wood-burning fireplaces were removed except the one in the library/den. The living room now has a beautiful mantel with gas logs due to the 'modernization' of the house when wood-burning fireplaces had fallen out of favor. Originally, the entry hall had a huge ornate iron fireplace with lion's feet and much detail, according to descriptions by those who had seen it, including a Mrs. Greer, a friend of the Florry girls who had lived with them for a short time. Backed up to this fireplace were two others: one in living room and the other in the dining room; they were backed up to each other catty-cornered so all three shared the same chimney on the East end of roofline that is seen in the old photographs of the house when it was still on Taylor Street. This chimney was removed when the house was moved. There was some kind of a small wood fireplace or stove in the kitchen and its chimney was also removed. Also, the fireplace in the master bedroom backed up to the one in the library/den and was removed on relocation. It shared the chimney with the library/den.

The dormer windows shown in old photos were all removed. The openings in the roof decking are still in evidence from the third floor even though they are boarded up under the wood shingles. The original fencing on the widow's walk on the roof was galvanized metal soldered into square tubing and made into very intricate design. This fencing was about halfway demolished in 1970. It is currently in third floor storage awaiting restoration. In the meantime, we had a wrought iron fencing designed and erected for the widow's walk.

The 15 or so wood columns that supported the wrap-around porch were incorporated into a wisteria arbor located in east part of the yard. The porch design was changed from a one-story wrap around porch to a tall two-story porch supported by four larger columns framing the small upstairs balcony with door and flanking windows. The living room was enlarged to approximately double in size and emulates the car port on the opposite side of the front of house. Floors are the original fir and pine and are either carpeted or covered with wood parquet (entry hall and master bedroom) and marble (powder room off from the kitchen).

The basement consists of a knotty pine recreation room with bar and still has original tile from 1945 as well as another room used for utility room and heater/air conditioner. It still has a boiler in it as we still used steam heat until just a few years ago.

The old steam lines became unreliable. We started up the heaters that were put in when we added central air conditioning in about 1984. Some of the old radiators have been removed to allow more livable space but we have preserved some for history sake. The downstairs radiators had been replaced with 'new' modern designs which were installed in the walls, thereby making more usable floor space when the Rogers updated the house. However, the long low radiator in the dining room under the big windows is still there. It is covered with a cabinet that matches the woodwork in the house and is used for a low cabinet top. Some of the original light fixtures remain in the house. Two bedrooms and the study upstairs have originals that are the antique copper with 'Lalique' globes. One bedroom has a matching wall light with the 'Lalique' looking globe. The huge antique copper four-armed chandelier in entry has four round enclosed globes.

There is a bell system on the wall from an upstairs bedroom and from the master bedroom as well as from the recreation room that rings in the kitchen. The Rogers kept a maid who had a small room at the top of the back stairs. It is currently used as an out-of-season closet with extra chests, files, luggage, etc. There was also an intercom/phone for house-to-servant's quarters over the garage with. The Rogers lived in the upstairs apartment while the house was being finished before it was a servant's quarters.

The front porch rails and posts were much neglected when we came in 1970. Berry F. and our son, Berry D., lovingly turned all the posts on a wood lathe in the garage. But with the weather and the constant moisture from the sprinkler system, they began to deteriorate again so Berry F. replaced them with all white Portland cement posts and rails. The brick pavers on the front porch were replaced in 1985 and the original directional compass made from a colorful ceramic tiled piece was put back on the porch.

The house originally had a sitting porch upstairs with a small railing off the back stair landing with a door leading outside to it. When the house was on Taylor Street facing West, this porch was on the Southeast and made for a nice comfortable sitting room. However, when the house was moved to 9th, the house faced the North, thereby shifting the sitting porch to the Southwest. Hence, it was very hot and totally unusable. After a few hail storms destroyed the flat roof of the sitting porch, we had the area enclosed as a solarium with tinted thermo pane glass, and the roofline was tapered down from the existing roofline to shed the water.

The third floor is unfinished with only the floor being done. The area is nice and light with the windows on the East and West sides as well as the small oval window over the porch. In the third floor unfinished attic space, we found a stack of magazines of various brands; each with at least one picture of a feature that Mrs. Rogers had incorporated into her interior, architectural, or landscaping designs. One offered a lovely English garden design fish pond. Another showed a greenhouse attached to the side of the double garage. Of course, the wisteria arbor and garden and orchard spaces were evident. Included in Mrs. Rogers' dream home landscaping was a summer house complete with large wood-burning fireplace for outdoor gatherings. It is constructed of rock and is enclosed by screen wire on most of two walls for protection against mosquitoes and flies during cookouts.

We spend many evenings in the summer house, especially when the weather turns cool or rainy or in the fall or spring of the year. We are told that Mrs. Rogers introduced millions of red night crawlers throughout the yard and gardens to further enhance the soil conditions as Amarillo is known for its non-fertile soil. These worms are still evident today. With her private well she included an oversized storage tank encased in a brick well house to support the large sprinkler system to ease the watering of such a large yard. In 1994, we put all the sprinklers on automatic timing systems to make it easier for us to be gone on long trips. She also had a sunken rose garden which was not salvageable. The English style fish pond had been filled in with soil sometime during the years. The Berry F. Smiths emptied the soil and repaired a large crack in the pond and have added a fountain, fish, aquatic plants, lights, and other ornamental items.

In 1970 when we arrived, there were still all the heavy wooden window screens on every window. They had regular screen wire plus heavy hail screen as well, making the inside of the house very dark and dreary. Most windows had heavy cornices and drapes with flannel linings. Since the home is located on the original Highway Route 66, the Rogers may have been interested in safety as well as dangers from hail with all the heavy screens. The first thing we did was to remove all screens and strip away the drapes and cornices letting in the light. The Berry F. Smiths were able to purchase a small rocker and an oak server from the Rogers' daughter, Marcella Rogers Lanham. These were originally in the house when the Rogers purchased it. It was a wonderful feeling to have the two pieces of furniture 'back in their home' where they belonged. There was also a sterling silver tilting water server with the original glass, also finished outof silver, with the initials or name of the James Lowry Smith beautifully engraved on it. Unfortunately, the Berry F. Smiths did not buy the water server and we have regretted it ever since. It went to a relative of the Rogers who was an antique dealer and it subsequently disappeared. We understand the Bynum family gave a large very ornate and floor-standing tilting mirror with pawed feet and heavy carving to the Junior League of Amarillo for their headquarters in the old Houghton House located at 1700 South Polk Street.

The past 40 years have been filled with loving care and our conce rn to protect the legacy of the James Lowry Smith House. Amarillo has lost so many of their old lovely historical homes through the years. We are proud to be able to preserve one of the 'grand and oldest nice homes' for history sake. When a historical structure has been moved, it is required to be at the new location for over 50 years to be able to be re-designated a "Texas Historical Home;" also when a property is so designated, there are restrictions on selling the property after it is designated a Texas Historical Landmark. We submitted paperwork and the designation was approved in 2008. The Dedication ceremony was held on August 15, 2009 when the cast plaque was unveiled on a pole at the front of the house showing the Smith-Rogers Home as being a Texas Historical Landmark.

The plaque reads:

THIS HOUSE WAS BUILT FOR EARLY AMARILLO SETTLERS JAMES LOWRY AND MARIE BYNUM SMITH CA. 1904, AND WAS ORIGINALLY LOCATED AT 1101 SOUTH TAYLOR STREET. THE HOME WAS PURCHASED IN 1945 BY JESSE A. AND DORIS ATTEBURY ROGERS, WHO PLANNED TO MOVE HIS CAR DEALERSHIP TO THE SITE. INSTEAD OF RAZING THE HOUSE, THEY HAD IT MOVED TO ITS PRESENT SITE TO SERVE AS THEIR FAMILY HOME. AT THE TIME OF ITS RELOCATION, ARCHITECT C.W. BROTT MADE CHANGES TO THE ORIGINAL DESIGN. THE CLASSICAL REVIVAL STYLE HOUSE FEATURES LEADED GLASS WINDOWS, ROOF CRESTING AND INTERIOR WOODWORK FROM THE 1900s AND BRICK VENEER, BALUSTRADES AND FULL-HEIGHT COLUMNS FROM THE 1940s.

Abbreviations

COLLECTIONS:

BCDB Papers	Benjamin Chapman Dupree Bynum Papers, Ann Bynum Whittenburg, curator, Amarillo
CSA&BA Coll	Private Collection of Christine Smith Andrews and her husband, Ben Andrews
FBC Mins	First Baptist Church Minutes, Amarillo
JAW Coll	John A. Walker Collection, Southwest Collection, Texas Tech University, Lubbock
MCJ Coll	Mary C. Jones Collection, Center for American History, University of Texas-Austin
S-W Coll	Smith-Walker Collection, Panhandle-Plains Historical Museum, West Texas A&M, Canyon

LETTER WRITERS:

AG	Ardelia Graves
BW	Bessie Walker
DC	Douglas Coalson
EC	Earl Cobb
JB	J. Blackwell
JAW	John A. Walker
JLS	James Lowry Smith
KBC	Katherine Bynum Cobb
KWB	Katherine Walker Bynum
LB	Lucie Bennett
MBS [1886-1934]	Marie Bynum Smith
MEW	Mary Elizabeth Walker
MMB [until 1886]	Marie Motheral Bynum
SB [until 1909]	Sally Bynum
SBC [from 1909]	Sally Bynum Cobb
WJB	William Joseph Bynum
WJBJr.	William Joseph Bynum, Jr.

NEWSPAPERS:

ADN	Amarillo Daily News
ASNG	Amarillo Sunday News Globe
DMN	Dallas Morning News

NOTES

1. Salado 1863-1882

1.   Michael A. White, *History of Baylor University 1845-1861* (Waco: Library Binding Co., 1968), 77.   See also CSA&BA Coll: Rufus C. Burleson and Jas. L. Smith contract agreement, Jan 1, 1855.

2.   Lois Smith Murray, *Baylor at Independence* (Waco: Baylor UP, 1972), 384 and 397.

3.   C.Y. Early, *Walker-Smith Company 1894-1944* (Dallas Holson-Spotts Co., 1944), 17.   See also CSA&BA Coll where Professor Smith is listed as a Captain for his Company.

4.   Charles Turnbo, *Salado, Texas: Frontier College Town* (Matton (IL): United Graphics, 2007), 36.

5.   Murray, 129.

6.   CSA&BA Coll: Ltr John G. Batte to Prof. J. L. Smith, Dec 16, 1876.

7.   Turnbo, xiv.

8.   Malcolm D. McLean, reproduction of Robertson's letter to Col. J. M. Morphis, Feb 18, 1874. McLean has edited a multi-volume *Papers Concerning Robertson's Colony in Texas*.   He kindly sent me a typed copy of Robertson's letter to Morphis contained in McLean's edited copy of *Sterling Clack Robertson's History of Salado, Texas*, published by the Salado Historical Society.

9.   Diary, James L. Smith, Salado, TX.   Subsequent references are incorporated parenthetically by date.

10.   George W. Tyler, *The History of Bell County*, 2d ed. (Belton: Dayton Kelley, 1971), 303-304.

11.   See Archibald Johnson Rose in *The Handbook of Texas Online*.

12.   Tyler, 390.

13.   "Rules, Regulations and Premium List of the Third Annual Fair of the Central Texas Fair Association To Be Held at Salado, Bell County, Texas, Beginning on the 26th day of October, 1875, and Continuing Four Days." Belton: Printed at the Journal Office, 1875.   Copy from original owned by Geneva Hiken, Stagecoach Inn, Salado, TX. The copy is stored at the Bell County Museum in Belton.   The program, exclusive of ads, is 19 pages long.

14.   J. P. Madole, "A History of Salado, Texas," MA thesis, University of Texas, 1952, 4.

15.   Smith Sr. and Jr. visited Julia Smith's maternal relatives since a later list of wedding invitations to Jimmie and Marie's 1886 marriage went to several McDowells in Edna, TX, in Jackson County.

16.   CSA&BA Coll: Christine Smith Andrews has confirmed that Julia McDowell Smith's mother married a John Bolling on Oct 4, 1859 after the death of her first husband.

17. CSA&BA Coll: William Henry McDowell (1852- ?) and Catherine Louise McDowell (1840-1885) were Julia Smith McDowell's brother and sister. Edwin Clary (1832- ?) was married to Mary Emma McDowell (1836-1908), the older sister of Julia Smith McDowell.
18. Ruth Garrison Francis, "Old Water Mills," *DMN*, Aug 12, 1928.
19. Welborn Barton in *The Handbook of Texas Online*.
20. Charlene Ochsner Carson, *Building His Kingdom: 140-Year History (1864-2004) [of] First Baptist Church, Salado, Texas* (Austin: Nortex Press), 7.
21. Orville Thomas Tyler in *The Handbook of Texas Online*.
22. Tyler, 286.
23. Carson, 8.
24. Carson, 4.
25. George Washington Baines in *The Handbook of Texas Online*.
26. Madole, 37.
27. Wilson T. Davidson, "Many Memories Cling about Old Salado College," *DMN*, Feb 18, 1934.
28. Turnbo, 64.
29. Turnbo, p. 210 notes a list of grave markers at Salado Cemetery, including one for a McHenry Smith showing a birth date of Sept 20, 1878.
30. William Evander Penn in *The Handbook of Texas Online*.
31. Autograph albums were to the late nineteenth century what high school yearbooks were to the mid and late-twentieth century. These specially designed stitch-bound albums could be purchased in stationery stores and their smooth blank ivory sheets paper offered plenty of room for friends to write goodwill messages. An additional requirement for each entry was the inclusion of the actual date it was made.
32. Felda Davis Shanklin, *Salado, Texas: Its History and Its People* (Belton: Peter Hasborough Bell Press, 1960), 31.
33. E. M. Hutchens, *Tales of Old Salado: An Unusual History*, ed. Carl R. McQueary (Austin: Sunbelt Media, 1999), 37.
34. MaryBelle Brown, "James Lowry Smith, 1827-1883," unpublished article produced for the Salado Historical Society in 2011.
35. CSA&BA Coll: All four tax receipts exist in this Collection. They are dated Feb 23, 1865, Sep 12, 1869, Sep 24, 1870, and Oct 5, 1872. Another document in the Collection, a November 9, 1874 contract between Professor Smith and a J. A. Upshaw, reveals that the Salado College head was even more astute in his real estate ventures: he purchased 100 acres of farm land for $1,600.

2. Horn Lake, MS and Winchester, TN 1864-1884

1.	Personal genealogy notes of Marie Bynum. Also, the information is recorded in the Family Bible by William Joseph Bynum. The eldest Bynum-Walker child, Thomas Joel Bynum, died shortly after his second birthday in 1862.
2.	The handwritten discharge papers, with accompanying endorsements up the chain of command, are still extant and constitute a cherished family heirloom.
3.	Information on Dr. Drew W. Bynum, an 1855 graduate of medical school, exists in the Bynum family papers.
4.	James E. Thorogood, "First Real College for Women Was in Tennessee," *The Nashville Tennessean*, Sep 16, 1934.
5.	Considerable information on Z. C. Graves is available on the Internet at *www. knoxcotn.org/tnbaptists/graves-zc.htm* and at the Zwinglius Calvin Graves (1816-1902) Papers at the Tennessee State Library and Archives in Nashville.
6.	Thorogood, "First Real College…".
7.	WJB to MMB, Oct 19, 1879
8.	KWB to MMB, undated, but internal references indicate it was written just after Mary arrived at college.
9.	KWB to MMB, Jan 12, 1881.
10.	LB to MMB, Oct 23, 1880.
11.	LB to MMB, Jul 10, 1880.
12.	LB to MMB, Sep 30, 1880.
13.	LB to MMB, Dec 18, 1880.
14.	LB to MMB, Jan 7, 1881.
15.	J. M. Moore to Etta Moore, Apr 6, 1880.
16.	J. M. Moore to Etta Moore, Nov 26, 1879.
17.	Mattie Morgan to MMB, Nov 6, 1879.
18.	Mattie Morgan to MMB, May 27, 1880.
19.	The costs are gathered from various extant tuition receipts and from family letters sent to Marie at Mary Sharp.
20.	These details revealed in two letters: KWB to MMB, Oct 9, 1881 and MMB to WJBJr., Jan 29, 1881.
21.	WJB to MMB, Dec 22, 1879
22.	WJB to MMB, Feb 22, 1880.
23.	WJB to MMB, Jun 14, 1880.
24.	WJB to MMB, Jan 16, 1881.
25.	AG to KWB, Nov 18, 1879.
26.	AG to WJB, Dec 1, 1880.
27.	AG to KWB, Feb 15, 1881.
28.	AG to KWB, May 15, 1881.
29.	MMB to WJBJr., Jan 29, 1881.
30.	MMB to WJBJr., Mar 27, 1881.

31. BCDB to MMB, Apr 29, 1881.
32. BCDB to MMB, Oct 5, 1881.
33. BCDB to MMB, Jan 6, 1882.
34. Program, "The Argonauts will anchor their good ship, the Argo, off Winchester, Tenn., Friday night, Dec 23, 1881.
35. "The Argonaut's Reception." A copy of this newspaper review was found in Marie Bynum's scrapbook. No source is given.
36. MMB to parents, Dec 25, 1881.
37. KWB to MMB, Dec 18, 1881.
38. MMB to parents, Dec 25, 1881.
39. WJB to MMB, Jan 6, 1882.
40. JAW to WJBJr., Aug 8, 1881.
41. WJBJr. to MMB, Oct 22, 1881.
42. WJBJr. to MMB, Dec 4, 1881.
43. WJB to WJBJr., Jan 19, 1882.
44. JAW to WJBJr., Feb 21, 1882.
45. S. D. Lee, undated Resolution adopted at a joint meeting of faculty and students.
46. E. Nehus and R. M. Caruthers to WJB, Mar 21, 1882.
47. The Certificate is pre-printed with all information filled in.

3. Colorado City 1882-1888

1. MCJ Coll: R. H. Looney, "A History of Colorado, Texas," 32.
2. Omar W. Cline, "History of Mitchell County to 1900," MA thesis, East Texas State Teachers College, 1948, 1.
3. MCJ Coll: John G. Rix, "Early History of Colorado City, Mitchell Co., Texas," 9.
4. Mrs. J. Lee Jones and O. W. Cline, "Frontier Days in Mitchell County and Colorado City, 1876-1885, WTHA *Yearbook*, 16 (Oct 1940): 40-43.
5. This letterhead occurs in an early letter written by James Lowry Smith, the firm's bookkeeper, on Dec 4, 1884.
6. Cline, "History," 62. Were it not for Mary C. Jones and her own copious notes and requests for reminiscences from early Colorado City residents in the 1930s and early 1940s, much of the City's early history would have been lost. These valuable materials are stored under her name at the Center for American History at UT-Austin.
7. *The Colorado Clipper*, ed. Alf Tolar. This undated article was located in Marie Bynum's scrapbook. The other competing newspaper, *The Graphic*, was edited by George Bailey, and several of Bailey's articles are referenced below.
8. Letterheads depicting these captions come from Smith's correspondence of Feb 16, 1885, Feb 25, 1885, and Apr 29, 1885. At least four more letterhead

variations occur in numerous extant letters Smith wrote from Nov 1884 to Feb 1886.

9. Several times Smith refers to conversations he has had with the "telephone man." The earliest is in a letter from Jan 14, 1885. The Colorado City exchange may have been installed as early as 1883.

10. Sherrie S. McLeRoy, *First in the Lone Star State: A Texas Brag Book* (Plano: Republic of Texas Press, 1988), 204-205.

11. The Sanborn Map Company of New York produced numerous maps of early Texas communities, mainly for fire insurance purposes. The earliest for Colorado City is May, 1886 and it contains detailed plots, street diagrams, even the names of some important buildings.

12. Numerous accounts exist of the population surge, from "The Founding of Colorado City" historical marker downtown to innumerable estimates in the documents contained in the Mary C. Jones Collection.

13. S. B. McAlister, "Building the Texas and Pacific Railroad West of Fort Worth," WTHA *Yearbook*, 4 (1928): 53.

14. Mrs. J. Lee Jones and Rupert N. Richardson, "Colorado City, the Cattleman's Capitol," WTHA *Yearbook*, 19 (Oct 1943): 54.

15. As shall be seen below, in his early letters to Marie, Jimmie discusses his salary and frequently refers to his writing to her between 10 pm and midnight because of all the bookkeeping tasks at the end of each workday.

16. Mutual letters of JLS to MMB (or vice versa) are hereafter referenced directly in the text or parenthetically by date to avoid excessive footnoting.

17. This article from Bailey's *Graphic* and several others like it were pasted in her scrapbook.

18. George M. Bailey, *The Graphic*, Dec 21, 1884.

19. Bailey, *The Graphic*, Dec 21, 1884.

20. Ivy H. Burney to MMB, Dec 20, 1884.

21. Julia M. Smith to JLS, Dec 30, 1884.

22. All 90+ letters of JLS to MMB survive. All 90+ *envelopes* of MMB to JLS survive, but *only* 13 of the letters she wrote. My daughter, Kate McCarron Head, is probably correct when she says that women keep all their love letters, but men tend to get rid of them.

23. Marie was present, of course, for New Year's Day, 1885, but one of Smith's letters a year later (Jan 2, 1886) mentions, perhaps with some hyperbole, "We made, I believe, fifteen calls and ate fourteen suppers."

24. George M. Bailey, *The Sunday Graphic*, January 4, 1885.

25. P. C. Coleman, Autograph Album, Jan 12, 1885. Coleman's sentiment is part of a 12-line poem, fortunately far less flowery than Bailey's.

26. The information on Bailey and Tolar comes from the Alfred H. H. Tolar obituary, available online at several sources and courtesy of the Hood County Genealogical Society.

27. There is an excellent summary of Coleman's importance in Jim Baum, *Bootleggers, Braceros & Bronc Busters* (USA: Four Seasons Books, 2001), 174-186.
28. *The Colorado Clipper*, Jan 17, 1885.
29. All songs are mentioned in the Jan 21, 1885 letter.
30. Information obtained from a letter written by Drew Pruit to Marie, Jan 19, 1885, and later conveyed to Smith.
31. Cline, "History," 71.
32. Rix, 13-14.
33. "Barbed Wire" in *The Handbook of Texas Online*.
34. MCJ Coll: Personal notations of Mary C. Jones.
35. William Robert Smith (Jr.), *Random Notes on the History of Mitchell County, Texas through 1918*. Colorado City Texas Bicentennial Celebration, July 3, 1976, 254.
36. Looney, 14.
37. Smith recounts both moves in letters to Marie dated Feb 27, 1885 and March 9, 1885.
38. Smith mentions how he scrimped and saved in several letters and the $30 a month fee comes from a July 16, 1885 letter to Marie.
39. Cline, "History," 59.
40. "Bone Business" in *The Handbook of Texas Online*.
41. MCJ Coll: A. J. Payne, "A Resume of the Early '80s of Colorado City," 3.
42. "Bone Business."
43. "Rodeos" in *The Handbook of Texas Online*.
44. For the most part, Smith's demeanor and correspondence were honest but polite. When he did *see* something dangerous or amiss, he wrote letters that are very pointed and explicit.
45. Jones and Richardson, 51.
46. Rix, 12-13.
47. Rix, 13.
48. More accurately, the program cover is likely a "proof sheet" run off by the Colorado Steam Press because there are no inner contents about the actual events. The sheet was mailed to Marie on Feb 23, 1885.
49. Cline, 109-110 claims the town had a very primitive electric light system, but that the system was very unreliable.
50. JLS to MMB, Mar 9, 1885.
51. JLS to WJB, Mar 9, 1885.
52. WJB to JLS, Apr 27, 1885.
53. During my own research, I sent several letters from Commerce, TX (65 miles northeast of Dallas) to Colorado City and received several in return. The average was three days per letter even though the distance is far less than half that from Horn Lake to Colorado City.

54. "Adding Machine," *Wikipedia*, p. 2

55. Cline, 66.

56. "Mitchell County, Texas, Newspaper Clippings & Newspaper Links" from the web site: rootsweb.com/~txmitche/newsclips.htm   The article on Colorado, TX, appeared in *Fort Worth Gazette*, Dec 6, 1884.

57. MCJ Coll: H. R. Solomon, "Account of early Colorado history" published in *The Clipper*, Jul 4, 1883. Typescript copy in MCJ Coll, p. 6.

58. Jones and Richardson, 42.

59. Smith, *Random Notes*, 254.

60. George M. Bailey, undated newspaper clipping found in her scrapbook.

61. Jim Baum, "Standpipe," in *Rodeos, Romeos & Radios* (Colorado City: Jimlin Books, 2002), 11-13.

62. The weekly entries are quite detailed and provide a solid look at the widely divergent views in the town discussions for the year 1885.

63. Looney, 12.

64. MCJ Coll: Mrs. John W. Mooar, "Recollections of Colorado and Mitchell County from 1880 to 1885," 5.

65. Rix, 2-3.

66. Baum, "Seven Wells," in *Rodeos*, 33-36.

67. This standpipe functioned fully for 111 years before "the grand old lady" as Jim Baum calls it, went into retirement.

68. MCJ Coll: Mary C. Jones, "The Town of Colorado," 21.

69. Rix, 20.

70. J. W. Williams, "A Statistical Study of the Drouth of 1886," WTHA *Yearbook*, 21 (Oct 1945): 85-89.

71. "Dengue Fever." National Institute of Allergy and Infectious Diseases. Web site: niaid.nih.gov/factsheets/dengue.htm.

72. "Mitchell County Texas Marriages." Web site: rootsweb.com/~txmitche/marriages/marriages_to_1965.html.

73. Bessie Peacock was perturbed, as was Smith, by Bailey's peremptory announcement of the Smith-Bynum engagement and imminent marriage in the *Graphic*, an offense made even more egregious by Bailey's failure to ask their permission to make such an announcement.

74. CSA&BA Coll: Evidently, Smith's change in plans came in the nick of time. The wedding invitation to one of the Smith sisters shows the pre-printed March 4th date crossed out and the February 25th date printed over it in red ink.

4. Amarillo and Temple 1888-1902

1. BCDB Papers: James S. Bynum, typescript history of James Lowry Smith, undated.
2. John Crudgington, "Old Town Amarillo," *PPHR*, 30 (1957): 92.
3. Della Tyler Key, *In the Cattle Country: History of Potter County*, 2nd ed. (Wichita Falls: Nortex Offset Publications), 1972, 48.
4. Mrs. C. May Cohea, "Her Memory's So Long," *ASNG, Golden Anniversary Edition* (1938), 22.
5. Katherine Bynum Cobb Baker (1912-1999) repeated this anecdote on numerous occasions during her lifetime.
6. Cohea, 22.
7. Della Tyler Key, *Potter County Land Records, 1875-1890*, Amarillo: Tyler-Berkeley, 1962, pp. 268-269. Cf. also John Arnot, "A History of Potter County Texas, 1876-1935," unpublished manuscript, presented to Amarillo Public Library by Henry R. Hertner, 16.
8. Crudgington, 107. Whether the original Old Town home of the Smiths was renovated or torn down or removed in 1892 is uncertain. An *ADN* article from June 27, 1926 refers to a "new Smith home [being] completed in 1892." Whatever the case, the Smiths lived at the Pierce St. address from Spring 1889 until May 1895 when they moved to Temple for four years before relocating to Amarillo in March 1899. The details of the moves are addressed later in this chapter.
9. Key, *In the Cattle*, 48.
10. Key, *In the Cattle*, 121.
11. Frank A. Paul, "Early Day Banking in the Panhandle," *PPHR*, 37 (1964): 70. Cf. also Jennie Harrell, "First History of Old Town Amarillo," typescript of a 1925 address in Mary E. Bivins Memorial Library, 2.
12. G. A. F. Parker, "Early Days in the Panhandle," typescript of address to annual Panhandle-Plains Historical Society in 1924 [or 1925], 2.
13. *ADN*, Special Edition, Nov 9, 1922, containing a reproduction of a daily paper printed in Amarillo, Dec 26, 1889.
14. S-W Coll: This collection contains several sales ledgers from 1898-1903 and 24 onionskin ledgers of copied business correspondence for various years, ca. 1893-1904.
15. *Amarillo Northwest* [newspaper], July 10, 1889.
16. "Morrison Brothers" in *The Handbook of Texas Online*.
17. B. Byron Price and Frederick W. Rathjen, *The Golden Spread: An Illustrated History of Amarillo and the Texas Panhandle* (Northridge, CA: Windsor Publications, 1986), 71.
18. Key, *In the Cattle*, 130. A recollection of the town fight and the club's formation survives in Marie's own handwriting; the article was published in printed form in the *ADN*, Oct 19, 1923.

19. Key, *In the Cattle*, 117.

20. *The Grand March: A Pictorial History of the First Baptist Church, Amarillo, Texas, 1889-1989.* comp. & ed. Mrs. Maston C. Courtney and Mrs. James B. Franklin (Whitney Russell Printers, 1989), 4.

21. Obviously, letters between spouses are usually only written when they are separated for long intervals.

22. JLS to MBS, Aug 5, 1893.

23. JLS to MBS, Aug 8, 1893.

24. Statement of Carol Brian, Secretary, First Baptist Church, Amarillo, May 15, 2008.

25. J. S. Calloway, *ASNG, Golden Anniversary Edition* (1938), 8.

26. FBC Mins: "History of the Beginnings of the First Baptist Church," anonymous undated typescript, 2.

27. FBC Mins: Gilbert Carter Matthews, "Thumbnail History of the First Baptist Church," undated typescript, 2.

28. JLS to MBS, Jul 30, 1893. The letter mentions his Sunday School class and that Mrs. Ware was covering Marie's class in her absence.

29. "Palo Duro Baptist Group Organized in 1891," *ASNG*, Jan 18, 1976.

30. FBC Mins: Numerous references to Smith's work in this area dot the handwritten pages between 1899 and 1926.

31. Paul H. Carlson, *Amarillo: The Story of a Western Town* (Lubbock: Texas Tech UP, 2006), 41.

32. Crudgington, 93.

33. Key, *In the Cattle*, 132.

34. Key, *In the Cattle*, 94 and Carlson, 59.

35. JAW Coll: JLS to JAW, Jan 12, 1894.

36. S-W Coll: JLS to Bosworth, Dec 4, 1894 and Dec 6, 1894.

37. S-W Coll: JLS to Farewell, Dec 4, 1894.

38. S-W-Coll: JLS to G. J. Worth, Dec 5, 1894.

39. *DMN*, Aug 6, 1894.

40. JAW Coll: JLS to JAW, Dec 29, 1894.

41. Dick Breen, "Born Leader," *ASNG, Golden Anniversary Edition* (1938), 4.

42. S-W Coll: J. S. McLaren to JLS, Dec 21, 1894.

43. Miss Addie Whitcomb, interview by Mrs. L. E. Moyer, 19 May 1958. Transcript available at Amarillo Public Library.

44. BCDB Papers: J. S. Bynum, undated handwritten biography of his father, 2.

45. ADN, "Woman Who Planted First Tree in City Is Taken by Death," March 17, 1934.

46. JAW Coll: JLS to JAW, Jan 12, 1895.

47. JAW Coll: M. C. Nobles to JAW, Mar 6, 1895.

48. Key, *In the Cattle*, 94.

49. JAW Coll: JLS to JAW, Dec 22, 1894.

50. Early, 104-105.

51. JAW Coll: Financial Documents File, 1892-1898.

52. Early, 25.

53. JAW Coll: JLS to JAW, Dec 22, 1894 and JLS to JAW from NYC, Feb 17, 1895 and Feb 25, 1895.

54. JAW Coll: JLS to JAW, Jan 14, 1895 and JLS to JAW, Jan 25, 1895.

55. JAW Coll: JLS to JAW, Mar 28, 1895.

56. JAW Coll: JLS to JAW, Mar 31, 1895.

57. JAW Coll: JLS to JAW, Dec 4, 1894.

58. The massive John A Walker papers at Texas Tech's Southwest Collection stand at 70,369 leaves. Nearly 27,000 of these are devoted to Rosario Mining Company operations in Chihuahua. An empty envelope bearing a New Walker Hotel address is dated Nov 22, 1894. A telegram from Smith dated Dec 21, 1894 indicates Smith's preference for Temple and Brownwood locations for their emerging wholesale grocery business. Other papers in the Walker Collection reveal John A. Walker as a man who never missed lucrative bank, stock, and oil and gas investments.

59. S-W Coll: JLS to Mr. Fitzhugh, Mar 11, 1895; JAW Coll: JLS to JAW, Mar 29, 1895.

60. JAW Coll: Embree-McLean Carriage Co. receipt from St. Louis, Missouri, Oct 23, 1895.

61. JAW Coll: JLS to JAW, Jun 4, 1896.

62. JAW Coll: Embree-McLean Carriage Co. receipt from St. Louis, Missouri, Mar 19, 1900.

63. BCDB Papers: J. S. Bynum.

64. Katherine Bynum Cobb Baker, "The House at 1101 Taylor Street," undated typescript in Baker family papers. She also reiterated same orally on many different occasions.

65. The two great nieces were granddaughters of Sissie's brother, Wade Bynum. As far as the author knows, these two women are the last survivors who knew Sissie when she was alive. Information obtained from Kay Coleman, interview by author, Richardson, TX, Jan 11, 2004 and follow-up phone conversation on Dec 6, 2008; and from LeBecca Paddock, interview by author, Austin, TX, Mar 17, 2004. The recently deceased Kay Coleman (1917-2010) spent the entire summer of 1933 visiting her aunt during the last full year of Sissie's life. LeBecca Paddock (1917-2010) visited her great aunt in Amarillo on several different occasions as a teenager.

66. *The Amarillo Evening News*, Sep 25, 1900, contains an excerpt on the donation based on an article in one of the Temple newspapers.

67. Patricia K. Benoit and Weldon G. Cannon, *To Lend a Hand: The History of the King's Daughters Hospital, 1896-1996* (Temple: King's Daughters Hospital, 1996), 45.

68. MBS to J. Walker Peebles, Mar 20, 1896.

69. SB to MBS, May 15, 1898.

70. Numerous copies of the Smith & Walker business letters from this period are preserved in Letter Copying Books in the Smith-Walker Collection at the Panhandle-Plains Historical Museum. Impressions of original letters about to be mailed were made via a wet-copy method involving oiled paper and a pressing device placed down on the onion skin pages of the copy books. Few of the copy books had ever been opened since being placed in the PPHM archives years ago. Thus, during my research, all the onion skin pages tended to stick together.

71. S-W Coll: S&W Co. to Dallas Mercantile Co., Feb 26, 1897; S&W to Mr. Highsmith, Amarillo, Feb 27, 1897; S&W to JLS, Feb 27, 1897.

72. S-W Coll: S&W Co. to Third National Bank, Apr 7, 1897; S&W Co. to Gauss Shelton Hat Co., St. Louis, Apr 8, 1897.

73. S-W Coll: S&W to JLS, Jun 15, 1898.

74. S-W Coll: S&W to Messrs. Sidden & Faringer, Gage, OT, May 3, 1898; S&W to Englehart Davidson Merc. Co., St. Joseph, MO, May 2, 1898; S&W to James A. Kirk & Co., Chicago, IL, Aug 1, 1898.

75. S-W Coll: S&W to Western Wheel Works, Chicago, IL, May 18, 1898.

76. S-W Coll: S&W to M. M. McKeen & Co., St. Louis, MO, May 4, 1898; S&W to Excelsior Flour Mills, Denver, CO, May 10, 1898.

77. Early, 107.

78. JAW Coll: JLS to JAW, Mar 10, 1899.

79. JAW Coll: JLS to JAW, Apr 27, 1899.

80. JAW Coll: JLS to JAW, Jul 5, 1899.

81. JAW Coll: JLS to JAW, Dec 20, 1898.

82. JAW Coll: JLS to JAW, May 15, 1899.

83. FBC Mins: Jul 16, Oct 4, and Oct 25, 1899; Nov 11, 1900; Jul 14 and Sep 8, 1901; and Jun 1, 1902.

84. *The Evening News*, Aug 26, 1899.

85. *The Evening News*, Nov 8, 1899.

86. *The Evening News*, Dec 12, 1899.

87. S-W Coll: Ledger entries for Jan 6 and Jan 27, 1900; May 2, 1902.

88. *The Evening News*, Jul 5, Sep 25, and Oct 11, 1900.

89. *The Evening News*, Dec 13, 1900.

90. *The Evening News*, Jun 11, 1901.

91. Laura V. Hammer, *Short Grass and Longhorns* (Norman: Univ. of Oklahoma Press, 1943), 9.

92. JAW Coll: JLS to JAW Jan 25, 1901.

93. JAW Coll: JLS to JAW, Mar 27, 1901.

94. BCDB to WJB, Mar 5, 1902.

95. Key, *In the Cattle*, 94-95.

96. JAW Coll: JLS to JAW, Feb 20, 1902.

97. JAW Coll: J. C. Paul to JAW, Jul 3, 1901.

98. JAW Coll: Letterhead of Buffalo Oil Company in J. C. Paul to JAW, Jun 19, 1901.

99. JAW Coll: J. C. Paul to JAW, Jul 2, 1901.

100. JAW Coll: J. C. Paul to JAW, May 11, 1901.

101. JAW Coll: Buffalo Oil Company, Announcement of Stockholder Meeting, Mar 18, 1902.

102. JAW Coll: J. C. Paul to JAW, Jun 14, 1901.

103. JAW Coll: J. C. Paul to JAW, Jul 1, 1901.

104. JAW Coll: Conclusions drawn from Buffalo Oil Company's Report to the Stockholders, Apr 15, 1902.

105. JAW Coll: Announcement of Buffalo Oil Company Stockholders Meeting, March 18, 1902.

106. All descriptions here and the statistics that follow are drawn from Buffalo Oil Company's announcements of stockholder's meetings for Mar 18, 1902 and Sep 24, 1902.

107. JAW Coll: D. O. Lively to JAW, Oct 22, 1901.

108. JAW Coll: F. M. Parish to Buffalo Oil Stockholders, Apr 11, 1902.

109. JAW Coll: JLS to JAW, Dec 20, 1902.

110. Paul H. Carlson, pp. 1-118, offers a superb summary of all three phases of Amarillo's growth.

5. Amarillo 1903-1914

1. Key, *In the Cattle*, 165.

2. Joseph L. Grant and Lawrence L. Crum, *The Development of State-Chartered Banking in Texas* (Bureau of Business Research: UT-Austin, 1978), 30; also, *DMN* articles on May 21 and May 26, 1903; and Key, *In the Cattle*, 94.

3. Avery Luvere Carlson, *A Monetary and Banking History of Texas from the Mexican Regime to the Present Day, 1821-1929* (Ft. Worth: Ft. Worth National Bank, 1930), 53; also, National Bank of Commerce letterhead.

4. *City Directory of Amarillo, Texas* (1903). A copy of this directory is in the Amarillo Public Library.

5. BCDB Papers contain this bank note.

6. Glenn G. Nunn, *Encyclopedia of Banking and Finance*, 8th ed. (Boston: Bankers Publishing Company, 1983), 100. Most banks started abandoning private bank notes with the passage of the Federal Reserve Act of 1913.

7. JAW Coll: *Hereford Brand*, May 5, 1927. Also, short biography of J. L. Smith provided by Ethel Mann Dawson from an Oct 17, 1930 Colorado City newspaper.

8. JAW Coll: Western National Bank statement, March 28, 1904. An undated

newspaper clipping in JAW Collection also indicates 1903 as date Smith converted the Hereford institution from a private to a national bank.

9. Duane F. Guy, *A History of the Panhandle Bankers Association*, monograph, 4. To date, the author has been unable to locate an extant copy of Smith's paper.

10. JAW Coll: Financial Documents file, 1899-1906.

11. JAW Coll: JLS to JAW, June 30, 1903.

12. JAW Coll: JLS to JAW Mar 26 and Mar 28, 1904.

13. JAW Coll: Details on the Smith's house plans come from letters written by Smith to his business partner dated November 2, 1904 and February 6, 1905.

14. Key, *In the Cattle*, 235.

15. Key, *In the Cattle*, 296-300 gives a solid account of the battles for control of Ellwood Park.

16. *ADNG*, Apr 22, 1928, contains a review article on Ellwood Park's development and some of Mrs. Smith's contributions.

17. Key, *In the Cattle*, 200 and the aforementioned *ADNG* article.

18. C. C. Cunningham is listed as a salesman for Texas Nursery in the 1909 Amarillo phone directory.

19. *ADNG*, Apr 22, 1928.

20. JAW Coll: JLS to JAW, June 2, 1902.

21. JAW Coll: JLS to JAW letters in mid-1904 cover these matters, including a particularly lengthy explanatory letter of JLS to JAW on Sep 12, 1904.

22. *Grand March*, 6.

23. The author is indebted to Stephanie Hayes, great granddaughter of Highfill, who has recently researched the Cornelius-Highfill matter, including newspapers from Clarendon, TX, in 1907; papers from the Earl Vandale Collection at the Center for American History at UT-Austin; and her own family accounts. I will leave the full disclosure of the incidents to Ms. Hayes, but I have obtained her permission to use her shared materials in my own study.

24. The summary of the shooting is based on Hayes' account and that of C. A. Crudginton, a typescript entitled "The Cornelius-Highfill Killing," 5 in the Vandale Collection.

25. BCDB Papers: a printed article exists entitled "The Battling Baptist," but with no date or publication information. Information on Smith's position as secretary-treasurer is based on listed entries in the Amarillo Phone Directories for 1907, 88, and 1908, 249.

26. JAW Coll: JLS to JAW, Mar 27, 1901.

27. JAW Coll: Power of Attorney document Walker to Cobb, Jun 18, 1904.

28. EC to SB, Mar 11, 1907.

29. Information gathered from a series of 1907 letters, EC to SB: Mar 13, Mar 15, Apr 23, Aug 21, and Oct 9. Luckily, many joint letters between the two survive for the years 1904-1912.

30. FBC Mins: Jul 12, 1904 and Oct 9, 1904 and passing references in numerous succeeding meetings.

31. FBC Mins: Jul 9, 1905.

32. FBC Mins: Feb 6, 1910.

33. JAW Coll: JLS to JAW, Dec 21, 1906. The handwritten expenses on the deposit slips were in a separate set of the Smiths' surviving papers and letters.

34. Early, 139.

35. JAW Coll: JLS to JAW, Feb 21, 1903.

36. Early, 141.

37. JAW Coll: JLS to JAW, Feb 17, 1904.

38. Early, 144.

39. JAW Coll: J. B. Garnett to JAW, Apr 2, 1906, based on Smith's records audit; also, J. B. Garnett to Walker, May 31, 1906.

40. JAW Coll: JLS to JAW, Jan 13, 1904.

41. JAW Coll: JLS to JAW, Feb 11, 1904.

42. JAW Coll: JLS to JAW, Jun 4, 1907.

43. JAW Coll: JAW to JLS, Jan 22, 1906.

44. JAW Coll: JAW to JLS, Feb 20, 1906.

45. JAW Coll: JLS to JAW, Mar 10, 1906.

46. JAW Coll: JLS to JAW, Mar 22, 1906.

47. JAW Coll: JB to JAW, Aug 29, 1916.

48. JAW Coll: JAW to JB, July 29, 1914.

49. JAW Coll: JLS to JAW, Jan 31, 1906.

50. JAW Coll: JLS to JAW, Feb 11, 1908.

51. JAW Coll: Information from tax return and a letter, JB to JLS, Jun 22, 1918.

52. JAW Coll: JLS to JAW, Feb 20, 1908.

53. Early, 121.

54. Early, 150-151.

55. Early, 168 and A. C. Greene, *Sketches from the Five States of Texas* (College Station: Texas A&M UP, 1998), 103.

56. JAW Coll: JB to JAW, Feb 17, 1913.

57. Early, 168.

58. JAW Coll: JLS to BW, Jan 2, 1911.

59. JAW Coll: Smith's advice following Temple Sanitarium to BW, Jan 1, 1912.

60. JAW Coll: JLS to JAW, Jan 25, 1913.

61. JAW Coll: JLS to JAW, Apr 22, 1905.

62. JAW Coll: JLS to JAW, Feb 5, 1907.

63. Key, *In the Cattle*, 163.

64. Key, *In the Cattle*, 248-250.

65. Guy, 41.

66. JAW Coll: JLS to JAW, Mar 6, 1909.

67. Potter County Register of Automobiles, June 12, 1907-June 22, 1917. This

unofficial typed registry is housed in the Amarillo Public Library. Makes of cars are numbered in order by buyer and purchase date.

68. SB to MBS, Apr 24, 1908.
69. "Program of the Forty-Third Annual Meeting," 6 and 9.
70. "Body of Boyce Brought Home," *ADN*, Jan 16, 1912. The so-called Boyce-Sneed Feud went on to become front-page news in Amarillo and across the United States and Canada for nearly the next six months.
71. For a thorough account of the Boyce-Sneed Feud, see Bill Neal, *Vengeance Is Mine: The Scandalous Love Triangle that Triggered the Boyce-Sneed Feud* (Denton: UNT Press, 2011).
72. Information derived from 1974-75 Esther McCrory DAR Chapter history and numerous sources elsewhere.
73. Louise M. Spencer to BW, Dec [?], 1909. Letter forwarded to MBS.
74. The Chapter affiliation and date come from Marie's DAR membership Certificate.
75. MBS to SBC, Nov 2, 1910.
76. The pen-and-ink duplicate copy of the original application is also in Marie's handwriting.
77. Information taken from an undated newspaper clipping noting May 9 "for the first regular meeting of the McCrory Chapter."
78. *ADN*, Apr 17, 1912.
79. Two newspaper articles from *DMN*: Nov 10 and Nov 11, 1912.
80. Emma Bynum to JLS, Dec 29, 1906.
81. *ADN*, Oct 26, 1911.
82. BCDB to WJB, Apr 23, 1903; Potter County Register of Automobiles, Sep 3, 1907, car #25.
83. *The Daily Panhandle*, Aug 27, 1907 and *ADN*, Jun 4, 1912.
84. *ADN*, Nov 5, 1912 and *ADN*, Jun 12, 1913.
85. *The Daily Panhandle*, Sep 25, 1909.
86. *ADN*, Jun 13, 1912 and *ADN*, Feb 9, 1913.
87. *ADN*, Jan 11, 1912.
88. JLS to MBS, Mar 12, 1913.
89. *ADN*, May 5, 1912.
90. The diary totals 148 onionskin pages, with only pp. 1-9 and 92-99 missing, an amazing feat in and of itself since Marie mailed 10-12 page segments from various stops along her tour.
91. MBS to JLS, Feb 4, 1914; Diary, 9, Feb 7. Where possible her diary entries are henceforth included parenthetically by page and date.
92. News of his travels are all conveyed in numerous letters sent to his wife at various ports of call where she was scheduled to visit.
93. MBS to JLS, Feb 10, 1914.
94. MBS to JLS Feb 25, Mar 8, and Mar 12.

95. MBS to JLS, Apr 6, 1914.
96. JLS to MBS, Mar 25, May 6, and May 13, 1914.
97. FBC Mins: Apr 8, 1914.
98. SBC to MBS, Feb 8 and Apr 8, 1914.
99. JLS to JAW, Jan 2, 1914.
100. BCDB to MBS, Feb 9, 1914.
101. Several JLS letters from late 1913 and early 1914 show this increased capitalization.
102. JLS to MBS Apr 2, Apr 7, and May 25, 1914.
103. Mary Walker had actually revealed her father's plans in a letter to Marie on Apr 27, but Marie wanted to hear the outrageous announcement from Walker's own mouth.
104. Among the artifacts Marie saved from her trip is the "1914 Souvenir Program of Long Spring Tour of Europe," with the Paines listed as directors.
105. Indeed, further research confirms Marie's careful observation; see *New York Times*, Oct 12, 1913.
106. MBS to SBC, Jun 28, 1914.
107. SBC to MBS, May 12, 1914.
108. JLS to MBS, May 25, 1914.
109. MEW to MBS, May 30, 1914.
110. Foregoing information derived from the following letters: MBS to JLS, Jun 5, 1914; SBC to MBS, Jun 18, 1914; and JLS to MBS, Jun 18, 1914.
111. Information pieced together from three successive JLS to MBS letters: Jun 11, Jun 12, and Jun 17, 1914.
112. Information derived from three different letters: JLS to MBS, Jun 18, 1914; BW to MBS, Jun 21, 1914; and JLS to MBS, Jun 21, 1914.
113. SBC to MBS at her NYC hotel, Jul 5, 1914.

6. Amarillo 1915-1927

1. Roxalee Smith Andrews to MBS, Jan 27, 1915.
2. MBS to JLS, Jan 31, 1915.
3. BW to MBS, Feb 7, 1915.
4. Mrs. B. W. Lewis to Hon. R. W. Hall, Amarillo, Feb 19, 1915 and Mrs. J. W. Robbins to Judge & Mrs. R. W. Hall, Amarillo, Feb 24, 1915.
5. ADN, Apr 15, 1915.
6. Texas State History of the Daughters of the American Revolution, 1929 comp. & ed. Helen Dow Baker (Abilene: Abilene Printing and Stationery Co., [reprint edition, 1991]), 30.
7. A copy of this song (lyrics and music) is still extant.
8. ADN, Oct 7, 1916.
9. Texas State History, 31.

10. Mrs. J. W. Cheney, "Early Activities of the Esther McCrory Chapter, DAR." This paper, delivered on Apr 10, 1939, consists of eight, double-spaced, legal-size pages.
11. *DMN*, Mar 17, 1918.
12. FBC Mins: Jan 6, 1915.
13. FBC Mins: Feb 14, 1915.
14. FBC Mins: Mar 24, 1915.
15. FBC Mins: Jun 2, 1918.
16. FBC Mins: Jun 11and Sep 27, 1919.
17. Early, 182-183 and JB to JAW, Aug 23, 1915.
18. Early, 185.
19. Early. 192.
20. JAW Coll: JB to JAW, Aug 16, 1916.
21. JAW Coll: JB to JLS, Jun 22, 1918.
22. JAW Coll: JAW to JB and JLS, Jun 29, 1918.
23. JAW Coll: JB to JAW, Jul 12, 1918. Blackwell's lengthy letter to Walker thoroughly explains the accusation and the favorable resolution.
24. JAW Coll: JB to JAW, Aug 17, 1914.
25. JAW Coll: JAW to JB, Aug 10, 1915.
26. JAW Coll: Telegram, JB to JAW, Oct 1, 1913.
27. JAW Coll: Buyer's Order and Agreement to JAW in Brownwood for August 26, 1914 and April 12, 1915.
28. JAW Coll: JB to JAW, June 24, 1916.
29. Early, 203.
30. JAW Coll: Subscribers' Agreement, Jan 15, 1917.
31. Early, 204.
32. JAW Coll: JLS to JAW, Jul 13, 1920.
33. JAW Coll: JLS to JAW, Aug 9, 1921.
34. Information gathered from *ADN*, Jun 11, 1916 and JAW Coll: Guaranty State Bank, Second Monthly Report, Aug 18, 1916.
35. Grant and Crum, 85.
36. JAW Coll: Second Monthly Report.
37. *ADN*, Jun 24, Jul 4, and Jul 28, 1916.
38. *ADN*, Jan 10, 1917.
39. *ADN*, Feb 22, 1917.
40. Roy Franks & Jay Ketelle, *Amarillo, Texas –The First Hundred Years, 1887-1987: A Picture Postcard History* (Amarillo, Roy Franks, 1987), Card #32. See also *ADN*, "Guaranty's Stock Raised Two Times," Feb 20, 1921.
41. Potter County Register of Automobiles shows that Smith purchased a Ford, #1016, in the name of Walker-Smith Co. on Nov 6, 1915 and the Franklin, #1020, six days later. According to Kay Coleman's recollection, the Smiths owned an Essex sometime in the early 1920s.

42. The forgoing anecdotes derive from a variety of sources, including verbal recollections of the Smith's favorite niece, Katherine Bynum Cobb Baker, and of B. C. D. Bynum's granddaughter, Ann Bynum Whittenburg.

43. JAW Coll: JLS to JAW, Jul 31, 1920.

44. KCB to EC, Aug 4, 1920.

45. *Texas State History*, 30.

46. "Proceedings of the Thirty-First Continental Congress," *DAR Magazine*, 56:1 (Jan 1922): 341.

47. Report of the Twenty-fourth Annual State Conference, Texas DAR, Paris, TX, Nov 7-9, 1923, 85.

48. "Proclamation to Regents and Daughters of Texas." Beaumont, TX, Sep 12, 1919.

49. "Proceedings" (1922), 341.

50. "Proceedings of the 29th Congressional Congress," Apr 1920, 157.

51. "Nearly Every Chapter Represented at DAR Convention," *ADN*, Nov 9, 1922.

52. *History of the Texas Society, National Society, Daughters of the American Revolution: Commemorating the Bicentennial Era in Texas, 1929-1974* (Texas, 1975), 49.

53. The page one newspaper death notice for Marie in 1934 reads, "Woman Who Planted First Tree in City Is Taken by Death," *ADN*, Mar 17, 1934.

54. "Tree Planted by Mrs. J. L. Smith 34 [38] Years Ago Felled to Make Room for Big Hotel," *ASNG*, Jun 27, 1926.

55. JAW Coll: JLS to JAW, Sep 21, 1921.

56. Early, 217-218.

57. Early, 214.

58. JAW Coll: JB to JAW, Jan 24, 1921 and JLS to JAW, Nov 17, 1921.

59. JAW Coll: JAW to JB, Dec 14, 1922.

60. JAW Coll: JLS to JAW, Dec 15, 1922.

61. JAW Coll: JLS to JAW, Aug 23, 1923.

62. Early, 211.

63. JAW Coll: JLS to JAW, Oct 6, 1924.

64. Early, 223, 234, and 237.

65. JAW Coll: JLS to JAW, Apr 3, 1925.

66. *ADN*, Jan 1, 1922.

67. JAW Coll: JLS to JAW, Mar 29, 1922.

68. *ADN*, Nov 5, 1922.

69. *ADN*, Jan 6, 1924.

70. *Amarillo*, comp. Clara T. Hammond (Amarillo: George Autry Printer, 1971), 215.

71. Grant and Crum, 124.

72. Grant and Crum, 140.

73. A. L. Carlson, 63.

74. JAW Coll: Financial Documents file, 1920-1924.

75. David Warren to EC, Jun 2, 1949.

76. BCDB Papers: J. S. Bynum typescript on Smith.

77. Ann Bynum Whittenburg, interview by author, 21 May 2008.

78. B. Byron Price and Frederick W. Rathjen, *The Golden Spread*, 88.

79. Information on Badger Oil Company comes from Jim Bynum's typed bio and longer handwritten account of his father in the BCDB Papers; from extant letterhead of Badger Oil Company; and the Mineral Deed no. 115575 closing Badger Oil on Aug 1, 1957.

80. This entry and those that follow come from Diary, Jan 1-11, 1924. Entries appear in a small pocket-sized notebook with a leather cover.

81. *ADN*, Jan 18, 1924.

82. FBC Mins: May 18, 1924.

83. *Golden March*, 36.

84. FBC Mins: Nov 12, 1924.

85. FBC Mins: undated entry.

86. FBC Mins: Doc 2, Jul 31, 1924.

87. KBC to EC, May 14, 1912.

88. JAW Coll: The entire rescue package has been a fortuitous find because the documents only came to light in a John Walker file from 1933 when he had contacted Smith's executor, B. C. D. Bynum, to send the Smith file copies because he, Walker, had lost the originals from 1924. References: B. C. D. Bynum to JAW, Jul 18, 1933; JLS to National City Bank, NY, Jun 28 1924; W. M. Woods to JLS, Jul 3, 1924; JLS to National City Bank, NY, Jul 4, 1924; JLS to W. M. Woods, Jul 7, 1924; telegram Forward to JLS, Jul 7, 1924; telegram W. M. Woods to JLS, Jul 9, 1924; "Consent of J. A. Walker Subordinating Debt" agreement, Jul 9, 1924.

89. JAW Coll: JLS to JAW, Sep 3, 1924.

90. *ADN*, Nov 14, 1924.

91. FBC Mins: Aug 11, 1926.

92. *Directory of Amarillo*, 1925, 523, and 1926, 637.

93. JAW Coll: DC to JAW, Dec 29, 1926.

94. JAW Coll: DC to JAW, Mar 24, 1927.

95. *PPHR*, 1 (1928): 125.

96. Joseph A. Hill, *The Panhandle-Plains Historical Society and Its Museum* (Canyon: West Texas State College Press, 1955): *37-38*.

97. JLS to Cobbs, Feb 28, 1927.

98. MBS to SBC, Mar 17, 1927.

99. JAW Coll: JAW to JLS, Mar 19, 1927.

100. JAW Coll: JLS to JAW, Mar 25, 1927.

101. *Golden March*, 50.

102. Information drawn from several newspaper accounts: *ADN*, Apr 30, May 1,

and May 3, 1927.
103. G. L. Yates, "An Appreciation of J. L. Smith," *Baptist Standard*, May 29, 1927.

7. Amarillo 1927-1934

1.   Early, 34-37.
2.   Early, 242.
3.   Early, 29.
4.   *Amarillo Phone Directories*, 1927, 227; 1928, 204; 1929, 204; and 1931, 476.
5.   KBC to MBS, Jul 29, 1927.
6.   MBS to KBC, Sep 26, 1927.
7.   The author's wife, Adele, inherited the ring upon her mother's death in 1999.
8.   Details for this event and others that follow are based on a diary Katherine kept from May 28, 1928-January 9, 1929; then, after a nearly year-long hiatus, from December 12, 1929-April 8, 1930.
9.   LeBecca Wills Paddock, interview by author, Mar 17, 2004.
10. KBC Diary entries, Dec 23, 1928-Jan 2, 1929.
11. MBS to SBC, Nov 24, 1929.
12. KBC Diary entries, Dec 23, 1929-Jan 1, 1930.
13. KBC Diary entries for Feb 20 and Apr 8, 1930.
14. Several JAW letters to Walker-Smith Vice-president Douglas Coalsen from mid 1932 reflect Walker's directions in behalf of Marie to set up this academic scholarship.
15. Yates, *Baptist Standard*, May 19, 1927, 7.
16. An envelope only, addressed to Marie c/o Roxalee, is the indicator. 17. *Amarillo Globe*, Nov 20, 1931. Kay Owens Coleman, interview by author, Jan 11, 2004.
17. *Amarillo Daily Globe*, Nov 20, 1931. Kay Owens Coleman, interview by author, Jan 11, 2004.
18. *Texas State DAR History*, 95.
19. *DMN*, May 6, 1928.
20. Ethel N. Nichols to MBS, May 21, 1928.
21. Newspaper clipping dated Galveston, Nov 9, 1928.
22. *ADN*, Nov 7, 1930.
23. *Amarallo Globe*, Nov 10, 1931.
24. *ASNG*, Nov 13, 1932.
25. *Amarillo Globe*, Apr 10, 1934.
26. Dedication Program, James Lowry Smith Memorial Chimes.
27. Chester Meneely, at the request of Earl Cobb, sent a letter dated May 1, 1934, which contains the inscriptions on all four bells and a personal note that Mrs. Smith was "exceedingly kind and attentive to me while there and I consider this transaction one of the most pleasant during my experience in

the bell business which has extended over forty years."
28. Kay Owens Coleman, interview by author, Richardson, TX, 11 Jan 2004; also, telephone conversation with author, 6 Dec 2008.
29. B. Earl Cobb to MBS, Mar 2, 1934.
30. CS&BA Coll: Christine Andrews Smith has added an undated article to her Andrews Family Tree web site: Gwen Smith McJunkin, "Dr. Arthur C. White, Marie Bynum Smith's Doctor."
31. Will of Marie Bynum Smith, April 10, 1931.

Index

Moore, J.M., 42
Morgan, Mattie, 42, 44
Morrison, Tom W. and James Newton, 98
Morrow-Thomas Hardware Company, 123

Naples, 145
National Bank of Commerce, 116-117, 122, 128, 131, 136, 138-139, 143-144
National City Bank (New York), 171-172
Navidad River, 22
New Orleans Exposition, 76
New Orleans, LA, 178
New Walker Hotel (Brownwood), 106
New York, NY, 101, 105, 127
New York Sun, 57
Nichols, Ethel N., 179
Nobles, H.A., 104, 155
Nobles, Mrs. H.A., 169
Nobles, M.C., 104, 116, 123
Norvell, Mrs. Lipscomb, 160
Nueces River, 22
Nunn, Bertha Kate, 118
Nunn, Dr. J.E., 122
Nunn, J.L., 176

Oates, G.E., 124
Ottoman Empire & Turks, 142-145
Owens, Mrs. Mary Bynum, 179, 182

Pacific House Hotel (Colorado City), 55, 66-67, 72
Paddock, LeBecca Wills, 11, 108, 178
Paine, Dr. & Mrs. Howard, 145
Paine Tour itinerary (1914), Naples, Roma, Pisa, Coltano, Venice, Lido, Bueno, Mortigny, Chamonix, Mt. Blanc, Mer de Glace glacier, Interlaken, Germany, Berlin, Hague, London, Liverpool
Palo Duro Baptist Association, 101, 111, 143, 150
Palo Duro Canyon, 93, 94, 133, 136, 150, 178, 182
Panhandle Bankers Association, 131
Panhandle City, TX, 94, 131

www.ingramcontent.com/pod-product-compliance
Lightning Source LLC
Chambersburg PA
CBHW020510120726
47904CB00003B/767